# THE 1978 FASHION GUIDE

---

# Kaori O'Connor

CORONET BOOKS
Hodder and Stoughton

Copyright © 1978 Kaori O'Connor

First published in Great Britain 1978 by Coronet Books

Written and edited by Kaori O'Connor
Promotions and special projects by Farrol Kahn
Art by David Reeson

Filmset by Elliott Bros. & Yeoman Ltd., Woodend
Avenue, Speke, Liverpool L24 9JL

Printed and bound in Great Britain for
Hodder and Stoughton Paperbacks,
a division of Hodder and Stoughton Ltd,
Mill Road, Dunton Green,
Sevenoaks, Kent (Editorial office: 47 Bedford Square,
London WC1 3DP)
by Richard Clay (The Chaucer Press), Ltd.,
Bungay, Suffolk

ISBN 0 340 21798 7

# CONTENTS

# For the reader

The shopping section of this Guide is divided into seven geographical areas of London, with separate sections on Menswear and clothes for children. Within each area the shops are arranged alphabetically.

Prices include VAT (Value Added Tax) except where stated.

Some addresses or times of opening may have changed, so if in doubt ring up in advance.

Prices are correct at time of going to press, but subject to change.

*All information contained herein is correct to the best of our knowledge at the time of going to press.*

# Preface

*by Farrol Kahn*

During the past four years of publication, we have inspected over 2,000 shops and stores and examined over 50,000 garments and accessories, and still stand firm over our initial decision to only make positive recommendations. When you buy a tin of beans and make a mistake on price or type, you merely consume the contents. But when you buy clothes and make an error, it can be a serious one. You are stuck with a negative image which you go on presenting until you discard those clothes. Making positive images is easy if you know what shops you can depend on and what lifestyle suits you. And that's what The Fashion Guide is all about. It is not enough for a shop or store to be good in parts—it must be consistently good, to get into the Fashion Guide year after year. This means buying at the right prices, looking for style and quality and improving on service and presentation.

**There is no charge for entries and shops cannot advertise in The Fashion Guide. Thus The Fashion Guide maintains its objectivity.** It has been succinctly described by the *Daily Express* as doing 'a marvellous, Michelin-type job on London's shops.'

It is worth stressing that each shop has been personally visited and is carefully described in detail—ambiance, stocks, prices, specialities, sizes, opening hours, credit cards and other useful information.

The grading system used is designed to give readers a balanced view of shops and also to highlight various areas in which shops excell—style, value for money, service and presentation.

# The Fashion Guide Shop Awards

The first awards were organised three years ago to encourage shops to improve their standards because the great traditions of shopping, like service, were rapidly declining. Shopping for clothes can be an exciting activity and all shops in The Fashion Guide reflect this. The awards merely highlight a small number at any one time in a city which has probably the best shops in the world. The criteria for judging the shops are value for money, style, service and presentation and all shops in The Fashion Guide are eligible.

This year the awards were presented at the **Italian Embassy** with **His Excellency The Italian Ambassador and Mme Ducci** as patrons of the Gala Soirée. **Gucci** showed their Autumn collection at the presentation and the evening was held in aid of **Action Research for the Crippled Child.**

The panel for **The Fashion Guide Shop Awards** included **Margaret, Duchess of Argyll; Ricci Burns; Brian Green** of **Windsmoor; Anne Price,** Fashion Editor of *Country Life*; **Jean Rook,** Assistant Editor of the *Daily Express*; and **Adel Rootstein** of Adel Rootstein Models. The awards, which were designed by Steven Hurst, were decided upon at Dukes Hotel, St. James's, London S.W.1

## Winners of The 1977 Fashion Guide Shop Awards

| | |
|---|---|
| The Best Woman's Shop | LUCIENNE PHILLIPS |
| The Best Man's Shop | TURNBULL & ASSER |
| The Store with the Best Service | HARRODS |
| The Store with the Best Presentation | HARVEY NICHOLS |

## Past Award Winners

| | | |
|---|---|---|
| 1975 | The Best Shop in London | BROWNS |
| 1976 | The Best Man's Shop | TAKE SIX |
| | The Best Woman's Shop | HARDY AMIES |
| | The Best Speciality Shop | GUCCI |
| | The Best Multiple | C & A |

## Explanation of symbols

★     Shop with a distinctive look or style

⚖     Shop with value for money

🎁     Shop with outstanding presentation

👔     Shop with outstanding service

# *Starred Shops*

## Four Stars

Ebony, Medina

## Three Stars

Bill Gibb, Paul Smith, Take Six, Turnbull & Asser

## Two Stars

Arabesque, Asprey, Apropos, Bally, Bentalls, Babyboots, Browns Men, Browns Women, Browns Shoes, C & A, Chic of Hampstead, Chic of Mount Street, Charles Jourdan, Clive Shilton, Cosmetics a la Carte, Cue Shop, Gucci, Huntsman, Harvey Nichols, Kickers, Laura Ashley, Lucienne Phillips, Maxwell, M & S, Piero de Monzi, Ronnie Stirling, White House, Zandra Rhodes, Zapata.

## One Star

Ace, Acushla Hicks at Antiquarius, Adam Owen, Annabelinda, Art Needlework Industries, Bazaar, Bombacha, Brother Sun, Burberry, Button Queen, Butler & Wilson, Casablanca, Captain Watts, David Fielden at Antiquarius, Dance Centre, Dunhill, Essenses, Floris, Friends, Herbert Johnson, Herbert Johnson Ladies, Harrods, Howie, James Drew, Janet Ibbotson, Janet Wilson, Jeeves, Ladies Habits, Les 2 Zebras, Liberty, Liberty Prints, Michael Pruskin at Antiquarius, Midas, Night Owls, Neal Street Shop, N. Peal, Penhaligon, Pennyfeathers, Rive Gauche, Royal British Legion Shop, Rowes, Seditionaries, David Shilling, Simpsons, Smythson.

# Clothing sizes

**Men's suits and overcoats**

| | | | | | | |
|---|---|---|---|---|---|---|
| British | 36 | 38 | 39½ | 41 | 42½ | 44 |
| American | 36 | 38 | 40 | 42 | 44 | 46 |
| Continental | 46 | 48 | 50 | 52 | 54 | 56 |

**Women's suits, dresses and shirts**

| | | | | | | |
|---|---|---|---|---|---|---|
| British | 8 | 10 | 12 | 14 | 16 | 18 |
| American | 8 | 10 | 12 | 14 | 16 | 18 |
| French | 38 | 40 | 42 | 46 | 46 | 48 |
| Italian | 40 | 42 | 44 | 46 | 48 | 50 |

**Men's shirts**

| | | | | | | | |
|---|---|---|---|---|---|---|---|
| British | 14 | 14½ | 15 | 15½ | 16 | 16½ | 17 |
| American | 14 | 14½ | 15 | 15½ | 16 | 16½ | 17 |
| Continental | 36 | 37 | 38 | 39 | 41 | 42 | 43 |

**Women's shoes**

| | | | | | | | | | |
|---|---|---|---|---|---|---|---|---|---|
| British | 3 | 3½ | 4 | 4½ | 5 | 5½ | 6 | 6½ | 7 | 7½ |
| American | 4½ | 5 | 5½ | 6 | 6½ | 7 | 7½ | 8 | 8½ | 9 |
| Continental | 35½ | 36 | 36½ | 37 | 37½ | 38 | 38½ | 39 | 39½ | 40 |

**Men's shoes**

| | | | | | | | | |
|---|---|---|---|---|---|---|---|---|
| British | 7 | 7½ | 8 | 8½ | 9 | 9½ | 10 | 10½ |
| American | 8½ | 9 | 9½ | 10 | 10½ | 11 | 11½ | 12 |
| Continental | 41 | 41½ | 42 | 42½ | 43 | 43½ | 44 | 44½ |

**Children's shoe sizes**

| Approx. Age | 4mth | 10mth | 2yr | 3½yr | 5½yr | 7yr | 8½yr | 10yr | 11yr | 12½yr |
|---|---|---|---|---|---|---|---|---|---|---|
| British | 3 | 4½ | 6 | 7½ | 9½ | 11 | 12½ | 1 | 2½ | 4 |
| French | 19 | 21 | 23 | 25 | 27 | 29 | 31 | 33 | 35 | 37 |

**Socks**

| | | | | | | | |
|---|---|---|---|---|---|---|---|
| British | 9½ | 10 | 10½ | 11 | 11½ | 12 | 12½ |
| American | – | 10 | 10½ | 11 | 11½ | 12 | 13 |
| Continental | 39 | 40 | 41 | 42 | 43 | 44 | 45 |

**Stockings**

| | | | | | | | |
|---|---|---|---|---|---|---|---|
| British | 8 | 8½ | 9 | 9½ | 10 | 10½ | 11 |
| American | – | 8½ | 9 | 9½ | 10 | 10½ | 11 |
| Continental | 35 | 36 | 37 | 38 | 39 | 40 | 41 |

Editor's Note: Sizes vary according to manufacturers, so use this table as an *approximate guide*.

# A Special Note on Endangered Species

Tortoise-shell combs, ivory bangles, crocodile shoes and lizard-skin handbags have for many years provided some of the most tempting items for visitors to Britain and for British shoppers. In fact none of these products, and a host of others, should be on sale, as they are derived from animals threatened with extinction.

Over a decade ago, it was clear that one of the main reasons why nearly 1,000 animals and thousands of plants were threatened with extinction was the trade in, and demand for, wildlife products. To try and control this trade and improve the status of animals and plants in the wild, a Convention on International Trade in Endangered Species of Fauna and Flora was produced with the help of about eighty governments, in March 1973. To date, about thirty countries have agreed to control the trade in a wide variety of endangered live animals and plants and their products. The trade in some species and items has been effectively stopped, and others are now subject to licensing.

The following are among the many items covered by the Convention:

(1) Any furskin, rug, coverlet, coat, jacket, cape or stole made wholly or partly of any furskin of the following animals: cheetahs, genets, civets, palm civets, spotted hyaenas, leopard cats, pampas cats, mountain cats, ocelots, banded mongooses,

clouded leopards, jaguars, leopards, tigers, snow leopards, polar bears, vicugnas and Spanish lynxes.

(2) Yarn, fabric, or articles of clothing made wholly or partly of hair of any animal of the species *Vicugna vicugna* (vicugnas).

(3) The raw hide or skin, and the leather, of any animal of the class *Reptilia* (reptiles).

(4) The shell and scales, and the claws, of any animal of the family *Cheloniidae* (sea turtles).

(5) Any tusk of any of the following animals—elephants, pigs, narwhals and walruses.

Visitors to Britain returning home should contact their embassy here to discover whether their country is a party to the Convention, and what licences they require to export goods.

British shoppers should, if in any doubt about wild animal and plant products, contact the **World Wildlife Fund** to discover whether the sale of the product in question is presenting a threat to rare wildlife. In London, the offices of the World Wildlife Fund are at 29 Greville Street, EC1, telephone 01-404 5691.

# For Brides

Don't lose your head when you lose your heart. The most surprising people do, and there's nothing worse than a reproachful collection of follies staring you in the face after the confetti settles. The best rule to follow is **not** to dash off to 'specialist' shops, but to shop where you would normally, so here is a short list of the best wedding buys of the year. **Engagement ring:** if money is no object, you should have no trouble, but if every penny counts you can't do better than **Asprey's** elegant solitaire diamond, about half a carat and of superb quality, in a simple coronet setting, for £200. **Wedding gowns:** if you want to make it yourself, **Bentalls** of Kingston have an excellent selection of washable bridal lace from £1.25 to £3.25 per metre, and the **Craftsmith** shops have all the fixings for assembling a wedding bouquet. If price is immaterial, you can have a wedding dress made to order by **Bill Gibb**, in chiffon, silk, French lace and *moiré* satin, trimmed with crystal beadwork, bugle beads and pearls. You can choose from samples and sketches—the designs are all rich and romantic, and you can have them in cream, white or any colour you like. Allow two months for delivery, and £450 to £1200 for the gown. If you'd like something old, try **David Fielden** at Night and Day, Antiquarius, for antique wedding dresses and the **Phillips** lace and costume auctions for antique wedding veils; **Liberty** have Thirties-style wax flowers chaplets to wear with them from £15. Ring up the **fashion colleges** and see if you can buy wedding dresses made for the student Dress Shows; if not, you can often find Dress Show gowns and gowns by young designers at **Uniquity.** For simple summer weddings **Mexicana** have very pretty traditional Mexican wedding dresses in pintucked white cotton trimmed with lace, from £60—and if you don't want to wear a gown at all, you can get married in a silk harem outfit from **Arabesque.** Once you've got the clothes, go to **David Shilling** for fabric flower chaplets, satin caps with fingertip veils or a confection to match your dress. He'll also do hats for everyone in the wedding party, so you can be sure the bridesmaid's hats don't clash with yours, or upstage you—very important if you're having photographs taken. Now you can think about your **make-up.** Don't have a professional make-up done on the day, you'll be far too nervous. Instead, go to **Cosmetics a la Carte,** and have them design you a special make-up about a week before the ceremony. They'll show you how to do it yourself, and you'll have plenty of time to practice; a very good way of making sure you'll look your best on your honeymoon. Don't forget to splash out on some special **lingerie**—something from **Zandra Rhodes'** lavish new collection, or a stylish negligée set from the **Charles Grahame** range. All you need now are two very special touches—a blue satin bridal garter trimmed with lace from **The White House** for £3.15, and Orange Blossom eau-de-cologne from **Penhaligon**—the perfect scent for a bride to wear for her wedding.

# GUIDE TO
# SHOPS

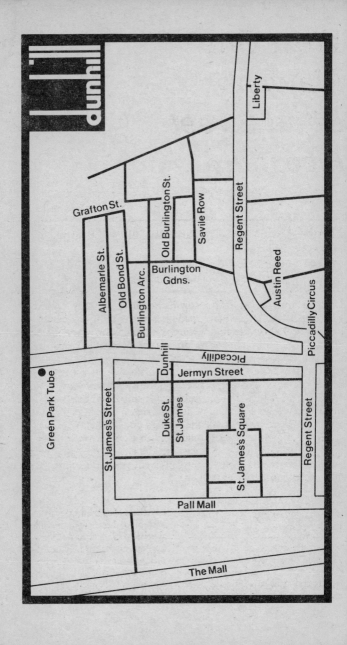

# West One
# Mayfair
# Bond Street
# Piccadilly

**Hardy Amies**  14 Savile Row, W1   01-734 2436
Mon.-Fri. 9.30-5.30
(Access, American Express, Barclaycard)
By appointment to Her Majesty the Queen, dressmaker

On the sunny side of Savile Row is the salon of Hardy Amies, whose taste and talents have made him many things to many people. Brought up to the couture tradition, Hardy Amies trained at Lachasse, designed evening dresses for Worth, and went on to establish his own couture house in 1946. This was the beginning of a career that has brought him many laurels, and little rest. His next success was through his semi-couture ready-to-wear collection, followed by a range of men's shirts that met with immediate acclaim. Today, he is couturier to Her Majesty the Queen, designer to many of the world's best-dressed women, creator of the international 'total look' in men's ready-to-wear international design consultancies. In the elegant Georgian town house where the dramatist Sheridan lived, you'll find three facets of this classics master of fashion.

## The Sportswear Collection

'Sport with style' sums up this collection of young-look classics—lots of knits, separates, jackets and coats in a mix and match range that will take you anywhere. Look out for the 'two-piece dress' long an Amies speciality and a wise fashion investment—worn together they make up into a classic shirtwaister dress, and if you get a toning skirt and top you'll have a perfect switch—around weekender wardrobe. Sportswear collection in sizes 8-16, sample range and prices:

**Knitwear:** co-ordinated knitwear making up into matching or contrast sets, all sold separately so you can put together your own look. Sweaters and cardigans in plain colours and tweedy-look yarn, all matching up to skirts. In acrylic, lambswool, and cashmere, from £18.49.

**Skirts:** in solid colours and softly smart checks, a range of styles including slender A-line, wrapover and pleated skirts, from £39.

**Shirts:** *Crêpe de Chine* shirts from £45, shirts in manmade fibre fabrics from £22.

**Jackets and Blazers:** all matching up to skirts and knitwear. Camel blazer from £69.

**Ensembles:** two-piece ensembles from £60; dresses from £49; coats from £79.

**Accessories:** *crêpe de Chine* scarves from £14.50. A selection of belts, bags and hats.

## The Boutique Collection

A semi-couture collection of classic styles for the sophisticated woman, exclusive to the Hardy Amies salon, 14 Savile Row. Models are made on the premises. The Boutique Collection comes in sizes 10-18, but you can arrange for other sizes by special order. Dresses from £120; coats from £150; suits from £160; evening dresses from £170.

## The Couture Collection

Hardy Amies couture models—orders can be completed within two weeks.

---

**Asprey** 165-169 New Bond Street, W1
01-493 6767
Mon.-Fri. 9-5.30, Sat. 9-1
By appointment to Her Majesty the Queen, goldsmiths, silversmiths and jewellers
By appointment to Her Majesty Queen Elizabeth the Queen Mother, jewellers

---

*An emporium fit for an Empress*, as Queen Victoria recognized when she granted them the Royal Warrant in 1861, this sumptuous treasurehouse is one of London's loveliest surprises. *Nothing is impossible at Asprey*, where crystal balls for clairvoyants, gold beard rakes for hirsute dandies and seven-piece luggage sets specially designed to fit in the boot of a Rolls are just the order of the day. Better still, *noblesse oblige* is the *comme il faut* of this true aristocrat of shops. Nothing is too much trouble and you'll be treated with the same courtly consideration whether you have a coronet or a pocket full of Jubilee Crowns. Best of all—money *isn't* everything at Asprey; £30 may not buy you a kingdom, but it will certainly buy you a truly princely present or a private fief of delight. A visit to Asprey is rather like weekending in a stately home—here a japanned Queen Anne cabinet, there an eighteenth-century spinning wheel, Fabergé bibelots, pony grooming kits in the boxroom, Great Aunt Charlotte's flatware on the table and trusted retainers everywhere. Five floors of delights await your attention, and from the downstairs room where purchases are wrapped in Asprey purple paper to the workshops under the roof where Asprey's craftsmen create their famous masterworks, nothing but the best will do. The crystal and silver sparkle majestically, little amusements are arranged as beautifully as the priceless pieces, and the jewellery salon was purposely designed to catch the constant north light that shows off fine stones and settings to perfection. You won't find Asprey's experts in Olympian offices—they're in every department, behind every showcase and table, happy to show you their treasures, explain the fine points, offer assistance and advice. And 'no' is not a word that exists at Asprey, where clients expect just what they please—and get it. A jewelled sword, a golden sturgeon to hold caviare, silver place mats in the shape of a fan—*anything* can be made to order. Brides marrying abroad can have Asprey prepare an international wedding list, and brides who place their lists in the Brides Book can choose from one of the best selections of china, crystal and silver in the world. You can take as much time as you like over your purchases, but if you're pressed don't worry—Asprey are used to people in a hurry, and if you leave them an order you can be sure your instructions will be carried out faithfully. So treat yourself to a few of life's little luxuries at Asprey—you won't know how good 'the best' can be until you do.

Sample range—all prices approximate:

## Fine Jewellery

Asprey are noted for their superb stones and fine settings; many special pieces are made in the jewel workrooms on the premises. Exceptionally fine use of beautifully coloured semi-precious stones like amethyst, citrine, tourmaline and peridot, coral in every colour. Rings, bracelets, necklaces, pendants and parures in classic and contemporary styles. Prices from about £200 to half a million pounds for a fabulous ruby and diamond parure. Gold Egyptian zodiac pendants, £198.50. Beautifully simple diamond solitaire, small choice stone in an 18ct gold coronet setting, *outstanding value for money*, £200. Chain necklaces in 18ct gold, plain or with semi

precious stones, from
£200-£2,000. Rich long ropes of
red coral beads, from about
£2,850. Fine 18ct white gold ring
set with deep green peridot and
diamonds, £345. Diamond collar
with a carved angelskin coral
pendant, £40,000.

## Silver

Modern silver in Queen Anne and
Georgian styles, including domed
Queen Anne style four piece tea
service, about £1,050. Large silver
crab to hold crabmeat, with gilt
interior and scallop shell serving
spoon, £1,350; caviar holder in
the shape of a sturgeon,
compartments for ice in the head
and the tail, £1,750; both made in
the Asprey workrooms.

**Christening presents:** silver
napkin rings, silver spoons and
forks, ivory and silver baby
rattles, all under £50. Silver plate
champagne buckets, £92.50.

**Small silver objets:** ingenious
corkscrew-cum-bottleopener,
£16.85; toothpaste tube squeezers,
£32.50; telescopic golf club
swizzlestick, £15.75; very smart
silver saccharin dispenser, £28.25.
*Large* selection of silver and silver
plated animals in all sizes.

## Gold

Golf markers in 9ct gold, £42.50;
small gold whistle, £25. Gold
collar stiffeners, made in the
workrooms, £29.75 the pair.
Travelling toothbrushes mounted
in 9ct gold, £285; 18ct gold
calculator, £725. Gold
swizzlesticks, pillboxes, key fobs;
*anything to order.*

## Antique Jewellery

A fine selection of rare and
beautiful things, including 1920's
*sautoir* of pearls and diamonds set
in platinum, £8,950. Georgian
topaz necklace, £1,450.
Gold-mounted ivory snuff-box,
French, about 1745, £1,750.

**Antique silver:** small selection of
antique silver snuff boxes and tea
caddy spoons from £50; rare
pieces by masters like Paul de
Lamerie; coasters, fruitbaskets,
winecoolers, antique cutlery and
flatware, occasion pieces in old
Sheffield plate.

## Russian works of Art

Always a selection of pieces by
Fabergé. Lapis shell snuffbox
with gold mount, by Henrik
Wigstrom, £6,300; varicoloured
gold snuffbox set with a portrait
of Czar Nicholas II, by Michael
Perchin; simple double cigarette
case with cabuchon ruby push
piece, by Anders Nevalainen,
£500: all workmasters to Fabergé.
Also, many fine examples of
Russian late nineteenth century
*cloisonné* work, *champlevé* and
*pliqué à jour*.

## Small Leather Goods and Handbags

Excellent department with
specialities from Asprey's leather
workrooms. Small leather goods
from £2.50 for a spool tape
measure in leather case the size of
a 10p piece. Good selection of
beauty cases: from £42.50 for a
black calf hide case with separate

tray and gilt locks to £150 for a
large calf hide case with suede
lining, three trays, suede flaps in
the lid and gilt combination locks.
Superb envelope-style document
case with flaps for passport,
currencies, tickets, luggage
tickets, travel documents and
papers, £25.50; *outstanding value
for money*. Strap and buckle jewel
roll in washable suede, beautiful
pastel colours, £13. Magnetic
travelling backgammon board
fitted into a leather case, £125.
Silver and leather photograph
frames; silver photograph frame
with Jubilee hallmark, eight by six
inches, £106. Handbags; classic
calf and kid bags from England,
Italy and France.

**Speciality:** crocodile bags made in
the Asprey workrooms: baby
crocodile evening bags, about
£600; crocodile beauty cases, from
around £1,300.

## Small gifts and Costume Jewellery

Small Royal Worcester thimbles,
popular presents for Nannies,
£3.20. Crocodile covered contact
lens cases, £13. Selection of
compacts, scent sprays,
handmirrors, Limoges eggs. Vast
selection of smart gold-plated
costume jewellery: in the unlikely
event that the plating wears,
Asprey will replate free of charge.
New Asprey umbrellas, £42.50; all
with scarves to match. French
hand-coloured silk flowers, about
£10 each.

**Pens:** all the best makes including
Asprey's own 18ct gold fountain
pen. £325, and 9ct gold felt-tipped
pen, £102.50.

## Cufflinks

Excellent selection, with full
engraving service. Classic Asprey
knot links in 9ct gold, £55; in
18ct gold, £130. Simple gold ovals
with twist bar fitting, perfect for
engraving, about £60 in 9ct gold,
about £130 in 18ct gold.
Cabochon tourmaline cufflinks,
£160. Lapis cufflinks set in 9ct
gold, £127.50; cabochon garnet
links in 9ct gold, £89.50.

**Blazer buttons** in 9ct gold, set of
four large and four sleeve buttons,
about £3.50.

**Evening links:** mother-of-pearl
with sapphire centre, about £300;
coral and onyx links, £465;
diamond and onyx links set in
18ct white gold, about £650. Also,
regimental links for Guards
regiments.

## Luggage and Accessories

Always a good selection of
Edwardian and Victorian **walking
sticks**, from about £100, including
silver topped ebony cane with
sovereign box in the top, £325;
Chinese silver-mounted sword
cane, £140; fine Malacca cane
with 18ct gold mount, made 1851,
£240. **New collection of swords**,
including Hungarian sabre in gilt
metal set with red stones on both
sides, presented to Louis Kossuth
in 1848, £1,750; French sword
with gilt handle and damascene
blade, late 18th century, £395.
Lots of fine hairbrushes, dressing
case fittings, shaving brushes and
shaving brush holders. Selection
of luggage lined with Asprey's
exclusive *Fleur de Lys* fabric;

seven piece luggage set designed
to fit in the boot of a Rolls, to
order, about £1,500. Best selection
of **wicker picnic chests** in town,
from £350 for wicker chest fitted
with earthenware, glasses, cutlery
and containers for eight, to a
*tête-à-tête* hamper for two, £65.
The **Beaufort Grooming basket**,
holding hoof oil, curry combs,
saddle soap, a fixture in all the
best stables, £59; pony grooming
kit in a leather-trimmed canvas
pail, £25. Binoculars including full
range by Leitz and Carl Zeiss.
Men's umbrellas, shooting, sticks,
hunting, shooting fishing and
sports bags.

## Antique Furniture and Treen

Exceptionally fine department
with treasures in every corner; a
massive mahogany bookcase
designed by Robert Adam, a late
18th century spinning wheel by
John Planta, and a glass fronted
Queen Anne cabinet.

**Treen:** new department with

delightful inexpensive antique
gifts in turned wood. Stoppered
glass scent bottle in wooden case,
£20; nutmeg grater, £26; whist
markers, £20 the pair.

## Top Table Room

The best selection of china, glass,
cutlery and flatware in London;
the complete Christofle collection
of silver plated cutlery, London's
biggest collection of Baccarat
crystal. Christofle silver plated
cocktail shakers in two sizes, from
£55.67; silver plated champagne
buckets, £97; single candle holder
in silver plate, very romantic,
£9.55. Fine English and French
china: exclusive to Asprey, Royal
Windsor dinner service in red.
Fine silverware in the best
traditional and modern patterns:
exclusive to Asprey, David
Melly's **Embassy** pattern
silverware, as used in British
embassies all over the world.
Seven-piece Embassy setting,
£233.65. Crystal ball, good
medium size, £102.

**Bally**  116 New Bond Street, W1   01-629 6501
Mon.-Sat. 9-5.30, Thurs. 9-7
(Access, American Express, Barclaycard, Chargex,
Diners, Masshercharge)

Like a fascinating woman, there are many sides to Bally's
charm—and if you've ever had trouble in narrowing down 'the
Bally look', it's because there isn't *just* one—there are four! One
thing is always the same—say 'Bally' in countries all over the
world, and they'll know you're talking about shoes of the very
finest quality. The Bally of France collection sparkles with
*prêt-à-porter* panache, and they do shoes for Yves Saint Laurent
under license. Bally of Switzerland make classic shoes with the

20

Cresta Run feeling—cool, exhilarating, terribly *terribly* smart. Bally of England specialize in free and easy leisure shoes, and good looks from every house go into the Bally International collection that is sold around the world. The houses work closely together, and this Spring the Bally collections are fresh, young and full of fashion personality. Colours and textures match up to golden tans, natural fabrics, summer flowers. The shoes show a strong sandal influence with lots of open toes, tiny straps, shot vamps—even the two-tone correspondent pumps have peep toes or sling backs. Bally of Switzerland's elegant D'Orsay range has fine gilt chains linking slender straps at toes and ankles—pretty and provocative. Mules come in open toe, classic and sandal styles, on heels of lacquered cork or wood bronzed in gunmetal and antique gold—just the thing to wear with this summer's linens and cottons. Hinged soles give high-heeled sandals a greater flexibility, low-heeled ripple soles cushion leather sport lace-ups. The schoolgirl sandal is everywhere—flat in all the season's colours, or on slender heels with the tiniest of straps over insteps, toes and ankles. Strappiest sandal of all—high evening heels in bronze, silver or gold, with *ten* tiny straps looped over the instep and around the heel. For the ultimate in bare beauty, choose the delicate flat-soled slave sandals that lace all the way up to the knee, and for fun in the sun pick the casual slip-on sandals trimmed with colourful clusters of fruit. Bally always make special shoes for Bill Gibb's collections, and the sandals and zori slippers in silver and gold that lit up the footlights at his fabulous autumn fashion show are now in the Spring range—don't miss them. As far as fashion goes, Bally is the house to watch. So hurry along to Bally's top salons, and get in on the start of something big.

Sample range—all prices approximate:

**Shoes:** in sizes 3-8, a few 2½'s. B & C fittings, with a few AA's. High heeled sandals on hinged soles, open-toe, classic and sandal mules, £32.50-£34.50. Low heeled sport laceups with ripple sole, about £34. Flat schoolgirl sandals, 'Finette', £42. Classic correspondent court pump with sling back, about £50; wear with matching handbags. High fashion zori slippers, £20. Young look sandals on high silvery or shiny white heels, wraparound ankle strap, about £23. Patent party shoes with open toe and sling back, perfect for the new cocktail dresses, £17. Slave sandals, £20. By Andrea Pfister, exclusive to Bally: schoolgirl sandals with finely plaited straps around the toes, in pale beige or almond green, about £55. Strappy openback snakeskin sandal, in cherry red or beige, about £55.

**Bazaar** 24 Brook Street, W1    01-408 1673
Mon.-Fri. 10-6, Thurs. 10-7, Sat. 10-4.30
(Access, American Express, Barclaycard)

The ethnic look may have passed like a caravan in the night, but it's left behind a legacy of new fashion classics that will never go out of style. Sheik meets chic in the wonderful collection of Folk Fashion that Betty Van Gelder has brought from all over the world. Some things have been adapted, others specially designed and made for Bazaar, and some are absolutely 'as worn' in exotic climes—but all are wonderfully right for today: wearable, well-priced, with that hint of 'something different'. Sparkle your way through summer in silk waistcoats, skirts and dresses lavished with gold embroidery and spangles. The designs come from India, Rumania and Afghanistan, and you can splash out on ensembles that shimmer from top to toe. There's a whole collection in cotton, perfect for this season's nonchalant natural good looks—big loose shirts in handwoven textured cotton, loose cotton jackets trimmed with hessian, sleeveless cotton waistcoats with wooden buttons and hessian pockets, off-the-shoulder tops and easy skirts in fine pastel cotton mull, a romantic white collection with ruffled tops and matching skirts. In winter you'll find special handknits, Bazaar's own collection of tweed skirts, culottes and knickerbockers, and there are folkloric caftans in stock all year round.

Sample range—all prices approximate:

Sparkly mirror skirts, £30; evening dresses in printed silk with gold embroidery, about £80; evening dresses in velvet with antique Afghani embroidery inserts, each different, about £100. Tunic length peasant style silk blouses with gold embroidery, £50. Pretty party and cocktail dresses, hand embroidered, from £25; big loose cottons shirt dresses, from £20-£30. Soft silky shirts with very fine pastel pencil stripes, gathered at front and back yoke, Peter Pan collar, about £24; pale cotton fatigues, under £15; dresses in pastel cotton mull, about £28.

## Burberrys   18-22 Haymarket, SW1   01-930-3343
Mon.-Fri. 9-5.30, Thurs. 9-7, Sat. 9-5
By appointment to Her Majesty the Queen, weatherproofers
By appointment to Her Majesty Queen Elizabeth the Queen Mother, weatherproofers

A foul weather friend indeed, Thomas Burberry introduced his weatherproof gabardine rainwear to the nation in 1856—and carrying on in the teeth of the storm has been the great British pastime ever since. But don't save Burberry for a rainy day, because the house has splashed out with a whole *new collection of fair weather fashions* that show the English tailormade look in a sparkling new light. You'll find everything you need for *le style Anglais*—soft single breasted jackets in smart Prince of Wales dogstooth or district check tweeds, lambswool, camelhair and cashmere, to wear with pleated or kilted skirts, shirts in silk and Viyella, waistcoats in suede and tweed. There are lots of two- and three-piece suits, all sold as separates so you can have the fun of putting together your own look. Start with a Viyella shirt in muted blue Dress Stewart, worn *under* a cream silk shirt with buttoned turnback cuffs. Smooth the tartan collar over the silk collar, and make sure a good inch of tartan shows at the wrist underneath the silk cuffs. Add a brown suede waistcoat, a kilted skirt in plain grey flannel and a tweed jacket. Finish with a long fringed silk cravat in cream or pearl grey, worn untied and tucked under the lapels—the season's smartest scarf, with a woven-in border of Burberry's nostalgic Thirties logo. This Spring you can look forward to lovely linens in pastel pink, *eau-de-Nil* and all the natural shades—soft skirts, easy jackets, shirts and waistcoats that will make your spirits soar like a barometer on a glorious day. But should the glass fall, and showers with it, rush to Burberry for the ultimate in weatherproof fashion—fine capes, coats and jackets, all trimmed with Burberry's international status symbol check—*just like clouds with silver linings*. The Burberry check now comes in *three new colourways*—olive with brown and rust, navy with red and royal blue, black with grey and red—and you can have scarves, skirts, shirts, brollies, luggage, hats and ties in all the new shades. Ladies should try the new Elgin rainjacket with check facing and a detachable check collar—just the thing to wear with trousers tucked into boots and a 'Burwester' reversible tweed and gabardine soft hat. And there are smart new styles for men as well—reversible tweed and gabardine safari jackets, and tweed

*At Burberry*

sports jackets with matching reversible tweed and gabardine topcoats. Londoners should look out for David Bailey's special photographs of Burberry's sunshine styles—a perfect Spring tonic. And if you need cheering up in the sodden season, don't miss Burberry's weatherproof witticisms, printed next to the Forecast in *The Times*. Samples: C. Dudley Warner—'Everybody talks about the weather, but nobody does anything about it.' Burberry—'**We beg to differ**'. Benjamin Franklin—'Some are weatherwise, some are otherwise.' Burberry—'**No comment**.'

Sample range—all prices approximate:

Jackets from £80, skirts from £37, suits from £105-140, kilts from £24.50, silk cravats from £18, suede waistcoats from £39, trench coats from £90 and ladies walking Burberry from £65.

---

## The Button Queen  19 Marylebone Lane

01-935 1505
Mon.-Fri. 10-5.30, Sat. 10-1.30

---

'**Rich man . . . poor man . . .**' Buttons may not be able to predict the future but as one of man's oldest forms of jewellery, they can certainly tell you a lot about the past. The romantic Edwardians doted on buttons in parma violet, the Victorians on sober buttons in cut steel. When the Ballets Russes took Paris by storm buttons blazed out in opulent jades and scarlets, and when Tutankhamen's tomb was discovered in the Twenties there was a flood of copper-finish fastenings tinted *eau-de-Nil*. Chanel and Schiaparelli designed buttons and had them made up specially for their collections, and up until the last war, pretty buttons in every shade, shape and size were something you could take for granted. With clothes becoming more expensive by the minute these little touches are worth their weight in gold, for they can transform a simple frock into something very special, turn a knit into a stylish novelty, add sparkle to the plainest shirt and give you a unique look for pennies. No modern buttons can top the stock of this tiny shop, brimming with antique buttons by the thousands—everything from rare Georgian collector's items to funky Woolworths buttons of the Thirties, showing Snow White and the Seven Dwarves. There are light blue grass flower buttons that make delightful fastenings for *broderie Anglaise* camisoles threaded with matching light blue ribbon, real horn buttons for tweeds and mother of pearl buttons for linens, burnished buttons to brighten your blazer and rare round pearlised glass buttons, perfect for wedding dresses. Twenties and Thirties buttons are a speciality—look out for novelty fastenings in the shapes of little bows, licorice allsorts and bright red fingernails. Don't feel you have to slip them through buttonholes—scatter them down the bodice of a blouse, around the hem of a skirt, or across the back yoke of a shirtdress. You can even adapt them into fun fashion jewellery or cufflinks, and trim a hat with what's left over.

Sample range—all prices approximate:

**Art Deco** button in all colours and sizes, from 10p each. **Blazer buttons;** fox mask, Royal Hussar, crown and anchor, crossed tennis racquets, pheasants, lots more, 70p each. Small Victorian dress buttons, 20-25p each. **Horn** buttons; from 10p for small, from 25p for large. Linen buttons, from 6p each. Twenties and thirties copper lustre buttons, 20p each. Round glass pearlised buttons, from 20-25p each. Light blue glass flower buttons, £1.50 for 6. Cut mother of pearl buttons, 25p each. Thirties red fingernail buttons, £1.50 for 3. Thirties cut wood buttons, 25p each. Also, antique hatpins, shirt studs, earrings, show buckles and cufflinks made of old buttons.

THE FASHION GUIDE
The Best Multiple Store 1976

**C & A**  (Marble Arch) 505 Oxford Street, W1
01-629 7272
Mon.-Sat. 9.30-6, Thurs. 10-8
(Access, Barclaycard)

When it comes to the multiples, C & A get top marks for style, and their Marble Arch store has great looks at really low prices. Because of their international fashion expertise, C & A can bring you super styles and fabrics from all over the world, and they're always quick off the mark in spotting new fashion trends. Some items are specially made for C & A, some have been bought from other houses—if you look through the rails, you're likely to find labels like Emesse and La Squadra for much less than you'd have to pay elsewhere. You can count on C & A to give you the cream of the season's fashions with tiny variations that make no difference at all to the look, but knock spots off the cost of a designer original. This summer ladies can look forward to *five* fashion collections from C & A—clothes for every mood and occasion. The romatic collection has flurries of lace, flounces of *broderie Anglaise*, Edwardian flourishes of smocking, *appliqué* and pleating. You can have a ladylike tea gown, a winsome camisole to wear with petticoat skirts, or gypsyish off-the-shoulder tops and swirling skirts, in pink, honey, yellow, black and white with touches of almond green and lilac. Then do a complete about-face with C & A's 'City look'—man-tailored jackets and blazers, front pleated trouser suits, classic shirts and ties. The go-anywhere-do-anything holiday collection has carefree clothes you can do what you like with —cotton pants to roll over the knee, shirts to roll over the elbow, shirt-styles jackets with big pockets to fill with sea-shells, lots of cotton and seersucker for breezy good looks. Last year's jungle-print theme is continued in a vivid collection of Caribbean prints—T-shirts kimono wrap dresses, sarongs, shirts and T-shirts, shorts and little skirts to show off lithe legs and limbo hips. And in the evening you can slip into C & A's new cool classics—fine jersey party dresses draped in the Grecian style. The children's collection repeats many of the women's themes and fabrics, and men can expect lots more daring colours, looser casual shirts, shorts in white, beige and khaki cotton, soft tops in rust and chamois velours. There's something for everyone at C & A—a Swim Shop with bibkinis, suits, coverups and robes, a seasonal Ski Shop with ski suits for men, women and children, departments for babies and under-fives, a juvenile department, an outsize department with dresses up to size 26 and the **Gear Cellar** where you'll find all the latest high fashion styles. And of course, there are changing rooms, so you can try everything on.

**C & A** other Oxford Street branches are at 376-384 Oxford Street, and at 200 Oxford Street, W1; same hours as Marble Arch store.

Sample range and approximate prices:

## For Ladies

**Ladies coats** from £19.95—£39 for Sixth Sense range, raincoats

from £11.95, skirts from £2.95-£13.95, blouses from

*By Giorgio Armani for Tiamale at Casablanca*

£2.95-£6.95, fashion knitwear from £6.95, standard knitwear from £2.50-£5; trousers from £3.95-£9.95, long dresses from £6.95—£35 for Sixth Sense range, two- and three-piece suits and dress and jacket ensembles up to £18.95.

## For Men

Raincoats from £14.95-£49; suits from £29.50-£80; sports jackets from £17.95-£49; jeans from £5.95-£8.95; trousers from £5.95-£19.95 for Westbury range; shorts from £3.95-£5.95 and sports shirts from £2.95-£7.95.

## For Children

**For girls:** ages 6-15 years: raincoats from £10.50; T-shirts from 75p-£1.05; summer tops from £1.75-£2.25; bikinis from £1.95-£2.50; shirt-style blouses from £1.95 and jeans from £3.95-£4.95.

**For boys:** ages 6-15 years: casual shirts from £2.95-£3.95; trousers from £4.95-£6.50; T-shirts from 75p-£1.05; swimming trunks, £1.15-£1.35 and jeans from £2.95-£5.95.

---

**Casablanca** 35 Brook Street, W1   01-493 0585
Mon.-Fri. 10-6, Thurs. 10-7, Sat. 10-5
(Access, Barclaycard, American Express, Diners)

*Casablanca plays it with style!* Today the *real* excitement in fashion comes from new young designers in Italy and France—**Gianangeli of Perugia, Swinger of Verona, Pepperone, Cloo Cloo of Milan, Boa and Monica, You Tarzan Me Jane.** The look is easy, fresh and natural—movement away from glass, chrome and hard-edged glamour. Exaggeration is out. Clothes are informal, wearable, fun—but with taste. That's the new mood on the Via della Spiga in Milan, the rue du Marché St. Honoré in Paris—and in Brook Street, where Casablanca have the cream of these stunning young collections. You can expect real originality, casual perfection, charmingly nonchalant ensembles that never look too put together. This season there are very special treats in store—**Giorgio Armani's designs for Tiamale**, Louis Avanez's Côte d'Azur cottons, unconstructed linen jackets and skirts in sensational prints by Gingerly of Milan and the complete collection of Danny Noble—Casablanca's choice as *the* young English designer to watch. Cut a dashing figure in his high summer smocks with cavalier collars, Pierrot shifts with ruffles everywhere, white brocade jackets over white velvet waistcoats and fuschia velvet skirts. The staff are exceptionally pleasant, and the prices are as good as the looks. Casablanca is one of the best and brightest shops in London, and you'll find yourself coming back often—as time goes by.

Sample range—all prices approximate:

Clothes in sizes 8-14, lots in size 6: dresses from £18; shirts from £11; trousers from £18; Fiorucci jeans from £20; summer knitwear from around £15; T-shirts from about £4; skirts from £18; evening dresses and separates from about £48; belts from £4, bags from about £15.

---

# Chic 100 Mount Street, W1  01-629 4960/5484

Mon.-Fri. 9.30-6, Sat. 9.30-1
(Access, American Express, Barclaycard, Diners)

---

This elegant salon has the *crème de la crème* of the British collections—fine designs by Jean Muir, Bill Gibb and John Bates—with shoes specially selected to complement the clothes. You can expect to be served with all the attention and personal service that Chic are famous for, and if there's anything you want that isn't in stock in Mount Street, they'll arrange to have it sent down from Hampstead. It's a wonderful introduction to all that's fine in British fashion, shown with the special Chic elegance and style. Clothes in sizes 8-14, some 16's. Shoes, sandals and boots in sizes 3½-9½. For full description, see listing for Chic of Hampstead.

---

# Chloé 173 New Bond Street, W1  01-493 6277

Mon.-Sat. 9.30-6, Thurs. 9.30-7
(American Express, Barclaycard, Diners)

---

London's new Chloé shop, full of beautiful designs for day and evening by Karl Lagerfeld. Also, Chloé perfume, luggage, accessories, shoes, scarves, and handbags.

Clothes in sizes 36-46, all prices approximate: **silk blouses** from £80; **day dresses** from £262; **evening dresses** from £320; **coats** from £262.

## Collingwood  46 Conduit Street, W1   01-734 2656
Mon.-Fri. 9-5

(Access, American Express, Barclaycard, Diners)

By appointment to Her Majesty the Queen, jewellers and silversmiths

By appointment to Her Majesty Queen Elizabeth the Queen Mother, jewellers

Collingwood have been personal jewellers to the Royal Family since the first year of Queen Victoria's reign, and you can rely on them for impeccable service, complete probity and jewellery that is exceptionally fine in every sense of the word. In times when both are rare, Collingwood's craftsmen have consummate expertise and *superb taste*, and since Collingwood have a team of house designers, you can choose from a splendid range of styles and specialities. Every Collingwood piece is beautifully balanced—the stones are well cut and chosen, the settings immaculate and the piece as a whole so beautifully designed that it transforms fine jewellery into art. Nothing is brash, gimmicky or startling. Collingwood pride themselves on craftmanship and refinement, and although their pieces always reflect contemporary styles, they also have pure and timeless beauty. The fabulous Collingwood *parure* is an excellent example of the more classical Collingwood design, and this, with a superb mid-nineteenth century diamond suite currently on display, reflects the expertise that has made Collingwood one of the great world jewellers. Consisting of a necklace of fine diamond clusters with pear-shaped diamond drops and joined by festoons and a large cluster brooch with drops and matching earrings, this at £150,000 is undoubtedly one of the most important suites of diamond jewellery in London. Collingwood are famous for two other timeless pieces—pearl chokers with fancy diamond clasps and the collection of rubies and emeralds. There is a ruby and diamond suite, which displays a collection of matching rubies of almost magical similarity of colour, for £190,000. A lovely Art Noveau butterfly made of horn, coloured precious stones and diamonds at £5,000 and an Art Deco flower of moonstone and diamonds at £3,650 are two delightful pieces in their current collection. The history of fine jewellery is second nature to Collingwood and it is possible to see examples of the last 150 years in their showroom. The sheer quality of settings is unique, and many people bring their pieces to be reset. The stones are set low to contribute to the harmony of the piece, the bracelets are beautifully linked, the ring settings are as lovely from the side as from above and the eternity rings are as comfortable as a simple slender band. A fine feeling for colour runs through the collection, every shade subtle and true. There are rich rubies, ropes of beads in rose quartz, smoky quartz and crystal, beautifully matched corals, pink, bronze and blue pearls, a large perfect peridot with that rare fine green shade and a wonderful ring set with yellow, white and green diamonds. Everything is shown with great care and attention—in that Collingwood are delightfully old-fashioned. At Conduit Street, you can also see a superb collection of fine and antique silver, and they will undertake commissions for pieces and cutlery in classic and modern styles.

Collingwood's elegant, exciting contemporary jewellery—displayed at Conduit Street and the showrooms at Harrods—will delight anyone who appreciates quality, taste and subtle imagination. Everything is beautifully designed and made, down to the smallest items like petite and highly fashionable diamond and yellow gold necklaces, earrings and rings, and diamond horses head cufflinks for gentlemen. When you buy from Collingwood, you know you are buying the very best. And that, these days, is a very reassuring thought.

Sample range and prices:

**Rings:** a fine large peridot ring with brilliant cut diamond surround and 18ct gold setting, £700. Diamond eternity ring, white gold set all the way round with marquise diamonds, £880. Ring of white, yellow and green diamonds set in white gold, £1,520. Modern band ring set with lapis, ivory and *pavé* diamonds, £200. Domed 18ct gold ring set with smoky crystal bound over with gold, £160. Superb 11.76ct Burma ruby, flanked by heart-shaped diamonds, £30,000.

**Pearls:** a rope of perfectly matched grape-sized South Sea pearls, with clasp of brilliant and baquette diamonds, £41,000. A rope of pearls with a diamond and pearl tassel, £7,800.

**Necklaces:** delicate chain necklace with gold and coral train, £200. Unusual gold collar necklace with gold lattice bib set with diamonds, £880. Rope of rose quartz, amethyst and smoky quartz beads with 18ct gold fluted caps, strung on silk, £475.

**Bracelets:** Three strings of smoky quarts and crystal beads with a tasteful gold plaque in the Adams style, £400. Nine diamond quartrefoils set in white gold, mounted on 18ct gold link chain, £630.

**Watches:** fine Delaneau watches and Collingwood watches with Delaneau movements. Collingwood watch with *pavé*, diamond dial and surround, crocodile straps, £2,750.

Collingwood fluted coral surround
watch with *pavé*-diamond detail,
on an 18ct gold link bracelet,
£4,120.

**Also:** a collection of fine jewellery
for gentlemen including watches,
rings, cufflinks, cigar cutters,
bracelets and cigarette boxes.

---

# Culpeper 21 Bruton Street, W1   01-629 4559
Mon.-Fri. 9.30-5.30, Sat. 9.30-1

---

Named for the 17th century herbalist, Culpeper is a physick
garden of delights, with herbs for every purpose under Heaven
and pure cosmetics for gilding the lilies that Nature forgot. You
can choose from a marvellous range that includes green lettuce
soap and red elm nourishing cream, nettle hair rinse, natural
henna powder, eyelash-growing cream and beauty pills; and if you
want to give your good looks a head start there are herbal teas
and tisanes, heady **potpourris** to carry all your cares away, pillows
filled with the stuff dreams are made of and natural seaweed
baths laced with iodine, bromide salts and the unmistakable tang
of the sea. At Culpeper life can be sweet—and good for you as
well—with pure brown cane sugar lumps rich in molasses, wild
forest honey, herb-flavoured honeycombs, honey from blossoms
of Greece and Brazil. And everything in the kitchen's nicer when
you add Culpeper's whole wild herbs and spices, special herb
blends for barbecues and salads, natural sea salt, green
peppercorns on the stem, and lively French and English
mustards. All Culpeper preparations are approved by the Society
of Herbalists, and if you are a herbalist yourself or interested in
the field, Culpeper have an excellent selection of books on the
subject, mortars and pestles for compounding your interest, and
stock 183 different herbs from Agar Agar to Yarrow. Mail order
forms and price lists are available on request, and interested
parties are invited to become members of the Society of
Herbalists by writing to the secretary at 34 Boscabel Place,
London SW1. **Recipe for a natural beautifying mask, courtesy
of Culpeper**: 'Take one egg and separate, keeping yolk if your
skin is dry and white if your skin is oily. Mix with fine oatmeal
and honey to form a paste. Apply to face and leave on for fifteen
minutes. Wash and finish with natural astringent.'

Sample range and prices:

**Cleansing creams:** elder flower
for normal and dry skin, lemon

for oily skin, in two sizes from
£1.05.

33

*By Lewis Gould for James Drew*

**Nourishing creams:** orange and red elm for normal skins, velvet for dry skin, from £1.25.

**Lotions:** *miel de mignonette*, *miel of white violets*, milk of lilies and mountain water, £1.15; balm, £1.85.

**Toilet waters:** elder flower, orange flower, rosewater, from 95p.

**Perfumes and essential oils:** *These are highly concentrated, and you need only one or two drops to perfume a bath.* All essences are absolutely pure, and prices are given for a half ounce. Lavender from France, £1.35; Patchouli from Indonesia, £1.10; Rose geranium from France, £1.95. Rosemary from France, use two or three drops for rinsing the hair, 95p.

**Hair preparations:** 40g of fair or dark shampoo, 30p; 20g of fair or dark hair rinse, 30p; 113cc of hair tonic or rosemary and bay lotion,

£1.25; 28g of herbal shampoo powder, 35p; natural henna powder, 70p a 100g.

**Bath preparations:** lemon verbena essence, £1.55; herb-gold pine needle milk, £1.65; lavender, stephanotis or rose geranium bath elixir, £1.95; seaweed bath, 75p; foot and bath salts, 55p.

**Pills and Tablets:** Alternative, Beauty, Catarrh, Cough, Chlorophyll, Circulation and Varicose vein, Comfrey, Herbal Aperient, Nerve, Passiflora, Pile, Rheumatic, Seaweed, Slim, Acidity pills, all 70p.

**Also:** Soaps from 45-75p, talcum powders from 75p, eyelash-growing cream and nail revitalizer, £1.15 each, Pomander oranges from £2.95; bags and boxes of lavender from 65p; boxes of potpourri in several scents, from £1.35; handmade *sleep pillows* in floral print cotton, £3.25; herbscented *sachets* from 50p.

---

**James Drew** 3 Burlington Arcade, W1    01-493 0714
Mon.-Fri. 9-5.30, Sat. 9-12.45

---

Paris may be busy rediscovering elegance, but it's never gone out of style at James Drew. This very special salon has an international reputation as discreet—and quietly devastating—as everything in designer Lewis Gould's exclusive collection. Pure simplicity and perfect luxury are the keys to the James Drew look—knit pullovers in pure silk, cashmere T-shirts, *dégagé* pyjama suits in spotted or striped silk, softly tailored tweeds, exquisitely cut skirts and trousers and *the finest shirts in the world*. It's the little touches that make all the difference in fashion, and no details have been overlooked—including specially designed cufflinks and charming white fabric gardenias to wear on the lapels. And here you'll get the kind of styling suggestions that have all but disappeared from *couture*. How to make the most of a pair of black *crêpe* trousers? For evening, wear them with a white silk Pierrot collar top and a length of spotted tulle tied round the waist in a bow. For day, team the trousers with a check jacket and spice with a white silk handkerchief in the pocket. The James Drew look is one of soft elegance, not severe chic. The lines are gentle, the figure suggested rather than defined. The clothes are meant to 'frame' and enhance unobtrusively, and they succeed so well that black—the most demanding background colour—never looks austere. Indeed, black is a house speciality and you can look forward to a host of dark delights including evening ensembles in black and gold *crêpe de Chine*, cut velvet evening suits, long slender cashmere cardigans, satin pyjama-style jackets, black silk jacquard tunics and black silk frocks for Spring, picked out in a pattern of cabbage roses. The new shirt collection is a *tour de force*—graceful silk shirts with Pierrot collars, wing collar shirts, lavish long band neck tunics and superb *crêpe* shirts with ruffled cuffs and a high ruffled neck held in place with a black *crêpe* bow. The favourite styles—classic, band neck, tie neck and Peter Pan collar—are back this Spring in softer shades with lots of flowing stripes, *ombré* tones, tiny prints and irresistible jacquards. All the fabrics, prints and colours are exclusive to James Drew, and all the silk shirts come with a generous sash to tie around the waist or wear as a cravat. A James Drew shirt is one of the best fashion investments you can make—and *don't miss the rest of the collection*!

Sample range—all prices approximate:

**Shirts:** in sizes 32-36. Cotton shirts from £16; silk shirts from £40. Pleated band neck tunic in voile, £30; long flannel tunics with shirt collar, to wear bloused with a belt, £30. Band neck silk tunics with separate scarf to wear as sash or cravat, £65. Pyjama type shirt with piping, £65. Wing collar shirts, Pierrot collar shirts and Alexandra collar shirts, all £50.

**Knitwear** in sizes 32-36, a selection including pure silk V-neck pullovers and cardigans, both £55. Classic V-neck cashmeres, £55; cashmere T-shirt in several colours, £35. *Day and evening wear*, a selection including silk dresses with box pleat skirt, tie neck and gathered back, from about £300. Smart pinstriped crepe skirt with kickpleat at back and plain wrapover front, £100. Crepe de chine blouson with small Peter Pan collar and tie neck, £75; matching skirt with stitched pleat to hip, £85. Tailored jackets in tweed, £165; in cashmere, £250; also in cut velvet for evenings. Black crepe evening trousers, about £95.

**Also:** white fabric gardenias, £1. Special cufflinks, all exclusive, £8

**Alfred Dunhill** 30 Duke Street, St. James's, SW1
01-493 9161
Mon.-Fri. 9.30-5.30, Sat. 9.30-4.30
Telegrams: *Salaams*, London SW1
(American Express, Diners)
By appointment to Her Majesty the Queen, suppliers of smokers'
requisites

Molière called tobacco 'the passion of all decent men', and no one has served the tawny temptress more diligently than these specialists in the fine art of smoking. Alfred Dunhill established his firm's reputation with tobaccos masterfully blended to order for clubmen who strolled up from Pall Mall to watch him at his work, and you can still come to the St. James's shop and have tobacco hand-blended to your order from a basic range of sixteen fine tobaccos from all over the world. All orders are recorded in a ledger called 'My Mixture', and if you want to savour the flavour of the past, you can flip back the pages and order yourself a mixture created for Rudyard Kipling or the Ameer of Bawaladur. Several of the founder's favourite mixtures are available in tins, including mild 'early Morning Pipe', stimulating 'Aperitif', and rich 'Nightcap'—real treats for smokers who like their tobaccos as carefully blended as fine spirits or perfumes. Upstairs you'll find the superb Cigar Room, scented with the fragrance of fine Havana tobacco and lined with cabinets that read like a roll of honour—Partagas, Hoyo de Monterrey, Ramon Allones, Romeo y Julieta, El Rey del Mundo, Montecristo Especial. More pleasures not to be sneezed at—Dunhill's special snuff, in six flavours. Dunhill provide the perfect accoutrements for each of their many delights—fine humidors and tobacco pouches, cigar cutters and holders, and the world-famous briar pipes and cigarette lighters. Look out for the new Dunhill 'S' lighters with angled flame, beautifully suitable for cigars, pipes or cigarettes. And to keep you company while the rich smoke curls upwards, Dunhill have a selection of fine writing instruments in precious metals, as well as chronometers, exclusively for them. There are also crystal goblets and decanters, luxurious ashtrays, and several amusing games.

Dunhill pride themselves on customer service. They are happy to store your cigar order in their large humidor and send them off to you in batches, will make any tobacco blend to order, and

Internationally acknowledged to be the finest cigarette in the world

dunhill The most distinguished tobacco house in the world

provide visitors with helpful advice on personal exports. **Dunhill's sumptuous catalogue is available free on request.**

Worth a separate trip in itself—Dunhill's **Pipe Museum**, displaying a selection from the founder's private collection of over two thousand pipes. There are elaborate carved pipes by the Maori of New Zealand and the Haida of British Columbia, Berber pipes from the North Sahara, eighteenth-century Staffordshire pipes and a host of others, watched over by an extremely rare carved snuff shop Scotsman. And look out for Sir Walter Raleigh's pipe and tobacco cabinet!

Sample range and prices:

**Tobacco mixtures:** a selection including Nightcap, Aperitif, Dunhill Light and Dark Flake, Elizabethan Mixture, Royal Yacht, Mr. Alfred's Own Mixture and the latest Aromatic from £1.59 for a 50gr. tin. **Dunhill Special Snuff**, in Menthus, Menthus Plus, Carnation, Oriental, French Carotte and Aperitif, £1.28 for a one-ounce jar. **Lighters:** new 'S' lighters for men and women in a nugget Line or Fine Line with Barley pattern, from £65 for silver plate, from £85 for gold plate. Classic oblong **Rollagas** models, textured in Square Tartan, Hobnail, Florentine, Chevron, Fine Barley, Basket, Line and Bark patterns, from £47 for silver plate, from £64 for gold plate. Slim dome **Rollagas** with laquered side panels from £79 for silver plate to £90 for gold plate. An 18ct gold lighthouse lighter mounted on an island of amethyst at £32,500. French-style **Sylphide** lighters, the ladies' favourite, in a range of textured patterns; £105 for sterling silver, £132 for silver gilt. In the impressive **Aldunil** range, textured lighters from £169.90 in sterling silver gilt. Also, a selection of table and desk lighters, including a textured Tallboy lighter in fine Barley pattern and a super satin-finished Rulerlite in silver or gold plate. **Pipes:** the renowned Dunhill briars, all bearing white dot trademark. Six briars—root, black, tanshell, redbark, shell and bruyère—in several styles and sizes. Prices from £21.10 for shell briars. Rare straight grain pipes from £75.10. Elegant gold-mounted pipes from £102 and with semi-precious bases and gold mounts from £450. For the connoisseur, seven Bruyère pipes in days of the week case, £398. **Cases and holder:** king-size cigarette cases in leather, £18.50 and in fine crocodile, £121. Shell cigar holder with 18ct gold band, £72 and 18ct gold cigarette holder with cabochon rubies, £217. Cigar humidors in various sizes and different veneers. **Pouches:** wrapover pouch in peccary hog-skin, £7.30; in club or school colours, £8.10. Rotator pouch, £5.85. Altogether pocket pouch to hold a pipe and an ounce and a half of tobacco, £6.50; vest pocket pouch, £5. Useful Box pouch that takes up minimum space in the pocket, £6.50.

**Elle**  92 New Bond Street, W1    01-629 4441
Mon.-Fri. 10-6.30, Thurs. 10-7.30, Sat. 10-5.30
(American Express, Barclaycard, Carte Blanche, Eurocard)

Top *prêt-à-porter* looks; cachet labels like Issey Miyake, Thierry
Mugler and Dorothée Bis; *très sympathique* English designers like
Bruce Oldfield and Salmon & Greene; accessories *à point* by
Mulberry and Herbert Johnson.

**Floris**  89 Jermyn Street, SW1    01-930 2885/4136
Mon.-Fri. 9.30-5.30, Sat 9.30-1
Telegrams: *Florissima*, London SW1
By appointment to Her Majesty the Queen, perfumers

Perfumers to the Court of St. James since 1730, Floris offer all
the scents of an English garden distilled into essences as rich and
rare as the Crown Jewels. Rose Geranium, Stephanotis, and
Jasmine bloom with Lily of the Valley and Red Rose—high
summer captured in crystal, royally displayed in gleaming
mahogany fittings. The Floris formulas are a carefully guarded
secret and the perfumes are compounded by members of the
family, for Floris is still very much a family firm and clients have
the unique benefit of an expert knowledge of scent that stretches
back for six generations. For gentlemen, Floris have toilet water
in the splendid 'Special No. 127'—created for a Russian Grand
Duke who lived in Paris during the *Belle Epoque*—and a range of
preparations scented with light citrus and sandalwood 'Floris No.
89': talc, toilet water soap, after shave and **charming hand-turned
elmwood bowls full of shaving soap.** Ladies will find dressing
table delights aplenty—the flower perfumes, Ormonde and
Sandalwood scents, toilet waters and powders, hand cream, fine
hair brushes and swansdown powderpuffs. There are pomanders
and *pot-pourris*, extravagant cut-glass decanters filled with scent,
scented candles and a dramatic perfume vaporiser that fills a room
with rich perfume seconds after you switch on the lights. Best of
all, Floris have all the trimmings for the great English bath—bath
cubes, bath essences, Bathofloris Bath Salts, long handled

beechwood pure bristle bath brushes, nail brushes, honeycomb and Turkish sponges and bath soaps in six of the flower fragrances. Floris's rich superfatted soaps are of exceptional quality, and they suggest you enjoy them to the full by removing the wrappers and using the soaps as sachets until required. Christmas is a very special time at Floris, and there are always lots of delightful presents like the new Ironstone china dish filled with *pot-pourri* and the new oval pomander pendants and key fobs with a pretty floral design. The service is impeccable, and although Floris scents are now available throughout the country and abroad, there are many things like the popular Rose Mouthwash and Thamar preparations you will only find here in Jermyn Street.

Floris catalogue and mail order particulars available on request.

Sample range and prices:

**Perfumes:** in Jasmine, Lily of the Valley, Malmaison (Carnation), Red Rose, Stephanotis, Ormonde, Sandalwood. Handbag size, £2.75; other sizes from £5.45. **Toilet waters:** in the perfume scents and Limes, Rose Geraniums, Special No 127 from £2.90. **Bath essences:** in all the scents above except Red Rose and Sandalwood, from £2.25. **Bath cubes** in Stephanotis and Ormonde, £1.25 for a box of six. **Toilet powders:** in all the bath essence scents. In flask, £1.20; in box with puff, £2.75. **Toilet soaps:** lovely superfatted preparations in Jasmine, Lily of the Valley, Ormonde, Rose Geranium, Stephanotis and Verbena. Individually boxed toilet-sized tablets, 65p and bath-sized tablets, £1.09.

Verbena or No. 89, £1.95. Refills, £1.30. Preparations in Floris No. 89 scent: after-shave from £1.75; roll-on deodorant, £1.20; brilliantine and hair lotion, both from £1.75. Brilliantine oil, £1.35; toilet boxes from £2.90; toilet soap in boxes of three, £2.55; lather or brushless shaving cream, £1.30.

## Also

Paper *sachets* in a choice of six scents, £1.65 for three; lace-covered satin sachets, £1.50. Long-handled natural bristle *bath brushes*, several sizes from £8.10. *Pomanders* in bone chine, from £3.60; miniature pomander pendants, £2.95 and key fobs, £1.95. Packs of *potpourri* from £1.65; ironstone china dish of potpourri, £3.45. *Perfume vaporisers* in Jasmine, Ormonde, Sandalwood, Stephanotis. Complete set, £2.45; refill essence, £1.85. *Scented Candle* in ceramic lantern holder, £5.95; box of three candles, £2.85.

## For Gentlemen

**Shaving soap:** in wooden bowls, scented with Rose Geranium,

*Beaded by Hand.*
*Pure Silk Crepe de Chine*

*By Les Lansdown at Fortnum and Mason*

# Fortnum & Mason 181 Piccadilly, W1  01-734 8040

Mon.-Fri. 9-5, Sat. 9-1: longer hours at Christmas
(Access, American Express, Barclaycard, Diners)

If you come just before the hour, you can glide through the main entrance to the tune of 'The Lass with the Delicate Air', played on the bells of Fortnum & Mason's unique clock as the clockwork figures of the founders bow to each other with gentle *bonhommie*. Inside you'll find Fortnum's legendary larder—brimming with delicacies like marrons in vanilla syrup, Beluga caviar, Bradenham hams and a princely panoply of curries and chutneys—that give real zest to Brillat-Savarin's maxim *'Tell me what a man eats, and I'll tell you what he is.' Where* he eats is just as important, and Fortnum's famous picnic hampers always add relish to Derby Day, Ascot and Glyndebourne. You can recognize the assistants by their black tailcoats, but don't be put off by their formal appearance. Fortnum and Mason pride themselves on personal service, so you can ask them to pack up a box of Fortnum's own chocolates or a litre bottle of Guerlain's Imperiale *eau de cologne* to be sent along with your hamper of goodies. And don't stop at the pickled crabapples and brandied peaches, because many more treats are in store. Just inside the main entrance you'll find Fortnum's own soaps, bath preparations and *superb eau de cologne* in two scents—perfect as presents, and very well priced. Go on to the upper floors for clothes, perfumes, shoes, hats, lingerie, a large selection of classic handbags, a toy department ranged around a miniature carousel and a luggage department—*the only place in London where you can buy pieces by Louis Vuitton*. You can make a whole day of it at Fortnum's—there's a ladies hairdressing salon on the second floor, a men's hairdressing salon on the third, and five restaurants serving everything from morning coffee to afternoon tea. Try a trasty brioche, croissant or pastry from Fortnum's bakery on the premises, and watch the *house model* showing clothes and accessories from the fashion and leather departments. Christmas is a lovely time at Fortnum's and you can take a Dickensian delight in Fortnum's fabulous Christmas hampers, plum pudding and brandy butter and *the most elegant crackers in the world*.

Sample range—all prices
approximate:

## Restaurants

St. James Restaurant, Mezzanine, Buttery and Spanish Bar open 9-5 Monday through Friday. Fountain Restaurant, separate entrance in Jermyn Street, long a favourite with theatregoers, open until 11.30 pm Mondays through Saturday.

## Toiletries

Specially made for Fortnum & Mason. Soap in lemon verbena, stephanotis, violet, jasmine, hyacinth or tea rose scents, box of six in hand size, £1.85. Box of four violet soaps, hand size, 80p. Fortnum's soap for men, smart black and gold box, chamois scent, £1 for box of four hand-sized. Fortnum's fine eau de cologne for men, £1.25, and eau de cologne, £1.85. Fortnum's soap in Rose Geranium, Verbena and Woodland Fern, boxes of six; hand size, £3.50; guest size, £2.85. Also, bath essence, talc, bubble bath, feather bath salts and hand lotion in the same three scents.

## Cosmetics and Perfumes

Cosmetics by Dior, Guerlain, Germaine Monteil, Elizabeth Arden, Lancôme, Clinique, Estée Lauder, Ultima II and Revlon. *Three very special perfumes created by Stanley Hall as a tribute to his friend, the late Sir Noël Coward.*

The scents are Easy Virtue, Blithe Spirit and Conversation Piece—*the Master's own favourite was Easy Virtue.* Also, perfumes by Hermes, Guerlain, Lanvin, Givenchy, Balenciaga, Dior, Gucci, Rochas, Carven, Balmain, Caron, Gres, Yves Saint Laurent, Jean Desprez, Jean Patou, Mary Chess, Taylor of London, Paco Rabanne. *Exclusive* to Fortnum: 1 litre bottle of Guerlain's Imperiale eau de cologne, first created for Napoleon III and the Empress Eugenie, £45. Also, sunglasses by Oliver Goldsmith.

## For Ladies

**Separates and day wear** in sizes 8-16 by Jean & Martin Pallant and Tiktiner, **coats** and **raincoats** by Jobis. **Knitwear** by Luisa Spagnoli, Nucci D'Angio, Valerie Louthan and Ballantyne. **Evening wear** by Jean Muir, Leonard, Les Lansdown, Bessi and Salvador. **Cruise and resort wear** by Tiktiner, Rosemarie Reid and Armonia. **Hats** by Graham Smith, Phillip Somerville and Frederick Fox. Also, *lingerie*, shoes, scarves and belts. *Fine handbags by S. Launer, and Launer leather cream to keep them at their best.*

## For men

Suits by Chester Barrie in sizes 38-46, long short and regular fittings. Also, velvet jackets, blazers, trousers, knitwear, nightwear, shoes and accessories.

## Bill Gibb 138 New Bond Street, W1

01-629 3579
Mon.-Fri. 10-6, Sat. 10-4.30
(Access, American Express, Barclaycard, Diners,
Masterchage)

Bill Gibb is the master magician of fashion and his sea-change
shop is pure enchantment—mother-of-pearl walls, tables made of
seashells bound with ropes of pearls, mirrors frosted with delicate
sea foam, iridescent shimmers everywhere. Bill Gibb's are the
ultimate evening dresses—sparkly shiny hand-embroidered
fantasies, the favourite dresses of the most beautiful women in the
world. Bill Gibb turns knitwear into something very special too.
Full of colour and imagination, the knits look perfect from
morning to evening and come with matching accessories so you
can put yourself together in lots of different ways. This Spring
you can slip into Bill Gibb's new pure silk knits, or wrap yourself
in fine light *bouclé*—easy coats, skirts, off-the-shoulder and halter
tops—patterned with a trellis and flower motif devised by Kaffe
Fassett. Frocks are soft and feminine, in pastel cheesecloth and
*broderie Anglaise,* lots of full skirts and cap sleeve tops trimmed
with white embroidery, silk and brocade waistcoats to wear over
double lace skirts. The graceful smock shape appears as a long
Pierrot blouson in Harlequin motley print silk, and there are
smock-style linen jackets with old-fashioned flower stitching down
the front and soft full skirts to match. Evening brings spectacular
creations in handpainted *panné* velvet, silk and net—each painting
evokes a romantic time or season—sunrise, sunset, summer,
spring. And after the ball you can look forward to the delights of
the luxurious new lounging collection—lace-trimmed silk and
satin camisoles, kimono wraps, pyjamas, nightgowns and
negligés—in *lingerie* shades of blush pink, celeste blue and *eau de
Nil.* The clothes are lovely, and the atmosphere is lovelier
still—easy, warm and helpful. The girls are the best-looking,
friendliest staff in London—all best-dressed by Bill Gibb of
course. Beautiful clothes deserve beautiful personal service, and
that's exactly what you get here—right down to the Bill Gibb
Cocktail served to special visitors, a wonderful concoction of
orange juice, mandarin brandy and Beefeater's gin. You can take
all the time you want—and advice, assistance and smiles are freely
given. It's hard to walk out of Bill Gibb—but when you do, you'll
walk out happy.

45

Bill Gibb's evening dresses can be made to order in standard sizes for no extra charge: allow six weeks to two months. There is a nominal charge for special sizes that require fittings. Wedding dresses also made to order, allow two months.

Sample range and approximate prices:

Clothes in sizes 8-16. **Knits** from £34-£130, average price, £42. **Dresses** for daywear from £120. **Suits,** average price £146.

**Evening wear** from £180. **Lingerie:** embroidered camisole top and matching shorts, in silk satin, from £194. **Scarves** from £24.

**Gucci**  27 Old Bond Street, W1
01-629 2716/7
Mon.-Fri. 9-5.30, Sat. 9-5
(Access, American Express, Barclaycard, Diners, Eurocard)

Gucci's GG monogram and green-red-green stripe are international status symbols, their fine shoes and scarves badges of membership in the good life. Now established in forty-eight cities around the world, Gucci have gone beyond the shoes and fashion accessories that were their first specialities, and the Gucci shops now offer everything you need for a total Gucci life style—tableware, towels, umbrellas, jewellery, game sets, perfume, and a complete collection of men's and women's ready-to-wear designed by Paolo Gucci. A special presentation of the Gucci autumn ready-to-wear collection was the highlight of the Fashion Guide's 1977 Awards held at the Italian Embassy. As always, leather was a focal point—peccary, suede and exotic ostrich, teamed with toning knits and herringbone tweeds, textured cord and fine wool, boots in tweed and leather. The GG motif linked smart day and evening styles—there were raincoats lined in blanket-look GG fabric, dark suits with tiny red stripes and GGs, new Gucci ties, Gucci bulldog pullovers, black silk satin shirts embossed with GG's. Everything had the Gucci look to perfection—well-balanced, well-matched and well-made. Every season Gucci has more to offer, and whatever you choose will pass as good taste anywhere in the world.

Sample range—all prices approximate:

# For women

Shirts and blouses in cotton from £35; in silk from £75. Trousers from £63. Jeans in blue denim with leather trim and GG motif in studs, and leather-trimmed jeans in a range of colours, £42-£48. Skirts in tweed, suede and gabardine, from £110. Dresses in wool from £105; silk day and evening dresses from £170. Shoes: from £32; shoes with gilt and enamel motifs, from £39. Also, evening shoes in GG satin.

# For men

Shirts in sizes 14½-16½, some 17½'s; in silk from £59. Trousers in sizes 30-38, all with unfinished bottoms, from £34. Jackets in formal, evening and sporty styles, in tweed, calf and cashmere, from £180; overcoats from £240; raincoats from £170. Sweaters in camel hair and cashmere, from around £95. Shoes from £48, slippers from £35.

# Also

Classic Gucci open top shoulder bags with GG monogram clasp, in leather and canvas, from £62. Formal leather bags from £70; evening bags from £45. Belts for men and women from £17; smart reversible belts, £28. Printed silk scarves from £22; cotton scarves from £10. Wallets from £23. Gucci pens, £25, and electronic lighters, from £35. Desk sets, seven to nine pieces, from £350.

---

# Hermes 155 Bond Street, W1   01-499 8856
Mon.-Fri. 9.30-6.30, Sat. 9.30-5.30
(Access, American Express, Barclaycard, Carte Blanche, Diner's Club)

---

'Cocher, aux Bois et au trot!' In the golden days of the Second Empire, the dressings of the most elegant equipages and *calèches* came from Hermes, in the Faubourg St. Honoré. Nearly a century and half later, Hermes still makes the finest saddles in Europe—and 'Hermes' still means elegance, uncompromising quality and the best brass, leather and silk in the world. Hermes have always been *handmakers*, not producers—and their workmanship is straggering in this day and age. *At Hermes, every handbag is made by a single craftsman, start to finish.* The pieces are cut individually on a slate block, and literally sculpted into shape. A Hermes bag is really two bags, the outer—and the inner fine lining, tailored from the inside into the curve, caught and pulled, so the flaps always fall back with a movement of their own. Handwork of any sort is rare today, and other *ateliers* now work on a production line basis, handing pieces on down the chain until they are finished. Only Hermes can say that a handbag 'made by Hermes' is made by Hermes. The workmanship is what makes Hermes unique. Small pieces are not much cheaper than the large, because they involve nearly as much work. Even the canvas bag piped and lined with leather shows little appreciable price difference because the workmanship is, if anything, more demanding.

Hermes scarves are *not* the most expensive and yet the sheer quality and weight of the silk are unsurpassed. Introduced in the Twenties, Hermes scarves are the loveliest pieces of colourful silk in the world—superbly-made pieces of drapery. Don't just knot it under your chin—twist it into a rouleau and wear it low on the forehead, wear it round the hips tied at one side, tie it like a turban, knot it over your shoulder, wear it as a bandeau on the beach! The first Hermes scarf is always a great moment, and many people collect them like first editions. The traditional association of horses and harness work has been carried through into Hermes' collection of jewellery and *objets*—stirrup cufflinks and bracelets, scissors and corkscrews with horsehead handles, acajou calf bracelets and silver link bracelets with buckle clasps. Hermes brass work has always been superb—the perfect clasp, the tiny link, the elegant buckle are all Hermes hallmarks. Hermes clocks and watches are particularly fine—the workings are made by the best Swiss specialists, but the cases and carrying cases have been made in the Hermes *atelier*, and show the unmistakeable house style. There are Limoges ashtrays, furs by Berger Christiensen specially made for Hermes, a choice selection of ladies' clothes, a menswear collection downstairs, towels and dressing gowns, luggage and toilet cases, and toiletries from Hermes' Equipage, Caleche and Amazone ranges.

**Jaeger**  204-206 Regent Street, W1   01-734 4050
Mon.-Sat. 9.30-5.30, Thurs. 9-7
(Access, American Express, Barclaycard, Diners)

Contemporary classic clothes for ladies, for description see separate listing under 'Knightsbridge' section.

# Herbert Johnson Ladies 80 Grosvenor Street,
W1 01-439 7397
Mon.-Fri. 9-5.30
(Access, American Express, Barclaycard, Diners, Carte Blanche)
By appointment to Her Majesty the Queen, hatters

**Close your eyes and think of England**—walking the course at Badminton, Eights Week on the river, picnics at Smith's, race meetings at Newmarket, weddings in the village church and, always, hats by Herbie J. The distaff side of the famous men's hatters, this cosy shop is the place to find just the sort of things a chap likes to see—classic tweeds, big soft berets, simple stetsons and, best of all, the summer garden fantasies that roses wear so well. This is *real English millinery*—floral trimmings scattered and coaxed with a gardener's instinct, patted and pruned with a florist's spry touch, tied up with ribbons and love. It's flowers, flowers, flowers from the end of April through July—not stiff mean shapes with single brittle blossoms but real wide-brimmed panamas, glossy straws, woven sisals and pretty boaters, trimmed *all the way round* with fine fabric blooms that would turn Nature green if she weren't so already. Gather daffodils, poppies, magnolias, violets, handmade organza roses—anthing you like. Hats can be made to order, or to match your outfit, in ten days—at no extra cost. It's tweeds galore from August onwards, quite the nicest in England—soft tweed Peatmore pull-ons, trilbys and stylish flat caps, in scores of subtle shades. The town hats are paragons of pure simplicity—velours and felt stetsons, graceful felts with rounded crown and brim—always trimmed with restraint: just a grosgrain band, and, perhaps, a tasteful spray of feathers. There are lots of useful knits, *the best selection of cotton scarves in London*, and charming specialities like the souwester hat in proofed gabardine, *so* useful for young mothers caught in a downpour while pushing prams or carrying shopping. And don't forget the riding collection—*sidesaddle veils*, and riding hats to order: this is the only place where you'll find ladies grosgrain top hats for four in hand driving! Herbie J. hats are available at top London stores and from the travelling hat shop that visits Burleigh, Badminton, the Game Fair and the Wembley Horse Show, but *the irresistable millinery is only available* here. Mrs. Turk, Herbie J.'s milliner, has seen a generation of ladies through their finest hours—let her see you through yours.

Sample range—all prices approximate:

**Special summer hats** from £18.50-£25; fully flower-trimmed hats from about £22. Straw boaters, very nice on young girls, £12. Panama trilbys, £9.90; wide brimmed panamas, copies of the famous velours, £9.90. **Tweeds:** Peatmore pull-ons with belt-loop band trim, £17.50; plain, £9.90. Tweed trilby, £12.50. Tweed flat cap, from £7.50-£12.50: *tweed hats can be made to order in two weeks at no extra charge*. Also to order, tweed caps and matching scarves, £10.50-£17 the set. Wide or medium-brimmed **stetsons**, £25. Big soft berets with visors, in cord, £8.90: in velvet, £11.95. **Knits:** handknit seven foot scarf, £7.90; knitted hat to match, £4.50-£8.50. Knitted bowlers: in mohair, £10; in wool, £5.95. Stitched gabardine **souwester**, £9.90; velvet souwester, £15. **Sidesaddle veils**, £1.50 **Cotton scarves** from £1. Riding hats, to order only, prices on application. **Hatboxes**, £1.50 Also: reblocking, retrimming and *excellent personal service*.

---

# Liberty 210-220 Regent Street, W1   01-734 1234
Mon.-Fri. 9-5.30, Thurs. 9-7, Sat. 9.30-5
(American Express, Barclaycard, Diners, Mastercharge)
By appointment to Her Majesty Queen Elizabeth the Queen Mother, silk merchants ★

---

Liberty is the most romantic of London's great stores, a rambling reminder of the elegance of the Raj, the exotic delights of the East, the delicate charms of the Pre-Raphaelites and the Victorian heyday of an Empire on whom the sun never set. This charming establishment was the first store to create a *total life style*—they introduced London to soft Indian cottons, rich silks and cashmeres, commissioned designs from craftsmen like William Morris, launched the fashion for loose flowing robes, imported jade from their own jade mine, created the fabulous Liberty prints inspired by Eastern colours and textiles, and gave the world the magical 'Liberty look'. Today, Liberty is as bewitching as ever, and with romance and mystery flooding back into fashion, there's no better place to treat yourself to a lovely time. Start out with the Liberty prints on cotton, wool and silk—*the most ravishing fabrics in the world*. The collection includes everything from the original William Morris designs to masterful designs by Susan Collier. Look out for her swirling florals to make into frilled flounced skirts, new small feminine prints that look like rosebuds on caviar, and the superb new 'Pharoah' furnishing fabric design, inspired by an antique Egyptian tapestry. If you don't sew, Liberty have their prints made up into everything you could possibly want—bags, hats, dresses, skirts, tops, evening dresses, dressing gowns, bikinis, children's clothes, shirts and ties, and there's *a new linen department with Liberty print trimmed sheets and towels*, Liberty-print duvet covers and china that repeats the Liberty print motifs. To go with them, there are white Victorian-style nightgowns specially made for Liberty, Liberty-print nightshirts—and a few tiny pieces of Liberty print *lingerie*. The Liberty scarves are world-famous, more beautiful Liberty prints on silk, cotton and wool, but there's much more to Liberty than prints. The Oriental Jewellery department has the best selection of semi-precious stones in London—jade, rose quartz, amethyst, cornelian, malachite and many more—made up into lavish bead necklaces; wear four or five at a time for the Helena Rubinstein look! And make sure you see the antique carved jade, Mongolian silver jewellery and antique hair ornaments set with kingfisher feathers. Downstairs there's a Craftsman's Gallery that continues Liberty's artistic tradition, and here you'll find fascinating one-off creations—imaginative ceramics, fine leatherwork, whimsical wooden puzzles and stunning dressing table boxes; Liberty will also arrange for special commissions. The bridal department has antique bridal veils and wax flower chaplets to go with them, the millinery department has fine designer hats by Alan Couldridge, and there's a new Oriental Bazaar with the best of the East, from chopsticks to carpets. *Liberty is one of the best-loved stores in the world—don't miss it!*

Sample range—all prices approximate:

*On the lower and ground floors:*

# One-Offs

The Craftsman's Gallery, with a constantly changing selection of lovely pieces by top craftsmen, at very reasonable prices. Sample range: Large natural ceramic crock with growing grain modelled in relief along the bottom and a tiny fieldmouse modelled on the lid, by Ken Bright, £120. Mugs by Carol McNicholl, in the shape of a half-unrolled carpet, £5 each. Delightful wooden puzzles by Kathy Wilson, from £9.50. **The dressing table of today**—a superb cosmetics box in stripy zebrano wood with deep drawers, a jewellery tray, a mirror set into the lid and a matching hand-mirror, by B. W. Howard, £250. Droll china by Linda Gunn-Russell: strawberry teaset for six, £87.50; deep white bowls with colourful snakes draped along the rims, £8.25. Three-piece flamingo tureen: bottom, lid and ladle with flamingo head handle, six bowls to match, £139 the set.

'Pharoah' in Union Cotton

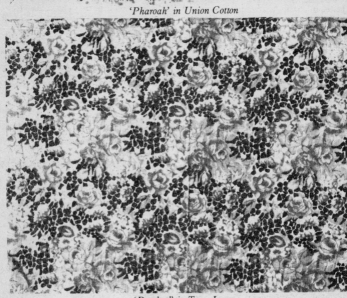

'Rosebud' in Tana Lawn

## Liberty scarves

**In silk:** £4.95 for 18″ square, £7.95 for 23″ square; £8.95 for 27″ square, £13.95 for 36″ square; £9.50 for long scarf. **In chiffon:** 36/36″ square, £9.50; long scarf, £9.95. **In wool:** £6.95 for 27″ square. Large Varuna wool shawls, about one metre square, £34.95; cashmere shawl, £70: in two paisley prints only. **In cotton:** Tana Lawn fabric squares, 23″, £2.75; 18″ square of Liberty printed cotton, £2.25. **Jubilee scarf,** modelled on the scarf that Liberty created to mark Queen Victoria's jubilee, in silk, 36″ square, £13.95.

## Oriental Jewellery

**Jade:** in shades that range from palest greenish white to deep spinach green. Jade bangles from £45.50; string of medium pale jade beads, £95; pendant necklace of three carved jade pieces and a pink tourmaline, £50. Jade pendant earrings from about £65. In **green aventurine:** strings of very large dark green beads, from £55. Strings of light green **bowenite** beads, £25. Strings of pearl-sized light green **agate,** £22.50. In **rose quartz:** long ropes of graduated beads, £80; small regular bead necklaces from £49.50. **Amethyst** bead necklaces from £49.50. In **cornelian,** shades from light to dark: bead choker necklaces from £22.50; long rope of pearl-sized beads, £135; necklaces of fluted cornelian beads and **cloisonne** enamel beads, £47.50. **Cloisonné enamel bead** necklaces, several sizes and

shapes, from about £70. **Malachite** bead necklaces, from £85-£175. **Turquoise:** from £10 for stud earrings to £200 for beautifully carved pendant, also: rings and necklaces. **Coral:** from £22.50 for a choker of cylindrical coral beads to £995 for long chunky necklace of antique coral. **Mongolian silver jewellery** from £7.50, antique hair ornaments with kingfisher feather inlay in **excellent** condition, and **small crystal balls** in three sizes.

*On the second floor*

## Fabrics

On the second floor, you will find Liberty's famous fabric department, with the complete collection of Liberty prints, the largest selection of fine silks in Europe, and a remarkable cotton collection with a constantly-changing selection of unusual cottons from all over Europe.

**Liberty prints: Country cotton:** a robust rustly weave in 100% cotton, 90cms wide, from £2.25 per metre. **Tana Lawn,** fine lawn in a 100% pure cotton. The new look is fields of flowers—asters, daisies, cornflowers, bluebells fresh as a summer morning. Tana Lawns, 90cms wide, £3.15 per metre. *Lightest of all,* **Liberty-print voiles,** 90cms wide, from £3.15 per metre. **Warm fabrics:** Liberty-print Jubilee, 82% cotton and 18% wool, 90cms wide, from £3.15 per metre. Liberty print Varuna, 100% pure wool, 135cms wide, from £7.75 per metre.

**Liberty-print silks:** Liberty print Richmond silks, 45in wide, from £7.40 per metre. Liberty print silk chiffon 36in wide, from £5.30 per metre. Tyrian Liberty print silk, from £4.50 per metre. Liberty print silk *crêpe*, 45in wide, from £12.50 per metre. Liberty print Honan silk, from £6 per metre.

**Cottons:** This department is a real find for do-it-yourselfers who love natural fabric with lots of unusual colour and texture interest. The selection is always changing and because there are plenty of one-offs and non-repeatable specialities imported from all over Europe, it is impossible to guarantee that particular items will be in stock. However, at the time of going to press, the range included Java printed Dutch cotton at £3.90 a metre; English shirtings, 90cms wide, at £4.20 a metre; Swiss hand painted voiles, 140cms wide, at £16 per metre; Austrian satins, 90cms wide, at £4.00 per metre; Swiss sheer jersey, 140cms wide, at £12 per metre; and Swiss voiles, 140cms wide, at £9.90 per metre. In the plain cotton range, Liberty's stock such things as Irish Linen, 115cms wide, at £5.60 per metre; self striped cheesecloth, 140cms wide, at £5.00 per metre; and velours from Germany, 160cms wide, at £12 per metre.

## Children's Clothes

A fine collection of Liberty print dresses for little girls from ages one to ten. Besides the classic smocked frock—with hand-whipped collar and cuffs and hand-smocking all the way

round—styles include simpler sleeveless sundresses and straight-cut dresses with dainty puffed sleeves. Prices depend on the amount of handwork involved and the size. Fully hand-worked smocked dresses for little girls aged one to two, in Jubilee or Tana Lawn, are from £15; simple sleeveless sundresses start at about £7.50. Liberty also do special prints for Cacharel and the Cacharel Liberty print collection for little boys and girls aged four to twelve includes short-sleeved button-up shirts for ages eight to ten, from £10.70; long sleeved shirts for ages four to six, £11; long-sleeved Jubilee shirts for ages eight to twelve, about £15; and quilted cotton dungarees for ages two to six, approximately £16.

## For Women

All sizes 8-16

**Model Room:** Dresses by Nettie Vogue from £100; Liberty print Tana Lawn dresses in exclusive styles from £60; Italian and French dresses and suits; Bonnie Cashin clothes; and beautiful pure silk and cotton jersey dresses by Pucci.

**Day Dresses:** Liberty print dress in Varuna or Tana Lawn with matching scarf or belt by Hildrebrand from £50; Jubilee print skirt and top from £40; Varuna Liberty print dress with smocked neckline by Sujon from £56. Also dresses by Taramina and Louis Feraud.

**Lingerie and Cruisewear:** Jubilee and Tana Lawn hostess and leisure dresses by Sara Fermi in several styles from £32-£40.

Victorian style nightgowns and Liberty print nightshirts, from about £26.

**Coats and suits:** Coats by Louis Feraud, Aquascutum, MicMac, Rodex, Burberry, Wetherall, Mansfield and Feminella in sizes 8-16.

**Separates:** Co-ordinates by Juliet Dunn, Daniel Hechter, Cacharel, Jeff Banks and a large selection of day and evening separates. Tana Lawn shirts from £13.50, Liberty print skirts from £15.

**Accessories:** Shoulder or clutch bags in Tana Lawn and leather from £12.25, Liberty print umbrellas from £10.75. Tana Lawn jewellery roll from £11.95, Liberty print double sided cosmetic bag from £3.95, folding tote bag in Liberty print from £5.95, Liberty print luggage from £17.95, purses, passport holders

and wallets in Liberty prints from £8.95, choker and wristband in Liberty print from £2.95.

---

## For Men

**Ties:** Summary Tana Lawn ties £3.45, pure silk ties from £7.50, Varuna ties from £8.50 and Lantana ties from £3.75.

**Shirts:** Tana Lawn Liberty print from £15.85.

**Dressing Gowns:** In a range of lengths and fabrics £22 to £78.

**Knitwear:** Cashmere slipover faced with heavy Liberty print silk in a selection of colours £33, cashmere pullovers £37, 100% camel hair jackets £45. Fashionable ready-to-wear by Tom Gilbey, Givenchy, Von Furstenberg, Cacharel and Piatelli.

---

# Long Tall Sally  40 Chiltern Street, W1   01-487 3370
Mon.-Fri. 10-6, Thurs. 10-7, Sat. 10-4

---

**Tall is beautiful** at Long Tall Sally, where long-stemmed ladies can really see themselves in the right perspective. Everything in this designer boutique is tall—rails, mirrors, even the assistants—and you'll start to stand up straight the minute you walk in the door. No short cuts have been taken with Long Tall Sally's exclusive collection—the height of style—specially commissioned from Maureen Baker, Jennifer Hocking, Dora Reisser, Georgina Loizou, Brigid Foley and Annie Gough, new young designers and houses like Emcar. There are lots of the things that tall ladies wear better than anyone else—culottes, blousons, long loose shirts and big chunky knits—plenty of hard-to-find basics like tailored blazers, silk shirts, trench raincoats and coats, all beautifully made in fine fabrics and colours. A good fit turns inches into assets, and nothing has been overlooked—the shirts and silky polos are long in the body as well as the sleeves, and *never* ride up; all the trousers come with unfinished hems, there are lots of sashed and tie-belted styles to break the length of the line, and day skirts really do come to the top of the boot. All the proportions have been carefully worked out so you can *think positive, walk tall and look great*. You can put together anything from a casual young jeans-and-handknit outfit to a classic day-in-town ensemble and you don't have to stop being stylish when the shadows lengthen because Long Tall Sally have a fine collection of evening wear, long velours and towelling robes, and lovely lace-trimmed satin nightdresses and *lingerie* by Charles Grahame. Service is warm and friendly and a *free mini mail order catalogue* is published three times a year, so if you're one of the 2,000,000 women in Britain over 5'8", this is the shop for you!

Clothes in sizes 10-18, sample range and prices:

**Shirts:** Polyester shirts from £10; Viyella and cotton shirts from £15. Fly-fronted silk shirts with scarf to use as cravat or tie belt, in lots of colours, from about £25. Cowl neck blousons, about £30.

**Trousers:** In gabardine, flannel, cotton and cord, French and English cuts, from £20-£25; also, jeans and jumpsuits.

**Skirts:** A-line wool skirt, fully lined, £16. Selection of skirts from £22, including full and tailored culottes in gabardine and tweed.

**Coats:** A selection, including classic doublebreasted coat in herringbone tweed, £82; check-lined proofed trench coat, £45; **tweed hacking jackets** and black velvet **blazers**, both from £45.

**Lingerie:** By Charles Grahame, lace-trimmed satin half slips in fondant colours, from £13.50; satiny nightgowns from £19; long satin nightgowns from £25. Also, kimono robes from about £17, long velours kimono robes from about £35.

**Evening Wear:** Long gathered *panné* velvet skirt in beige, in peonies and poppies in Chinese blue and red, £65. Long smooth six panel wool crepe skirt A-line skirt in brown or black, £52, to wear with cream jersey tie neck blouse, £22.

**Also:** Very special **handknits**, wool and silky polos, long line Chanel style shetland **cardigans, dresses,** Mulberry belts and *appliqué* suede pochettes.

---

**Marks & Spencer** 458 Oxford Street, W1
01-486 6151
Mon.-Fri. 9.30-5.30, Thurs. 9.30-7.30, Sat. 9-5.30

---

**'Do it big, do it right, give it class'** used to be the motto of

M.G.M. studios, and if anyone is following on in the tradition it's the remarkable Marks & Spencer retail chain. The best place to see the Marks magic in action is their showplace store at Marble Arch where crowds of shoppers queue up at opening time as eagerly as the cinemagoers of yesteryear, and buy more stock per square foot than in any other shop in the world. Every week the Marks chain serves 13,000,000 customers from many countries and all walks of life. Princess Anne and Princess Grace have popped into the Marble Arch store and many foreign visitors save up for an annual trip to Marks, knowing the wear they'll get from the clothes will significantly offset the cost of travel. Everything that bears Marks & Spencer's **St Michael** label is of excellent quality. Nothing reaches the floor until it has been subjected to exhaustive durability tests, and because they only run winners, Marks can count on a high turnover and you can count on Marks for the best of British value. With 254 stores in the U.K., three in France, one in Belgium and 70 in Canada, Marks are certainly doing it big and right—but shoppers will be more interested in the touches of class that are moving the chain steadily up-market. The Marble Arch shop is the place to find men's cashmere coats at £95 and men's leather trench coats at £75, ladies cashmere coats at £120, ladies cashmere fine ribbed pullovers at £25, big mohair and wool plaid travelling rugs for £17.99 and, at Christmas, special luxury *lingerie* sets—last year lace-trimmed satin slips with matching French knickers. The Marble Arch shop is also the place to find Mark's most up-to-the-minute fashion lines—last autumn there were ladies tweed hacking jackets at £30, tattersal check country smock dresses at £9.99 and cotton-backed sporty track suits for men at £10.99. Available in selected shops only, these high flyers give very good value for money, and all shops carry the down-to-earth basic range that includes lambswool pullovers from £4.99 and pure cotton bikini briefs from 59p. Originally known for their underwear and knitwear, Marks have expanded into ready-to-wear for men, women and children, shoes, accessories, home furnishings, luggage, tablewear, books, food, spirits, toiletries and cosmetics, so you can dress yourself at Marks from top to toe, and celebrate with Marks champagne drunk from Marks cut crystal goblets. There are no changing rooms but sizes and lengths are clearly marked in Imperial and metric measurements, and if you get back to your home or hotel room and decide you don't want something after all, you can take it back to any branch of the store for an exchange or cash refund, no questions asked. The Marble Arch store has a *bureau de change* in the basement, and all U.K. branches sell gift vouchers that can be used to purchase all St Michael goods, including food, in U.K. branches.

Sample range—all prices approximate:

## Knitwear

The champion department in the Marks & Spencer stable, bringing in the highest sterling value of all their clothing sales. Knits come in a vast selection of styles, colours and weights including: **For men**; in sizes 36-44: lambswool V- and crew-neck pullovers and botany wool pullovers, both from £4.99. Shetland nylon pullovers from £3.99; ribbed Shetland pullovers from £5.50. Patterned Shetland cardigans from £6.99; patterned slipovers, from £2.99. Cashmere jumpers with V- or roll-neck, from £17. **For women**: in sizes 12-18; long-sleeved acrylic jumpers from £3.50; Shetland jumpers in crew- and polo-neck styles, from £4.99. Smart lambswool cardigan with sporty shirt collar, £6.99. Cowl neck cashmere jumpers from £14.99; cardigans from £18.99. Fine ribbed cowl necked cashmere pullover, £25. Aran-look acrylic knits in sizes 10-16; pullovers, £7.95; matching toggle-fastened jacket, £12.99; matching long hooded coat, £15.99.

## Ladies Lingerie

This department sells more goods by piece than any other, including an astounding total of over forty million knickers a year. **Knickers** come in three basic styles—briefs,

bikinis and mini bikinis—with French style knickers in selected stores. Range includes cotton modal mini bikinis, 59p; patterned polyester bikinis, 89p; combed cotton bikinis edged with lace and candystriped bikinis in pure cotton, both 75p; nylon mini bikinis, 79p; nylon *lingerie* bikinis with lace insets, 85p; lace-trimmed nylon French style knickers, £1.99. **Nightwear**: **nightdresses** in polyester cotton, nylon and brushed nylon, many styles and colours in a total size range of 32-44, including mid-length polyester cotton nightgown with broderie Anglais sleeves and hem, £4.99; long boudoir style nightie with lace sleeves and ribbon-trimmed neck, £4.99; long polyester nightie with scooped gathered neck and three-tiered skirt, £6.99; pure flannelette **nightshirts**, £4.99; nylon **pyjamas** trimmed with lace, £6.99 **Dressing gowns**: a large selection including plush nylon gowns with mandarin collar or with tailored revers, piped with contrast trim, both £12.99. Washable kimono style dressing gowns in stripes and colourful peasant prints, £11.99. Quilted nylon dressing gowns, £9.99. Cotton towelling robes, wrapover or revers styles, with or without piping, £12.99. Summer-weight polyester dressing gowns with button through front, short sleeves and smock-look ruffled yoke, £4.99. **Leisure gowns**—a selection including caftans in solid colours with lace trim, or in prints with contrast trim, £8.99. Stylish shirt-style caftans with sleeves gathered from elbow to shoulder, £8.95. **Slips**: many styles and sizes including slips to fit up to size 44" bust. Nylon waist slips to fit 34"-40" hips, 99p. Bra-slips and 37" long polyester slips to wear under mid-calf skirts, both £2.99. Luxury gypsy-style waist slips, Flounced and trimmed with lace, selected stores only, £2.95. **Bras and girdles**: wide selection including crossover, front fastening, halterneck and plunge style bras; prices from 99p. Also, matching bra and bikini sets, and new range of pantie girdles and body shapers giving light and medium control.

## Ladies' ready-to-wear

A complete range, from shoes to cosmetics. **Jeans and trousers** in a total size range of 10-18, different lengths length fittings. Polyester jersey trousers from £2.99; denim jeans and new narrow leg jeans in sizes 11-16, from £8.99; corduroy jeans in sizes 10-18, £8.99. **Skirts**: gently flared wool skirts, fully lined, sizes 10-18, from £8.99 for prints, from £10.99 for classic styles, Kilts from £8.99; long kilts, £12.99. Acrylic jersey skirts, unlined, from £3.99 for prints, from £4.99 in plain fabric. Day length velvet skirts, printed or plain, £12.99. **Long skirts**: long kilts, £12.99. Long printed velvet skirts, £25 and plain velvet skirts, £16.99. **Shirts and blouses**: silky nylon polo neck in plain colours

and stripes, sizes 10-16, £2.99. Classic shirts in cotton modal, printed with stirrups, flowers, spots and stripes, £5.99; similar shirts in acrylic jersey, in sizes 10-18, £3.99. Big plaid shirts with military shoulders or blouson bottoms, £6.99. Warm handle brushed cotton blouses, £5.99. **Dresses**: a selection of budget dresses from £5.99. Velours dresses, several styles, from £13.99; printed polyester shirtdresses with zip front and long sleeves, from £6.99. Knit tabards, plain and patterned, from £7.99. Dropped shoulder pinafore dresses in sizes 12-20, £9.99. Styled dresses in corduroy, wool, flannel and donegal, from £14.99. Aran-look sweater dress with cowl neck, £10.99. **Jackets and coats**: cotton cord blazers in sizes 10-18, £16.99; velvet blazers, £22.50. Raincoats from £22.50; pure wool coats from £36. Classic double-breasted coat with belt and wide revers, in camel coloured wook, sizes 12-18, £27.50. Wool coat with real fur collar, £42.50. Selected branches only; classic llama coat, £65; sheepskin jacket, £99; pure cashmere coat, £120. **Suits** in sizes 12-18, from £14.99; classic velvet suits from £30. **Shoes** in sizes 3-8, from £6.99 in synthetics, from £8.99 in leather. Synthetic **boots** from £8.99; leather boots from £22.99; sheepskin boots from £17.99. **Also**: cosmetics, skin care and bath preparations, scarves from £1.25; silk scarves from £2.99-£4.99; selection of luggage including smart rigid frame suitcase covered in tan fabric, trimmed with red and green stripe, £25.

# Men's ready-to-wear

**Shirts:** vast selection in sizes 14½-17½ including polyester cotton shirts in prints and stripes, £4.99; in plain colours, £4.50. Cotton twill shirts in checks and small traditional prints, £5.99; nylon shirts from £3.50. **Sports clothes:** cotton-backed track suit, £10.99; pure cotton sweat shirt, £6.99. Zip front velours overshirt, £9.50; short-sleeved towelling shirts, £4.99; printed T-shirts, £2.50. **Jeans and trousers:** range includes cotton denim jeans, £8.50 and terylene and worsted trousers, £11.50. Half-lined wool and polyester trousers, in waist sizes 30″-40″ and 29″-33″ inside leg measurements, £13.99. Straight leg cavalry twill trousers, in waist sizes 32″-42″, inside leg 29″-31″, £12.99. Polyester trousers, £7.99; polyester and worsted trousers, £10.99. **Coats and jackets:** pure wool tweed sports jacket, £27; double-breasted velvet jacket, double breasted navy blazer and double breasted three-quarter length wool coat, all £35. Pure wool safari jacket, £22.50. Proofed parkas with flap pockets, £29.50. Raincoats, £18.50 unlined; lined raincoats from £22.50. At selected branches only: Classic raglan-sleeved tweed coat, £39.50. At selected branches only: three-quarter length pigskin coat and classic leather trench coat, sizes 38-44, both £75. In sizes 36-46, classic fly-fronted coat in pure cashmere, £95. **Suits:** range includes slim fitting suits in pure wool worsted and wool rich blends, styled in the U.K., Italy and Finland, in sizes 35″-44″ chest, £37.50. West of England

flannel suits, £39.75. **Shoes** in sizes 6-11: young fashion shoes with leather uppers, from £9.99. Lace-up brogues with punch detail, in black or brown, £13.50. Classic moccasins, £27.50; classic slip-ons with gilt trim, £27.50. Suede chukka boots with synthetic soles, £5.99; sporty leather shoes with synthetic soles from £9.99. **Underwear:** fine ribbed cotton slips in white and colours, £1.10; printed cotton briefs, £1.25; cotton trunks, £1.35; polyester and cotton stripy boxer shorts, £2.15. Pure cotton **pyjamas**, £6.99; flanelette **nightshirts**, £4.95; cotton towelling kimono style **robes**, £10.99.

# Children—Girls

**Dressing gowns:** modacrylic long tartan dressing gowns with hood, £8.50 for sizes 9-10 years, £9.50 for sizes 11 years-34″ chest and plush cossack style dressing gown with flower print yoke, shoulders and tie belt, quilted nylon gown with flower print trim on collar, cuffs and hem, all £8.50 for sizes 9-10 years, £9.50 for sizes 11 years-34″ chest. Quilted nylon nursery print gowns, £6.50 for ages 2-4, £7.50 for ages 5-8.

**Nightgowns:** printed polyester long nightdresses, from £3.25 for ages 2-4 to £4.50 for age 11-34″ chest. Fun polyester long nighties with colourful big transfer prints, £3.25 for ages 3-4, £3.50 for ages 5-8. Long lace-trimmed polyester nighties ruffled laced trimmed pinafore style bodice, three tiered skirt, £5.99 for sizes 32″-36″ chest (ages 9-14). **Underwear,** a good selection, including pure cotton briefs and matching vests: ages 3-8, 59p and 89p; ages 9-34″ hip, 33″ chest, 65p and 99p.

**Separates:** a large range, including top value permanently pleated acrylic and wool **kilts** in Dress Stewart and other tartans: ages 2-4, £3.99; ages 5-8, £4.25; ages 9-11, £4.99, ages 12-14 and 25″-26″ waist sizes, £5.75. French cut cord **jeans**, several colours; ages 2-4, £4.99; ages 5-8, £5.99; ages 9-11, £7.99. Cord **dungarees**, ages 2-4, £4.99; ages 5-8, £5.99. Also: dresses.

**Coats:** showerproof polyester/cotton coats and styled wool coats for ages 2-4 to ages 12-14, 34″ chest. Outstanding model from last winter's collection: pure wool doublebreasted six button coats with rounded collar, the classic 'Royal Children' look, from £11.99 for age 2-4 to £14.99 for ages 7-8.

## Children—Boys

**Jeans:** pure cotton denim jeans: for 23″-27″ waist, £6.99; for 28″-30″ waist, £7.99; inside leg from 20″-28″. Needlecord jeans: 23″-27″ waist, £5.99; 28″-30″ waist, £6.99. Cotton jeans in khaki, cream and light blue: 23″-27″ waist, £6.99; 28″-30″ waist, £7.99. Younger sizes, French cut cord jeans, ages 2-4, £4.99; ages 5-8, £5.99; ages 9-11, £7.99.

**Coats:** a range, including warm hooded duffle coats with toggle fastenings and two patch pockets, in tan: ages 5-8, £17.99; age 9-32″ chest, £18.99, 34″-36″ chest, £21.99.

**Shoes: Staff measure child's foot**

**properly,** leather shoes come in slim and wide fittings. In sizes 11-5½: suede chukka boots, £3.99; training shoes with leather uppers and synthetic soles, £4.50. Also: all-leather lace-ups, in sizes 4-10½, slippers and moccasins, plain or warmly lined.

**Knits & T-shirts and tops:** sporty hooded cotton top, from £5.99 for ages 9-11, £6.50 for ages 12-14. Long sleeved pure cotton shirts in football stripes; ages 5-8, £3.75; ages 9-11, £3.99; ages 12-14, £4.50. Long sleeved polo jumpers, plain colours: ages 2-4, £1.50; ages 5-8, £1.75; ages 9-11, £1.99; 32″-34″ chest, £2.25 in prints, from £1.99-£2.25. Lots of seasonal sweaters, including classic Scandinavian sweaters with snowflake patterns from £3.50 for ages 5-8 to £4.50 for 32″-34″ chest. Long sleeved Aran-look polo sweaters, ages 5-8, £3.50, ages 9-11, £3.99; 32″-34″ chest, £4.50. Knits in shetland wool and nylon blends, jumpers in crew and polo styles with matching cardigans; ages 5-8, £3.50 and £5; ages 9/10-10/11, £3.99 and £5.75; 32″-34″ chest, £4.50 and £5.99. For ages 3-4, cardigan only, £4.99. Polyester T-shirts with colourful transfer prints: ages 9-11, £1.75; 32″-34″ chest, £1.99. Machine washable velours tops, solid colours and prints; ages 3-4, £3.99; ages 5-8, £4.50; ages 9-11, £4.99; 32″-34″ chest, £5.50.

**Underwear:** range including pure cotton briefs: ages 3-8, 65p; 28″-29″ waist, 75p. Sleeveless vest from 85p for ages 3-8; and other sizes. Short sleeved vest from £1.10 for ages 3-8, £1.25 for ages 9-11.

## Toddlers

No complete baby and toddler department, but a choice selection of very useful articles for children ages 1-4. Look out for one piece **padded anorak suits**, ages 1-3, £6.99-£8.99; two piece padded suits, ages 1-3, £8.99. **Very good value:** cotton-nylon velours dungaree style **babygrows:** £2.99 for ages 6-12 months, 12 to 18 months; £3.50 for ages 2-4. Toddler's **shoes**, all leather, sizes 4-10½, from £4.50. Long sleeved **Jumpers** in amusing patterns for ages 1-4, prices from £2.25. Colourful long knitted dungaree and jumper **sets** for ages 1-4, from £5.75.

---

**Midas**  72 New Bond Street, W1   01-629 3633/4
Mon.-Sat. 9.30-6
(Access, American Express, Barclaycard, Diners)

Midas has the golden touch, and this is the place to come for shoes with such star personality that you'll never think of shoes as an 'accessory' again. Midas's shoes are the ones you buy *before* you buy a dress to go with them—the strappiest evening sandals, flat summer sandals—high, high fashion at good prices. The Midas collection is colourful, exciting and chosen with flair—feet have *never* been so fascinating! You'll find the best looks by all the top names, and many of the designs are exclusive. Midas has one of the smartest salons in London, designed by David Hicks, with niches displaying superb handbags, belts and little things like visors and legwarmers, specially chosen to set off the shoes. This is the favourite shoe shop of lots of London's top models, and if you stop in during the sales, held in January and June, you'll see some of the prettiest girls in town.

Sample range—all prices approximate:
**Shoes** in sizes 3-8; **espadrilles** from £5-£15; **flat sandals and strappy evening shoes** from £10-£30.

---

**N. Peal**  37-40 Burlington Arcade, W1   01-493 5378
Mon.-Fri. 9-5.30, Sat. 9-1
(Access, American Express, Barclaycard, Carte Blanche, Cooks, Diners, Mastercharge)

The classic British Look is misleadingly simple, for unless you have the very best in quality and design, you won't get the classic British style—the masterful mixture of understated tailoring, casual elegance, and completely relaxed assurance that show themselves so well in fine wool on wool separates. That's why discriminating people from all over the world come to N. Peal for classically up-to-date separates that show *le style anglais* at its best. The shop features the high fashion knitwear of designer Valerie Louthan, who uses cashmere as beautifully as it ought to be in sophisticated creations that include smoking jackets, soft draped tops and long evening ensembles. Downstairs, a room full of knitwear offers a choice of single and double cashmere in many styles and colours, including lace-stitch pullovers, fine-ribbed sports sweaters, and the Continental favourite hand-framed Shetland look cashmere pullover. Everything matches up to tailored shirts in cotton and pure silk, made by their own shirtmaker, and to an exceptionally stylish range of exclusive skirts.

---

## Phillips   7 Blenheim Street, New Bond Street, W1
01-629 6602
Telegrams: *Auctions*, London W1

---

Good things are worth waiting for—particularly the Phillips *Costume and Textile* sales, held six or seven times a year. The nicest of the big London auctioneers, Phillips do *not* charge a buyers commission: their premises make up in warmth what they lack in elegance, their viewings have the feeling of a friendly family shareout and they give you the chance to put in your bid for some of the best fashion bargains in town. Although all of the goods accepted for sale at Phillips are eminently collectable, most of them are bought and worn for pure enjoyment, which could have a lot to do with the prices—dependably at least a third less than you'd pay for the same thing in other sale rooms. It could also have to do with the fact that Phillips appeals as much to sellers as to buyers; eminently approachable, they tend to get the lion's share of goods from box room, attic and bottom drawer where the most interesting fashion treasures are to be found. If you follow the Phillips sales closely you'll get a crack at Twenties Porthault sheets and designs by Fortuny and Alix, Madame Grès, but the best buys are often the ones *without* labels. Lace is a Phillips speciality, and you can pick up all the trimmings you need for romance. Mixed lots of lace will provide the makings for superb petticoats and cavalier collars, and there are often fine antique christening robes for under £20 that look much nicer at the font and in photographs than modern versions costing three times as much. Brides-to-be will find antique wedding veils from about £20—you can easily pay £60 for similar antique veils in speciality shops, and you might be lucky enough to find a bridal flounce, six to ten yards long and one to two feet wide, to trim your wedding gown. Trunks of linen give wonderful value for money—hand embroidered organdie and damask cloths in perfect condition, at a fraction of modern prices—and there are always lots of white Victorian and Edwardian nightgowns and Twenties *lingerie.* Special fashion tips: look out for embroidered linen country smocks, perfect for this summer's pastoral outfits, and for large paisley shawls to wear draped over one shoulder. Sales are usually held on Thursdays at 11 a.m., with viewing two days before; for dates, ring Phillips. As a guide to what you can find, these are sample lots and the prices they fetched at recent auctions.

| Lot | Pric |
| --- | --- |
| **Vogue** Fashion Bi-Monthly, Spring, February-March 1926; a set of five buttons and a pin; another set of three; a pair of buckles and an enamel belt clasp. | £2 |
| A Ukranian costume, comprising full-sleeved and tucked bodice blouse with skirt and apron, each embroidered in red and green wools in flowers and leaves, with lace trim and an embroidered bonnet. | £3 |
| A Chantilly lace double collar designed with flowers and leaves. | £1 |
| A silk christening robe, having lace insertions, and an ivory cashmere christening cap. | £1 |
| A linen table cloth designed with squares linked with bobbin lace, 1.60 × 1.80m; another cloth, a bedspread with lace insertions, 2.70m × 1.92m, a quantity of lace and crocheted edged mats and pie frills. | £9 |
| A Chinese terracotta silk dragon robe, having coloured silk embroidery of flowers, dragons, fish, pheasants, cosmic and other symbols; and a black silk panel. | £2 |
| A 1930's ivory satin peignoir having *écru point de gaze* trim; an apricot satin and gold thread lace wrap, three pairs of camiknickers and a pair of French knickers of silk and satin. | £6 |

A Honiton *appliqué* bridal veil designed with florets and ferns; two Limerick ties; two stoles; a black embroidered net bonnet veil; a pair of mittens; and edgings of various 19th century laces. £28

A Japanese bridal kimono, pale aqua silk hand embroidered with cranes and flowers, lined, deep sleeves and padded hem. £42

A cotton nightdress, the bodice having whitework and tucked trim; another with lace collar; and four others, similar. £42

A 19th century ploughman's linen smock having deep embroidered collar and smocked bodice and cuffs, possibly Devonshire. £75

Art Deco trimming, including twelve hat clips and lengths of sequin braid, tortoiseshell and other combs and pins; and a quantity of feathers in brilliant, pastel and other shades. £50

Chinese skirt of pastel orange silk, the front, back and pleated side panels embroidered with Ho Ho birds, Dogs of Fo, flowers and blossom in coloured silks, lined. £42

A Norwich ivory silk gauze shawl printed with typical cone design; a Lyons shawl having lotus flower motif to the border and another shawl of cream and lilac gauze. £48

An Edwardian peignoir of fine white lawn, having gathered and flounced collar and sleeves, with whitework decoration. £80.

---

**Janet Reger** 33 Brook Street, W1   01-629 6504
Mon.-Fri. 10-6, Sat. 10-5
(Access, American Express, Barclaycard, Diners)

---

Want to bring out the best—or the beast—in your man? Choose your perfume with care—and leave *everything* else to Janet Reger. This is the place to come for ravishing designer *lingerie* and nightware—confections of silk, chiffon, *crêpe* and *satin de lys* that frankly set out to make you more attractive, and succeed beyond the shadow of doubt. The collection features *lingerie* sets in delicious shades like Orchid, Firebird, Ebony and Bamboo—perfect tints for trousseaus, trysts and lovely treats. Some sets come in a range of styles, so you can have the tiniest bikini briefs or lace-trimmed French knickers, slinky halter brassières or lacy underwire brassières with a delicate uplift—all matching up to suspender belts, camiknickers and slips. All pieces can be purchased separately, but Janet Reger always provides the total look. The nightwear collection has everything you'll need for *chaise loungerie*—long sheer chiffons trimmed with lace, long pintucked pinafores in lace-trimmed *satin de lys*, sophisticated scarf-tie halter gowns. The perfect backdrop to all this loveliness? Luscious *satin de lys* sheets in colours to match or handpainted pure silk sheets made to order. Don't forget to put the champagne on ice—Janet Reger's sheer delights send temperatures soaring.

Send £1.50 for lavishly illustrated mail order catalogue—price refundable on purchase.

Sample range and prices:

**Lingerie sets** in the following colours and fabrics:

**Silk:** Azure, Caprice and Bamboo. **Satin:** Snow, Oyster, Haze, Tearose, Ebony and Eau-de-Nil. **Crêpe:** Snow blossom, Shadow and Dusky Rose. **Lace:** Black and Palisander Rose.

**Sets:** brassières in sizes 32A-38C, from £11.50. Bikini briefs, in sizes S, M, L from £7.50-£10. **French knickers** in same sizes, from £12.60-£17. Suspender belts in same sizes, from £8.70-£10. Waist slips, size M only, from £16.20-£18.50. Full slips from £36; minislips, from £43. Camiknickers in sizes 32-38 from £30.50-£35.90.

**Nightwear:** nightdresses from £65; négligés from £81.

**Sheets:** *Satin de lys* sheets in all the satin *lingerie* colours. Single sheets from £40, double sheets from £55. Matching pillowcases from £15; duvet covers to order. Handpainted silk sheets to order—prices on consultation.

---

**Zandra Rhodes** 14a Grafton Street, W1
01-499 3596
Mon.-Fri. 9.30-6, Sat. 9.30-5
(Access, American Express, Barclaycard, Diners)

---

This is London's A to Z fashion shop—Z for Zandra everywhere, and the clothes aren't called clothes, they're called Art. The decor is spectacular, in shades of henna, copper and ripe peach, absolutely **full** of Zandra. Her fabrics cover the walls and pillars, her wallpaper glitters on the ceiling, her original design sketches hang over the clothes rails, the clothes hangers are covered in Zandra's signature prints—even the seats are shaped like big Z's. There's nothing like it anywhere in the world—but then there's no one like Zandra. The fantastical printed chiffons that have made her an international fashion personality are grouped together in the Works of Art Collection; when you buy one, you receive a certificate printed on silk recording the number of the dress, and this personal message from Zandra—**'This is one of my special dresses, I think of it as an artwork that you will treasure forever.'** And you will. This season, you'll find Zandra's most ravishing prints ever—new Mexican Firework, Mexican Brick, Mexican Border and Mexican Horseshoe patterns in spicy greens, oranges, purples, turquoises and pinks. There are new designs too, deliciously delicate dresses with plunge necklines, cape sleeves and fine four-panel apron skirts over slim jersey underskirts, scalloped cocktail length skirts and matching tops, strappy slim gowns with crystal pleated frill bodices or bodices made of a great big bow. Last summer there was a pretty pastel cotton collection that showed Zandra in a new soft mood—dropped shoulder V-neck long dresses in lighthearted sunburst prints, and smocks with ruched panels, back and front, in pink on *eau-de-Nil*—and this season there will be more cotton delights! For the **most original, exciting collection in town**, don't miss Zandra's stunning 'posh punk'—real masterpieces in black jersey, tattered in all the right places, scattered with sequins, contrast stitching, little chains and sparkly safety pins. If you aren't quite up to the full rig—and no one with style should have any trouble—you can buy the pins in pairs or in a special pack with six pins, two satin rouleau and a note from Zandra: **'These are my special beaded safety pins, yes-real safety pins. Wear them as . . .'** And that's not all. This season there's a sensational collection of irresistible luxury lingerie—in washable polysatin trimmed with wriggle and signature lace—boleros, pyjamas, camiknickers, kimono wraps, nightgowns, negligees, perfect peignoirs. This is Zandra at her best and brightest, her most beautiful summer yet!

Sample range and prices:

**From the Works of Art Collection:** evening gowns from £350. The 'Z' collection including 'posh punk' designs, from £55 upwards.

**Summer cotton collection:** ruched smock, £59; long V-neck dress, about £60.

**Lingerie collection:** black pyjamas with lace-trimmed kimono style top, £65. Lace-trimmed camiknicker in blush, ivory or black, £33.

Lounging robe with V neck, drawstring Empire-line waist, full kimono sleeves edged with lace, in pink, black or fuschia, £65. Slender nightdress with crystal pleated hem and bodice, slender spaghetti straps, with long crystal pleated wrap; gown, £59; wrap £125; in ivory, blush or black. Same design in lily lace border print: in black with yellow and orange, or in fuschia with turquoise and red: nightgown, £65; wrap, £165.

## Saint Laurent—Rive Gauche 113 New Bond Street, W1
01-493 1800
Mon.-Sat. 9.30-6, Thurs. 9.30-7
(American Express, Barclaycard, Diners)

Yves Saint Laurent's ready-to-wear collection of international
good looks—casual and sporty clothes, formal and evening wear.
The Rive Gauche total look is a real fashion plus—clothes and all
the accessories to wear with them, scarves to shoes, underscored
by the same design thinking. Spring collection in the boutiques
from the end of January, Autumn collection from mid-July.
Prices are the same as in Paris since duty came off last July.
Clothes in sizes 6-16.

Sample range and prices:
Blouses from £54, jackets from £94, skirts from £80, shoes from
£41 and scarves from £12.

## Royal British Legion Shop 49 Pall Mall, SW1 01-930
8131
Mon.-Fri. 9.30-4.45

Tucked into the heart of clubland like a poppy in a buttonhole,
this cosy shop is bursting with some of the best buys in town.
Everything has been made by ex-Service and other disabled
persons—you can expect fine hand-craftsmanship and
old-fashioned quality which are rare today at any price, and
nostalgic touches like wickerwork wastebaskets in boudoir pink or
*eau-de-Nil* dusted with gold, very Thirties, for only 90p! Pride of
place goes to bolts of *handwoven* Welsh tweeds from the Royal
British Legion's Cambrian Mill in Llanwrtyd Wells—shepherd's
plaids, houndstooth checks, herringbone weaves, Prince of Wales,
lively contemporary checks, lots of light tweeds, plain tweeds
with coordinated patterned tweeds for mix and matching, in fine
dress and heavier country weights. Prices start at only £3 per
metre—*just what you'd pay if you bought direct from the Cambrian
Mill!* With tweeds back in fashion, all you need is someone to run
up a coat, suit or skirt and the shop has *a dressmaker who will
make to measure in classic styles—the Mayfair couture look at a
fraction of the cost!* For weekends in the shires, order a hardy
country tweed skirt for about £10.50 and go on to choose from a

Standing needlework boxes, £7.50; nest of tables from St. Dunstan's, £15.

## Tailoring and Dressmaking to Measure

For ladies; day skirts, £4.50; long skirts from £5.50, coats from £13 not including the cost of the fabric. Also, trouser suits, capes and jackets. For gentlemen: suits and carcoats, £35; jackets, £24 not including the cost of the fabric.

---

## Sac Frères  45 Old Bond Street, W1  01-493 2333
Mon.-Fri. 9.30-5.30, Sat. 9.30-1

The hearts of sunken forests wait for you at Sac Frères—golden amber from the Baltic, rich brown amber from Persia, opalescent amber from Russia, scarlet amber from China, rare amber from Sicily—green as the sea. In past ages, amber was believed to bestow gifts of immortality, luck, inspiration, happiness and health. Even today, it works a special magic, for amber has a comforting warmth of its own, seductively pleasant to the touch. One old tale is certainly true—that amber enhances beauty. The patina of antique amber accents the shine of hair and eyes, draws clear colour to the cheeks, and bathes the wearer with a rich candlelight glow. Diamonds chill, rubies burn, emeralds mock—only amber kisses. Sac Frères are the only amber specialists in the world, and the best pieces and most discerning collectors find their way to these doors. The collection is treated with affection and care—beads from different necklaces are never mixed, necklaces are restrung onto silken cords chosen to compliment their colour, and every piece is hand polished frequently. Amber is still being carved and fashioned, but no modern pieces have the craftmanship and beauty of Sac Frères antique treasures. There are graceful Muslim and Buddhist prayer beads, necklaces of ancient cylindrical beads from the Middle East, long ropes of superb pieces the size and shape of an egg, sparkling strings of large hand-faceted beads, baroque carved amber set in rings of Russian silver, chokers of tiny beads from China and *objets* worked with exquisite carving. Ask to see pieces from John Hunger's own collection—the necklace from the Russian Imperial Court, the collar made for a Ming mandarin or the elegant strand of Sicilian green amber. Antique amber of this quality is not inexpensive, but you get unsurpassed value for money—particularly when compared to modern jewellery in a similar price range. It always seems to be a golden afternoon at Sac Frères—so come along and start your love affair with amber. For the interested collector there is now a book on amber by Rosa Hunger of Sac Frères called 'The Magic of Amber'.

Sample range and prices:

**Necklaces:** short necklaces from £65; long necklaces of tiny beads hanging 10in below the waist from £120; long graduated necklace of faceted clear Baltic amber, £250; Persian prayer necklace of round opaque amber beads, £300; Chinese madarin necklace of regal red amber, £350; exceptionally rare necklaces of large graduated or regular beads, from £450. Superb long golden opaque necklace with slight graduations, £450. Irregular string of rare brown Persian amber, £450. Magnificent necklace of egg-sized beads, £650. **Earrings:** drop, carved and stud earrings in all colours, for pierced and unpierced ears from £35-£125. **Rings:** unusually set with **cabochon** amber, sometimes with beautifully carved plaques. Rings of amber set in gold from £65-£150. Large baroque rings set in handworked Russian silver from £100. **Bracelets:** a selection, including clear amber plaques set in silver, £175, and plaques of red amber set in gold from £400. **Also Carvings:** from Eastern Europe and the Orient from £150; Muslim and Buddha prayer beads from £200, and a few pieces of fine, jade, including graduated chokers of small beads, from £350-£3,000.

---

# David Shilling  36 Marylebone High Street, W1
01-487 3179
Mon.-Fri. 9-6; other times by arrangment
(Access, American Express, Barclaycard, Carte Blanche, Diners)

★

At Ascot and the Derby, the horses win the guineas—but the Shillings sweep the hat stakes. David Shilling's fabulous Occasion hats have been front-page news since he began designing at the tender age of twelve. Occasions are a sometime thing, but now that accessory-dressing is *the* day-to-day way of making the most of yourself, the best fashion scoops are his hats for every purpose under Heaven—*the most exhilarating millinery in London*— displayed in his marvellous Marylebone salon. You've heard of a hat tree. David Shilling has a hat forest—branches and bushes hung with clouds of top hats, turbans, berets, Bretons, pillboxes, postillions—and you can't see the cloches for the caps. You can have *fedoras folles* and over-the-toppers to order, but the *ton* of the

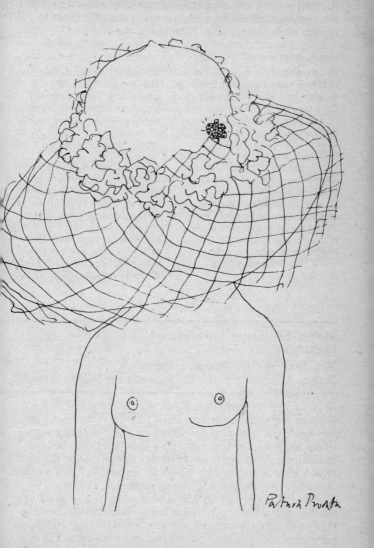

*David Shilling hat drawn by Patrick Proktor*

main collection is pure sophistication—laced with effervescent Shilling style. David Shilling did coolie hats before Saint Laurent, cavalier hats before Chloé, and his creations are pure *couture*. The shapes are exceptionally flattering—graceful mushroom brims, piquant saucers, flippantly aquiline felts—all handmade on the premises, carefully moulded on the designers own wooden forms. This is the only place in London where you'll find fur hats that are blocked instead of just draped; his fox and marabou confections never lose their shape, and they're so soft you can roll them up and put them in your pocket. Every hat can be pared down to the bare essential of a matching or contrast band and still look superb, but the trims are as important as the shapes, if not more so—and this is where you see the consummate Shilling magic. All the trims are antique, from the designer's own collection built up over the years—veiling, ribbons, flurries of feathers, puffs of plumes, elegant rapier quills, tulle camellias and carnations, poppies and snowdrops in silk. Many of the hats have already been beautifully trimmed, but you can have David Shilling confect a hat for you on the spot—*the most exciting fashion experience in town*! This summer when women want to look prettier, softer, more casual, David Shilling has a ravishing collection full of relaxed romanticism and *dégagé* delight. Flowers are sprinkled instead of placed, mixed with feathers and silk veiling on large-brimmed hats to wear to the beach—not just to Ascot. And Ascot hats are more like hats for the beach—wicker stetsons and bowlers, small finely woven saucer shapes. There are satin Juliet caps to wear with Pierrot collars, satin riding hats to go with jodhpurs, schoolgirls straws for the Gigi look trimmed with cascades of ribbons, sweet felts shaped like fondant candies, topped with icing swirls. Hats come in all the classic colours and an appetising palette of tints—vivid peppermint pinks and greens, lots of creams, naturals and blacks, delicious combinations like peach and avocado. If this romantic summer leads to wedding bells, you can come here for special bridal millinery that you'll cherish forever—tiny satin skullcaps with silk veiling that brushes the shoulders, fabric flower chaplets, fluffy marabou for weddings in the snow. Simple hats can be made to order in a matter of hours, but if you want something very special, allow as much time as possible. (This year's top dates : Derby, June 7; Royal Ascot, June 20-24.) Don't be shy—you can touch, browse, try on to your heart's content, and you can learn a lot about fashion just by looking around. DS initial hatpins come free with every hat, and there are always pretty pieces of fashion jewellery and little accessories like cream gloves and satin *pochettes*. The designer will put you at ease with his contagious charm and witty style. His creations took Paris by storm last season, so if you want people to take their hats off to you—pop in and see David Shilling!

Sample range—all prices approximate:

Main collection hats, from £20. Gold peaked caps, £9.95; woolly pull-on hats, £4.95. Matching scarves, £14.50. Feather boas, from £10. Gold and silver turbans, from £26. Ostrich feather tango fans, from £5.25. Glittery berets, from £9.95. Fur hats from £45-£480. DS initial scarves and cravats from £2.50; also, very special David Shilling T-shirts. Bridal flower chaplets, £14.50. Special hats to order; prices on consultation.

---

**Simpsons** 203 Piccadilly, W1   01-734 2002
Mon.-Sat. 9-5.30, Thurs. 9-7
Telegrams: *Simperos*, London
(Access, American Express, Barclaycard, Diners, Eurocard, Mastercharge)
By appointment to Her Majesty the Queen, outfitters
By appointment to His Royal Highness, the Duke of Edinburgh, outfitters

---

Three floors of women's fashions are the icing on the cake of this top men's store, where you'll find everything from Chessa Davies's designs to **London's best value-for-money buys in stylish camelhair and cashmere coats.** You can rely on Simpsons for consistent quality, but the sheer variety is what makes Simpsons so interesting—it's very much the sort of place where you're likely to come up with 'wonderful little finds', whatever your tastes. The entire sixth floor is given over to the Follow the Sun department, where a comprehensive collection of cruisewear and lightweight clothes is kept in stock all year round. There are jumpsuits, tailored classics, slim long skirts to match up to slinky halter tops, jeans and jackets and designer collections by Cherry Frizzell and Tiktiner. On the fifth floor, you'll find the *Separates* department, with clothes by Cacharel, Wahl, Clubman, Daniel Hechter and others—look out for occasional specialities like velvet jumpsuits or sporty jackets in the non-tailored styles. The **Knitwear** department has French fashion knits by Tricot Caroll, Italian fashion knits made exclusively for Simpsons, and an excellent selection of classic English knits with lots of superb cashmeres—**including those hard-to-find** ribbed **cashmere rollnecks**. Next comes the ladies DAKS **collection**, featuring the DAKS **look**—stylish classic separates in the smart DAKS house check, with toning shirts and polos, and capes faced with DAKS check to add the finishing touch. There are plenty of DAKS more traditional styles too, and sporty ladies shouldn't miss the DAKS golf shirt with straight front and back pleats to give movement to your swing, pockets with stitched-in tee-holders—and three tee fitted jauntily into place! On the fourth floor, the **Women's Tailoring department** has classic trenchoats by Invertere, raincoats, tailored suits and coats galore. Two new additions to this department, are suits and coats by Serge Perier and raincoats by Julie Latour. This is where you'll find Simpsons very special camelhair and cashmere coats—**look out for the new style cashmere coat with smart straight cut, deep revers and a half belt at the back**. There's a selection of coats and jackets in suede and leather and a shoe department with exceptionally stylish shoes and boots by Cesare Piccini of Florence—exclusive to Simpsons. The **Dress department** has day and evening wear by Maureen Baker, Diane von Furstenberg, Chessa Davies, Yuki, Chacok, Gordon Luke Clarke, Marcel Fenez, Marina Ferrari, Juliet Dunn and Mandy Pothecary. There's lots to see—and two restaurants where you can relax over luncheon and tea.

**Sales:** Simpsons sales, held twice a year in January and July give superb value for money. For the dates of this year's sale, ring Simpsons.

Sample range and approximate prices:

**DAKS** collection in sizes 8-16: jackets from £40-£70; skirts from £32-£50; cotton shirts from £22; silk shirts from £27; raincoats from £85; camel coat from £156; Harris tweed cape coat from £129; cashmere cape from £208; signature range of cashmere jackets from £140, hacking and blazer jackets from £95 and skirts from £36.

---

**Smythson**  54 New Bond Street, W1   01-629 8558
Mon.-Fri. 9.30-5.30, Sat. 9.15-12.30
By appointment to Her Majesty the Queen, stationers

★

---

The Summer Show, the Squadron lawn and shoots on the Glorious Twelfth—what would the Season be without Smythson,

stationers extraordinary and social arbiters plenopotentiary.
Whatever else has changed, the etiquette of stationery is still
firmly fixed, and Smythson's visiting card and watermarked
writing paper are the *sine qua non* of social perfection. The cards
are, of course, engraved—and Smythson's craftsmen are
renowned for the finest copperplate script in the world. You can
have black script on a white card, blue on white or white on blue.
If you want any other combination you will be gently persuaded
that it is not correct etiquette. Smythson's coveted invitation
cards have such *ton*—and cause such *frisson*—that they always
have pride of place on the mantlepiece. Apart from the
particulars, they're the one's with *no gilt* on the sides. Smythson's
superb writing paper comes in white, cream and all the right
colours—supplied in *Imperial* sizes. You can have a crest,
monogram or simple address—in beautiful die styles that bring
back the days where *all* telephone numbers began MAY-, BEL-,
WEL- and, sometimes FLAX-. Smythson's command of protocol
and etiquette is impeccable, and they advise visiting Heads of
State and Ambassadors to the Court of St. James. Should you
have an occasion to consult them, you may rest assured that
placement and precedence are always correct, 'pleasure' and
'honour' are never confused and 'H.R.H.', as it should be, is
Always Spelled Out. The atmosphere is clubby, and blue is the
house colour—Oxford, Cambridge, Burke's, Debrett's and true
shades in between. *Nothing* in good society happens without
by-your-leaves from Smythson's special leather bound
books—diaries come in twenty styles and a hundred different
bindings. Smythson were the first to do really light, slim pocket
diaries and the range includes the ever popular blue paper diaries
in the featherweight and wafer series. Smythson have the largest
selection of fine address books in the world. There are also pukka
Polo Books for recording your chukkas, executive clipboards
bound in buffalo calf, luxurious double binders to take the Radio
and TV Times and the Badminton Diary—the sporting man's
bible—with all significant fixtures past, present and future. The
Game and Hunting books are substantial, the Christmas List
books slim and the Bride's books are the same oyster shade as St.
Margaret's, Westminster. There are amusing miniature
Morocco-bound pocket books entitled London-Paris-New York,
Lovers & Losers, Blondes-Brunettes-Redheads, Yachting Notes,
Gymkhana/Show Notes and Bridge Notes—Smythson's version of
the social contract. Smythson have everything from photo albums
and press cutting books to hunting journals and menu and guest

registers, superb ladies accessories in *eau-de-Nil* shagrain leather, and they will undertake special commissions to order. It's a wonderful place to come for little gift items and novelties, and purists will be delighted to hear that Smythson's is one of the few places where you can still get sealing wax. In the words of Lady Troubridge—*'There is no greater opportunity to show good taste—or bad—than in the type of notepaper we use. It is as clear an index to one's individuality as the clothes we wear.'*

Sample range and prices:

**Stationery:** notepaper is still supplied in Imperial sizes—Duke (7 × 5½in), Kings (8 × 6¼in), Post Quarto (9 × 7in), Large Quarto (10 × 8in)—covering a range of ten of their own watermarked papers and in six colours, palin or bordered paper, from 90p per hundred sheets and £2.80 for the envelopes; handmade paper, £8.50 per sheets and 20 envelopes. Engravings include a simple address or a drawing of your house or your family crest, prices available on request. **Invitation cards:** all copperplate engraved, black on white, on average £14 per hundred excluding the plate which is about £45. **Visiting cards:** all copperplate, including the finest script, black on white, on average £6 per hundred plus the plate which is about £8. Other ranges include bookplates, yacht stationery, printed luggage tags, birth announcements, prices on application.

**Diaries:** available in twenty styles including prime names such as featherweight and wafer series and in a hundred different bindings, fancy silks, crocodile and other fine leathers, from £1.40-£120 for a refileable diary wallet in crocodile. Most famous diary is sportman's 'bible'—The Badminton Diary—which lists every important sporting event, past, present and future, from £1.45.

**Address Books:** the world's largest selection of address books, varying in size, bound and loose-leafed and in coloured leathers of which two unusual items include a double-indexed version titled social and business or home and abroad, from £3.20 and a tripled indexed address book headed London-Paris-New York or any three cities you care to name, from £3.70.

**Game Books:** a range of fishing, hunting, game books as well as polo record books, from £9.45.

**Leather goods:** a selection including visiting card cases, wallets and briefcases. Executive clip boards bound in buffalo calf, several colours, £16.50. For the boardroom, covers to take an A4 pad, bound in buffalo calf or long grain Morocco, with inside pocket to hold meeting papers, £25; available with company symbol or names blocked in gold. Hide-bound double cover for Radio and TV Times, £20.

**Leather goods de luxe:** a 'special commission collection' in hand-dressed black Morocco; briefcase, desktop equipment, personal leather goods such as cigarette case and diary, all with the same gold motif throughout. Over thirty items, making a princely gift for £760. All items can be bought separately. *Superb shagreen leather goods for ladies*, in coral pink or *eau-de-Nil*: a range of diaries from £1.85; also, jewel boxes, note pads, note cases, address books, credit card cases and visiting card cases.

**Specialities:** magnetic table plan in circular or rectangular shapes to help in planning seating arrangements. The plans, in hide, are from £27.50; magnetic name pieces are available separately in any quantity. Also individual pressed flower greeting cards, from £1.10.

---

## Ronnie Stirling 94 New Bond Street, W1

01-499 2675
Mon.-Sat. 9.30-6, Thurs. 9.30-7

---

**Snap!** These are the instant fashion specialists, always quick off the mark to give you what you want almost before you want it. Stirling Cooper always start trends, never follow them, and their talented young designers will give you the liveliest new looks in town, full of the very special flair and imagination that make student shows at top British fashion colleges so much more exciting than the **pret.** There are small capsule collections all through the year so you can be fashionably up-to-the-minute, and because they do their own manufacturing Stirling Cooper can rush a new look into the shops in no time at all. In fact, they take their fashion timing so seriously that they often sell pieces from month-old collections at reduced prices, and you can make some exceptional bargain buys if you don't mind being a few weeks behind, style-wise. With things moving so quickly, you'll have to be on your toes to make sure you catch the best of these exclusive designer collections, so keep alert this Spring. **You won't want to miss Annie Anderson's delectable layered ensembles**—a fascinating blend of feminine frills and boyish tailoring. The look starts off with a camisole dress—dainty top and pleated lace-trimmed tiered skirt. Tie on a drawstring open ruffled skirt in printed voile with ruffled pockets and piecrust frill waistband. Tuck in a ruffled voile blouse with full drawstring sleeves and embroidered flowers down the front. Add a boxy narrow-collared jacket in textured rough linen, and top with a panama hat! Beautifully romantic, in dusty pinks, creams and greens. You'll be swept off your feet, but keep your eyes open because **the new**

*By Annie Anderson for Stirling Cooper*

**Stirling Cooper India collection is being launched this Spring, and it's a stunner!** There are soft subtle blouses in handwoven **crepe** with attached knotted scarves instead of collars, all the edges embroidered in multicoloured pastel yarns, with embroidered three-tiered skirts or drawstring trousers to match. In voile, more beautiful blouses with scooped top-stitched yokes, misty shadow embroidery, full sleeves and peplum waists with matching skirts in pastel peach, *eau-de-Nil*, blue, sand, white and black. The satinised cotton collection has scalloping everywhere, and you can go on to a fourth collection in fine hopsack weave cotton trimmed with pretty raffia embroidery. Completely original, wonderfully stylish—and **the prices are the best surprise of all!** Stirling Cooper clothes are available at the Way In at Harrods and in Top Shop at Oxford Circus, but you'll get the best selection here. **Don't miss it!**

Sample range—all prices approximate:

## Stirling Cooper India collection

In sizes 1, 2, 3, (10, 12, 14). **In handloomed crepe:** dropped shoulder top with ruffled edge, two patch pockets, drawstring waist and pastel embroidery, £12.50; matching three-tiered skirt with embroidered trim, £12.99; top with soft knotted scarf collar, one knotted scarf at side, £13.99. **In voile:** top with soft knotted scarf-collar, £9.99; scoop neck top with shadow embroidery on pockets, elasticated peplum waist, £9.99; fully lined three-tiered skirt, about £10.99. **In satinised cotton:** scoop neck dress with illusion peplum top and two tiered skirt, embroidery trim, £21.99.

Top only, £11.99; drawstring trousers with embroidered pockets, £16.99. Cap-sleeved jumpsuit with scallop edges, scalloped Peter Pan collar, drawstring waist, £26.99; smashing little scalloped drawstring shorts, £8.99. **In hopsack weave cotton:** pastel blouson dress with dropped waist, long sleeves, raffia embroidery, £21.99; simple cap-sleeved dress with drawstring waist, plunge back tied behind the neck, £19.99; softly gathered skirt with embroidered pockets, £12.99; jumpsuit with woven raffia belt, raffia-embroidered Peter Pan collar and yoke, £25.99. Little long sleeved shirt with raffia trim, £11.99.

# Swaine, Adeney, Brigg & Sons  185 Piccadilly, W1

01-734 4277

Mon.-Fri. 9-5.30, Sat. 9-1

Telegrams: *Swadeneyne*, Piccy London

By appointment to Her Majesty the Queen, whip and glove makers

By appointment to Her Majesty Queen Elizabeth the Queen Mother,
umbrella makers

---

The salmon leap in May and June, the guns go out to the grouse
moors on the Glorious Twelfth of August, and the best thing to
pour into hip flasks is a mixture of brandy and madeira, or scotch
and ginger wine, in proportions to suit your taste. These truths
may not be all you need to know in the world at large, but
they're fairly fundamental in the huntin'-shootin'-fishin' life of
Swaine, Adeney, Brigg. There are superb wallets, attaché cases,
handbags and brollies for town, but practically everything else is
meant for the shires where the pursuit of happiness usually lies in
pursuit. Swaine, Adeney, Brigg have the finest whips in England,
silver hunting horns and everything for the well-dressed
horse—and if you prefer the course to coursing, you'll be
delighted with their wicker race hampers and special racing
umbrellas fitted with gold pencils for marking racing cards. Even
if you've never heard of the Quorn or Tattenham Corner, you'll
find lots to interest you in this jolly establishment. Now that the
country-tailored look is back in fashion, it's just the place to find
finishing touches to go with your tweeds. Look out for dog
whistles to hang on silver chains, foxmask studs to wear with
flowing stocks, hunting gloves to tuck into your belt and graceful
horsehair fly whisks to wave at the Guards in Rotten Row. And
don't forget the portable bars and backgammon sets—to while
away the time on country weekends.

## The Well-Dressed Horse

After a tasty breakfast from a two-horse nylon haynet (£2) shared
with his stable chum, the well-dressed horse begins the day with a
thorough veterinary check and grooming, his owner having
obtained all the necessary items from the comprehensive range of
products at Swaine, Adeney, Brigg. What fun! Our horse rather
likes the hoof oil, and thoroughly enjoys his session under the
jockey curry comb, body brush, and Wolseley Pedigree electric
clippers. Now its time for the morning canter, and we can hear

someone coming from the tack room. Will he have the all-purpose spring tree saddle with suede knee grips (£185) this time, or the Stubben Siegfried spring tree saddle? He doesn't mind which as long as he get his favourite pure wool numnah and Pelham complete bridle. After a run through the fields, he returns to be tidied up with a rubber sweat scraper, cuddles up in sweat rug (£16) and finally settles down to admire his name on the plate over the stable door.

Catalogues in full colour available on request—send 60p postage in the U.K., or the equivalent of $3 if writing from abroad.

Sample range and prices:

**Whips:** ladies and gentlemen's whips for hunting, riding and driving. Prices start at £9 for an ordinary whip and can go all the way up to £180 for a very special driving whip. Other models and prices: plaited calf polo whip £15; horsehair fly whip with malacca cane, £18; lightweight riding whip with lizard handpart and silver mounts, £25; crop with ivory hook and gold collar, £65. **Horns:** most American and British hunts have accounts here for their hunting horns. Countess of Lonsdale copper-nickel hunting horn, £25; Cotswold nickel-banded hunting horn, £45; all-silver Goodall hunting horn, £155. Also coach horns from £60.

## Riding Wear and Accessories

A large selection of ready-to-wear riding clothes for men and women of all sizes, with a large range of choice in the tweeds. **Jackets:** ladies tweed jackets from £36; ladies formal navy jacket, £36. Men's all-wool tweed jackets from £58; black formal jackets in cavalry twill, from £58. **Riding breeches:** for men and women, in two-way stretch fabric. In beige,

yellow, white, navy or black from £22.50. **Shirts:** hunting shirts in pure wool, yellow or white, £16. **Riding waterproofs:** for men and women, short from £35, long from £52. **Hats:** riding bowlers from £24; polo helmets from £16.50; fibreglass protective skullcap, £15.50; silk covers for skullcaps, £5.50; riding hats covered with velvet from £12.50. **Boots:** ladies rubber riding boots, normal sizes range from £15; ladies box calf riding boots from £71. Men's fully-lined rubber riding boots from £17.50; box calf riding boots from £80; box calf boots with mahogany tops from £86. **Also:** riding gloves from £4; hunting kit bag with black hide trim, £195; hunting flask in bridle butt case, £65; hunting appointment card holder, £40; and a range of stock pins, crop pins and foxmask studs, cufflinks and brooches.

## Umbrellas

An excellent collection of classic umbrellas for ladies and gentlemen, covered in nylon or silk. Specialities include extra-strong stick-umbrellas which combine the functions of umbrella and walking stick, and racing

83

umbrella with a gold pencil fitted into the crook. Ladies umbrellas include silk covered umbrella with malacca or whangee handle, £39 and nylon-covered racing umbrella, £40. Men's umbrellas come in short, medium and tall lengths, with handles that include crocodile, lizard, black morocco leather, pigskin and furze. Prices from £21 for nylon, from £39 for silk.

## Turak Gallery 5 St. Christopher's Place, W1 01-486 5380
Mon.-Fri. 10-6, Sat. 12-4

Earthy, sensuous and satisfyingly substantial, ethnic jewellery is one of fashion's most fascinating accessories. Turak travel the world for the fine pieces displayed in their showrooms like the works of art they are—intricate necklaces, belts, armlets, rings, earrings, fibulas and crosses in beautiful natural substances that have far more *richesse* and mystery than modern designs in diamonds and gold. The best examples come from the tribal peoples of Oman, the Yemen, Ethiopia, North Afghanistan and Tibet—magnificent family heirlooms that are rapidly becoming rare collector's items. Antique ethnic jewellery is a little known field and prices are still reasonable, so if you want to go in for exotic investment dressing, now is the time to start. Very few prices at Turak go above £500, and there are lots of lovely antiques in the middle range—a striking choker in baroque coral, amazonite, cornelian and silver from the southern Sahara for £259, a Somali necklace of ceramic beads overlaid with gold for £175, a silver Tibetan prayer necklace for £80.50 and Yemeni silver armlets for £56.25. For those who prefer modern ethnic pieces, Turak have an excellent selection that includes Ethiopian silver crosses from £10 and lion's claws set in Ethiopian silver from £20, and exceptional pieces in the ethnic vein made for the shop by young craftsmen. Look out for small scent bottles in silver, amber, coral and turquoise on a silver chain, by Andy Bye, for £50; slender silver rings set with turquoise, coral or garnet by Bob Roseberry for £5.50, and delicate necklaces of silver beads, garnets and antique ivory by Jean Davenne, £27. You'll also find lovely little *objets* like miniature glass bottles and jars by David Landsman, pillboxes in Mexican silver inlaid with abalone shell for £2.70 and small stained glass boxes from £4—perfect for thank you presents. And for those who care more about art than adornment, Turak have special exhibitions of designer and antique jewellery throughout the year.

Sample range—all prices approximate:

**Antique:** ethnic jewellery: museum-quality Yemeni wedding necklace of silver, coins and coral, £725. Rare Ethiopian silver bracelets, from £58.50. Heavy Ethiopian necklace of amber and chased silver beads, £323. Fine silver belts from India, from £55. Moroccan hand of Fatima, £27; antique Moroccan fibulas, from £17.50.

**Modern:** ethnic jewellery: Ethiopian silver chains from £66; necklaces of silver and malachite beads with antique silver cross pendants, from £35-£65. Indian plaited silver wire chokers in sacred thread motif, £47; Indian silver necklace with Paisley pattern pendants, £28.25; necklaces of West African trade beads and silver beads from Ethiopia and Rajastan, £26; earrings of coral, trade beads and silver, from £7.

---

# Captain O. M. Watts 45 Albemarle Street, W1
01-493 4633
Mon.-Fri. 9.5.30, Sat. 9-1
Telegrams: *Yachtnavi*, London W1
(Diners)

---

Set your sails for Captain Watts, on the port side of Albemarle Street. The Captain edited Reed's Almanac for many years, and he sees his world-famous establishment as a service to yachtsmen—a place where dedicated sailors will find everything they could possibly want for themselves or their yachts. The ceiling is rigged with brass lamps and anchors, and stowed on the shelves Bristol fashion, are sextants, shackles, burgees. belaying pins, charts to steer by, stoves to cook with—almost as many things as there are fish in the sea. But don't worry if you can't tell a bow from a stern—just go below to the clothing department for some of the best buys in town! There are classic heavy-knit ribbed crewneck sweaters in pure wool for only £13.50, and snappy striped French fishermen's sweaters with buttons on the shoulders for £15.50. For cheap chic, you can't beat the traditional fisherman's sailcloth smocks in boatnecked or dashing open-necked styles. Captain Watts smocks come in deep Breton red, brown and the classic navy—and unlike most other smocks, they have pockets as well. If you want a casual, warm, hardwearing wool coat, look no further than the rack of toggle-fastened duffles. They come in children's sizes too, at £10.50—unbeatable value when you compare them with the mock duffles in children's shops. There are sailcloth shorts and trousers, tailored reefer jackets and natty sailing shoes—if you use a bit of imagination, you can put together a whole new fashion look. Accessories include St Malo caps, real French Breton caps in navy canvas, and the smashing 'Maybe' belt with a buckle enamelled in a geometric pattern that combines the code flags for 'Yes' and 'No'—just £2.60! But the most marvellous accessories of all are pieces from Captain Watts's exclusive collection of hand-crafted enamelled yachting jewellery. There are port and starboard lamp charms, tiny ships wheel and anchor earrings, seahorse stickpins, reef knot cufflinks, gay bracelets enamelled with 26 code flags, one for each letter of the alphabet. They can make up bracelets that spell your name in code, supply brooches with the burgee of every yacht and sailing club in the world, or make brooches with your houseflag or personal flag to order. You can have great fun with their international code flag brooches—the pretty designs actually convey messages like *'Stop carrying out your intentions and watch for my signals'*, *'I wish to communicate'* and *'Keep clear of me, I am engaged in pair trawling.'* Now that fashion's full of sporty feeling, these unique and charming pieces are sure to start a trend. So scrape off your barnacles and hurry along!

Sample range and prices:

**Knitwear:** traditional tightly-knit Guernsey sweater with dropped shoulders, in navy only in sizes 32″-46″ from £11.95-£17.50. Ribbed crewneck whaler sweater in navy, cream, sizes small, medium, large and extra large from £13.50-£14. Children's whaler sweater, sizes 26″-32″, £8.95. Norwegian sailing sweaters and stripy boatneck sweaters, navy on cream, £14.95.

**Smocks:** traditional boatnecked fisherman's smock, sizes S, M, L, XL, from £5.95-£6.25. Open-necked sailcloth smock sizes, S, M, L, XL, from £5.95-£6.25. Jackets: ladies double-breasted reefer jackets in navy lined with red, sizes S, M, L, XL, from £21.90-£22.60. Men's double-breasted reefer jacket sizes, 32″-46″, from £29-£33.50. Duffle coats with toggles and deep patch pockets, sizes 30″-46″, £20.95. Children's duffle coat lined with plaid, sizes S, M, L, £10.50.

**Also:** sailcloth shorts with button fly, in navy, white and Breton red, sizes 30″-40″, £5.50. Sailcloth trousers, sizes 30″-44″, £8.95. St Malo cap in navy melton, £6.95, real French Breton cap, £4.95.

# The White House  51-52 New Bond Street, W1

01-629 3521
Mon.-Fri. 9.30, Sat. 9-1

Really luxury is above the vagaries of fashion—as is this world-famous establishment in which nothing but the very best will do. Since the *Belle Epoque*, this Anglo-French house has been celebrated for its exquisite handmade linens, lingerie and children's clothes—peerless creations fit for palaces, princesses and connoisseurs. Today, the White House remains a byword for sheer excellence, and its specialities travel out to royal establishments all over the world. The White House is full of beautiful treasures, many doubly so because they can never be made again. The handwoven lace used for trimming has not been made for thirty years, nor have the handspun linen ladies' handkerchiefs, as light as a sigh—but the White House has very much kept up with the times, and you'll find a vast selection of lovely things to delight the most modern of tastes. Start out in the fabulous linen department, where potentates come to furnish their palaces and pampered brides leave their wedding lists. The White House is the only place in London where you can treat yourself to linens by Porthault—the best sheets in the world—with matching towels, peignoirs, robes, trays, tablecloths and the **new Porthault breakfast services**, specially commissioned from Limoges. Go on to discover the delights of cashmere blankets, embroidered cotton voile sheets, handworked organdie table cloths—and the White House will accept special commissions for anything made to order. Why not have an elegant dressing table cover, a table cloth for a wedding breakfast, a table cloth for a banquet, wedding sheets that will be a joy forever? Then go to the lingerie department—if you're lucky, some of the White House's own exquisite pieces will be available; if not, you can have them to order, and in the meantime you can amuse yourself with some highly unusual silks. There are woven silk briefs, singlets, pure silk ski underwear, and fine **silk bloomers—just the thing to wear under jodhpurs and knickerbockers!** Don't miss the hot water bottle covers in quilted silk, silk lingerie covers, padded silk hangers and beautiful **bridal** garters—in blue satin trimmed with lace. Gentlemen will wish to acquaint themselves with the pure silk underwear in the men's department, and the ladies fashion departments offer knitwear, lovely printed silk dresses, Ascot parasols by Parsols Parisienne, classic clothes by Desarbe and the finest selection of ladies handkerchiefs anywhere in the world. If the White House had a motto, it would surely be, 'nothing is better than the best', and that is true of everything within its doors. Come to the White House—it's a place of privilege, and the privilege will be entirely yours.

Sample range and approximate prices:

**Linens:** exclusive selection of Porthault linens, the best in the world. **Sheets** by Porthault; printed kingsize sheet and two pillowcases, £165; cotton voile embroidered sheets with matching pillowcases, kingsize from £398. Blanket in quilted cotton, £190. **Towels** by Porthault: face cloth, £5.75; guest towel, £8.50; bath sheet, £38.75; bath mat, £35.50. Sheets and towels match up to Porthault's trays, table cloths, peignoirs, men's robes and new Porthault porcelain sets specially commissioned from Limoges. Fabulous selection of handworked applique and embroidered organdie and linen cloths, including organdie cloth 70″ × 90″, £147; cloth for large round table and twelve matching napkins, £155; handworked organdie tablemat sets in floral and classic designs, eight settings, £25. Special commissions undertaken. **Also,** fine blankets, including pure cashmere, kingsize, £349.

**Lingerie—in silk:** French woven Milanese brief, £9.50. English woven silk Milanese brief, in sizes slender to outsize, shell pink or white, £8; matching singlet with ribbon straps, £9.95. English silk Milanese bloomers in peach or white, reaches just to the knee, perfect under jodhpurs or with fancy garters, £9.95; to wear with

ribbed spun singlet, £9.35. Silk ski underwear, ankle length pants and long-sleeved boatneck top, in poppy red or navy, £25.50 each. Silk suspender belts in pure silk satin, in black, white, peach to order, £27. **Lingerie-in wool and silk:** bloomer and singlet, £7.45 each. **In pure wool:** bloomer and singlet, £6 each. In Swiss woven wool, shaped and fitted camisole style singlet, £9.75, and straight legged bloomer, £7.75. **Real spencers:** short and long sleeves, with button front and scoop neck with woven crochet trim, £9.50 and £11.50; other spencers from £9.75-£11.75.

**Silk Amusements:** hot water bottle covers in pure silk with quilting and embroidered flowers, in pink and blue, padded, £15.75. Padded pure silk hangers in peach, pink, white or blue, trimmed with lace, £3.75. **Bridal garter**—in blue satin trimmed with lace, £3.15. Silk lingerie covers, applique or trimmed with real lace, for covering drawers and top layers in suitcases, from £20.

**Robes:** excellent selection of gowns in velvet, pure cotton, poly cotton, pure silk, including towelling gowns by Porthault from £75-£195 and long tailored terry gowns with hood, £29. Negligee and nightgown sets in cotton and poly cotton, from £36-£114. Singl

cotton nighties, short, from £16.
Pure wool handknit bedsocks
from £6.35.

## For Women

Classic selection of bandbox-smart
models, lots of silk and pure wool
jersey. **Dresses**—the best
collection of Leonard designs in
London, also long and short
dresses by Desarbe, Bessi, Pucci,
Prince Carmina and others:
beachwear and cruisewear in stock
all year round. **Evening
Wear**—good cocktail and after six
collection, velvet evening skirts
and ball skirts. **Knits**—pure
cotton jumpers from £9.60, lots of
luxurious cashmeres including
cashmere and silk pullovers, £105
with zip front, £70 with cowl
neck. **Stoles**—a large selection,
including polyester stoles from
£15, pure wool stoles with
handknotted fringe from £42 and
silk St. Laurent stoles from £80.
**Also:** shirts in plain or printed
polyester or silk, skirts, suits,
coats, slacks, scarves in Swiss
cotton and Italian and French
silk, designer scarves by Leonard,
Pucci and others, costume
jewellery, parasols, perfumes,
crocodile handbags from £175,
French calf handbags from £75,
and evening bags.

## For Men

Shirts in sizes 14½-17½, some
17½'s in silk. In cotton and cotton
polyester, long and short sleeves,
button and French cuffs, from
£14. Silk shirts from £26 in
cream, from £31 in colours. Swiss
cotton knit shirts with short
sleeves, £24; long sleeved knit
wool shirts, £11.50. **Underwear:**
in silk, pure briefs, £9.50;
matching singlet, £11.50;
matching T-shirt, £13.50. English
wool and silk trunks, £9.10;
matching singlet, £8.30; matching
T-shirt, £11.50. Also pure silk
cotton underwear in similar styles.
**Handkerchiefs:** the best selection
in London, in snowy white and all
the colours of the rainbow. All are
hand-rolled, prices from £1.20 for
plain to £3.95 for coloured, and
specialities include the
increasingly rare pure white linen
handkerchiefs at £14.40 per
dozen, and women's handspun
linen handkerchiefs from
Northern France, which are no
longer made, £20 per dozen. **Also:**
a selection of classic cashmere
knitwear, including intarsias in
single and double weights, from
£45. Smart ties, including a fine
selection by Leonard, and belts by
L'Aiglon.

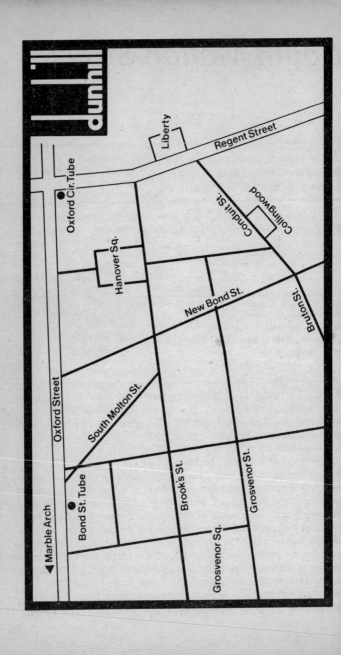

# South Molton Street

---

**Ace** 51 South Molton Street, W1    01-499 1469
Mon.-Sat. 9.30-6, Thurs. 9.30-7
(American Express, Barclaycard)

---

The **Kings Road look** in South Molton Street; for description and prices, see separate listing under 'Chelsea' section.

---

**Browns** 25-27 South Molton
Street, W1    01-491 7833
Mon.-Wed. and Fri. 10-6, Thurs. 10-7,
Sat. 10-5
(American Express, Barclaycard, Diners)

---

Living life to the full and enjoying it is what Browns is all about. Browns good looks depend on you—the clothes are subtle, undemanding, completely relaxed, never contrived or fussy. They give you the confidence of wearing something that is absolutely superb—and after that, it's up to you to make the most of it. Nothing could be easier, because Browns have created a look of their own, and a life style to go with it. Browns means *everything* working together—hair, makeup, clothes, shoes, the food you eat and the plates you eat off. You can spend a whole day in South Molton Street, have lunch at the Molton Brown restaurant, buy some new clothes and have a Molton Brown hairstyle to match. At the end of a Browns day, you'll be able to look in the mirror and see the person you always hoped was there. Showing you how to live is the first step—after that, Browns will teach you more about fashion than any other shop in England. Mrs. Sidney Burstein has magnificent taste and a rare imagination. She was the first to recognise Sonia Rykiel's potential, the first to bring the Missonis to England, and under her direction Browns will be having their most exciting season ever. There's a new upstairs salon, and the walls between the fashion, shoe and living shops have been taken away so you can see the clothes and accessories as total looks. The living shop has a whole new image—less obviously pretty, much more definite and natural, with lots of handwoven wool rugs, rush baskets, antique linen, needlepoint tapestries by Lilian Delevoryas and exclusive fabrics designed by Kaffe Fassett. Biggest news of all—the **Brown's Studio collection for women**, a wardrobe of easy jackets, trousers and skirts, cotton knits, stripy shirts, pretty schoolgirl sandals. And that's just the beginning. This spring Browns is **the only place in London where you'll find the exciting Giorgio Armani collection, Geoffrey Beene couture, Missoni, Sonia Rykiel, Alvear and Private Label designs by Pinky and Diane**. Look out for blazers, shorts and transparent voile vests by Armani, stripy blouson tops and fine cotton dresses in curry colours by Missoni, soft jackets and gathered skirts by Geoffrey Beene, pastoral charmers by Krizia and Chloé, simple linens by France Andrevie and Corine Bricaire, gym slip dresses and Pierrot styles by Pablo and Delia, easy shifts and shirts by Bulle e Pupe and brightly coloured layered ensembles by Sonia Rykiel, with two pairs of trousers, one worn over the other. The outfits are accessorised and shown exactly as they were at the collections, and the staff will tell you how to get the best out of the new looks. That's what makes Browns so special—where else could you learn so much about life and style and making the most of yourself!

Sample range—all prices approximate:

High fashion designs in sizes 6-16. **Browns Studio collection** for women: pure cotton *gilets*, about £20; spring Fairisle sweaters, sizes S, M and L, from about £28. Natural linen blazers, about £50; also, raincoats, skirts and trousers. **Shoes** by Rossetti and Maud Frizon, in sizes 34½-41½. Browns Studio shoes, in sizes 35½-39½, schoolgirl sandals, Nubuck sandals, sporty laceup training shoes, from £36-£40. **Living shop** needle point tapestry kits by Lilian Delevoryas, £36. Clarice Cliff ceramics, Thirties pottery, pieces by Charlotte Rhead, Carlton Ware and Radford. Quilted mugs, teapots and plates by Ray Saddington, rag rugs, antique linen and lace, Agraria *potpourri*, knit cushions and fabrics designed by Kaffe Fassett, Gianini diaries, Il Bisonte leather goods, Fendi luggage.

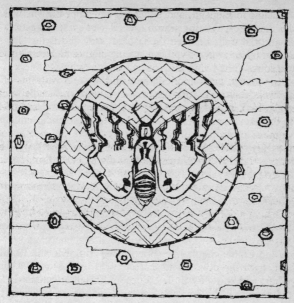

*Needlepoint design by Kaffe Fassett at Browns*

## Carolyn Brunn  4 South Molton Street, W1   01-629 1708
Mon.-Sat. 10-6
(Access, American Express, Barclaycard, Mastercharge)

Knitwear is a way of life here, and you can choose knits for all
seasons and occasions from an exclusive collection that includes
the *bouclé* classics that have always been a Carolyn Brunn
speciality, and superb new designs with panache to spare at a
fraction of Paris prices. All the pieces are sold separately, and the
collection has been keyed for perfect match-or-contrast
coordination in fine natural shades like pale grey, camel, beige
and mink lightened with bilberry for early spring, and soft
romantic peach, cream, biscuit and almond green for summer.
Look out for the new cossack-style band neck tunics to wear over
softly gathered dropped panel skirts on elasticated waistbands,
scoop neck pure wool blousons, waffle textured pullovers and
loose stripy blousons with big cowl necks. In the classic vein

you'll find all the old favourites—pintucked smock dresses, V-neck *bouclé* sweater dresses, lots of easy smocks that make excellent maternity tops. These are knits for modern living—completely comfortable, undemanding and specially designed so you can build up a whole wardrobe of looks from a few basic pieces. And you don't have to stick to knitwear, because there are Mulberry belts and accessories, a whole wall of silk, Viyella and cord shirts by Michel Axel, and cord and cotton skirts by Hardware Clothing Company. All the knits are made up under the Brunn's direction, so there are no middle-man markups and you get tremendous value for money. If you're lucky enough to find partner Paddy Campbell in the shop, you'll also get some of the best advice on dressing and accessories that London has to offer. Personal service, style and good prices are the reasons why Carolyn Brunn's customers come back again and again.

Sample range—all prices approximate:

Clothes in sizes 10-4. **Skirts:** dropped panel skirt, £22.50; skirts in wool and *bouclé*, in a range of styles, from £20. **Sweaters:** from £19.50, including waffle texture V-neck, £24.95; soft pure wool scoop neck blouson, £19.50; very heavy cream pole with ribbed cowl neck and ribbing at cuffs and hem, £29.95. **Tops:** stripy cowl neck blouson, £22.50; cossack tunic top, £24.95; pintucked smocks, £24.95. Dresses from £30-£38; *bouclé* V-neck dress, £35.50; pintucked smock dress, £35; new scoop neck bouson dress in pure wool, £32.50. *Bouclé* suits in classic Chanel style, about £55. Winter jackets from about £45; very stylish heavy kimono wrap coats with turnback contrast cuffs, about £75; also, knitted rouleaux, pull-on hats and long scarves to go with all the knits.

---

**Friends** 44 South Molton Street, W1    01-629 1552
Mon.-Sat. 10-6, Thurs. 10-7

A friend indeed to anyone in need of good looks at great prices, Friends have the complete French Connection collection of young *prêt-à-porter* styles with all the dash of Continental originals, at half the cost or less. A parallel of the Continental new look rather than a straight copy, the clothes are exceptionally wearable, undemanding and flattering—often more so than designs from top French and Italian houses. Most of the collection has been designed by Nicole Farhi, and everything has the casual young *dégagé* feeling that characterises her work. The look is easy, relaxed but always effective—the colours and styles are complimentary so you can easily build up several layered ensembles from a few pieces, and the shapes and details always capture the mood of the season perfectly. Last winter there were lots of big overshirts in soft brushed cotton, plaid and plain, to wear over silk shirts and cord skirts at £18.95, and superb shift dresses modelled on French jeweller's smocks for £16.95—unbeatable value for money. This summer, look out for lots of soft embroidered and *appliqué* dresses, full skirts and shirts, muted flower prints in cinnamon, sage, avocado, soft yellow and ruby port. Also at Friends, a choice selection of designs in rough silk and cotton blends from the Stephen Marks collection.

Sample range—all prices approximate:

In sizes S, M and L. **Shirts:** pretty feminine blouses with scalloped collars, £16; tailored shirts with flap pocket and small collars, £8.95; brushed cotton shirt in tiny check, with scalloped collar, £14.95; matching full skirt, £19.95. **Dresses;** a range, including jeweller's smock shift dress, £16.95. Stephen Marks smock dress in Prince of Wales plaid, £20. Jeans in sizes 10-14, from £14.95; jodphurs from £25.95. **Jackets:** tweed hacking jackets, £29.95; padded builted jackets with toggle fastening, about £30; heavy cotton sleeveless waistcoats, £15.50. **Knits:** Fairisle V-neck slipover, £11.95; Fairisle sleeveless cardigan, £12.95; Fairisle round- or V-neck pullovers, £16.95; chunky handknits from £30. Also, lots of skirts from £13.95. **Special note:** Friends also at 170 Kensington High Street, W8. 01-937 4665, Mon.-Fri. 10-6, Sat. 10-5.30.

# Kickers 66 South Molton Street, W1   01-629 1718

Mon.-Fri. 10-6, Sat. 10-5
(Access, American Express, Barclaycard)

What's summer white all over, with grass and daisies around the sides, a green dot under the right heel, a red dot under the left, and a heart under each instep? It's Kickers, the shoes of the Seventies. Where other shoes follow the fashions or ignore them, Kickers started a whole new look for men, women and children, and kicked off a life style to boot. It's the weekend look worn all

95

week long—sporty laceups to go with blousons, casual Nubuck slipons to wear wtih unconstructed jackets,—everything on springy soles to remind you with each step that life is a game, not a grind. The basic canvas Kicker is a game in itself—criss-crossed with contrast topstitching and scattered with so many tiny Kickers lables and logos that they look like a soccer strategy plan. Then come Snowballs and Kicksnows with snow caterpillar tread, Kick Rain boots and Kick's de Kickers—the Formula 1 sports shoes in Nubuck leather with soles treaded like a racing tyre and inward-slanting 'mudguard' heels that give a pivot for quick braking. They're all as much fun as they sound, but Kickers don't play games when it comes to quality and comfort. The edges that meet the ankle or calf are bound in softest leather to give a gentle grip instead of a chafe. The rubber and crepe used in the *pre-* and *après-*ski range will not crack in the cold, and Kickers crepe soles and Nubuck leather pass the demanding test of being firm and flexible at the same time. Every Kickers shoe has a raised padded instep for proper support, and every Kickers is completely washable with soap and water. This summer Kickers come in white for the first time, and there are new combinations like lemon with green, red with green, grey with white, new soft oxblood red, sage green and sandy beige colours as well as the bright primary shades, with new corrugated sole laceups and ladies Nubuck & leather boots. So many people have lost their hearts to Kickers that the new range is called the *J'aime Kickers* collection, and there are *J'aime Kickers* T-shirts, sweatshirts and shoebags, lots of new accessories, socks dyed in match the shoes, Kickers hats and satchels, legwarmers and boot tops, ladies long john Shetlands, the complete Hot Nitz collection, Kickers shoehorns—even Kickers skateboards, for those who want to move with the times. Feeling casual, colourful, comfortable and fun? If the shoe fits, wear it!

Sample range—all prices approximate:

**Shoes:** in sizes 18-47. Kickers sandals from £10.95, Kickers boots from £40; Kickers canvas lace-ups from £12.95; Kickers shoes in Nubuck from £34.95.

**Accessories:** large stars and stripes satchels, £12.95; Kickers polo shirts, £3.95; Kickers sweatshirts, £5.95, and T-shirts, £3.95. Kickers sunvisors, £1.95; sportscaps, £2.50; beanie hat, £2.50. Kickers skateboard, £29.95. Kicker shoebags, £1.95. Kickers pencil cases filled with coloured pencils, £5.95.

**Prestat**   24 South Molton Street, W1   01-629 4838
Mon.-Fri. 10-6, Sat. 9-5.30
By appointment to Her Majesty the Queen, purveyors of chocolates

Chocolates never go out of fashion, and this one place where
'good taste' is something you can really get your teeth into.
Prestat goes a long way toward giving South Molton Street its
unique flavour. Back in the Twenties, Prestat was the darling of
the Bright Young Things—and today, this delightful
establishment is everybody's sweetheart. The chocolates are made
on the premises, and if you pass by while a batch is in progress,
you will be drawn *irresistibly* to the door. Inside you'll find the
fabulous Prestat truffles, *the finest in the world*, made to an old
family recipe dating from the time of Napoleon III. There are
*bonbonnières* of plump Brandy Cherries wrapped in rich gold foil,
dishes of delicate chocolate wafers and Prestat's exclusive Coffee
Mints—coffee cream centres covered with luxurious peppermint
chocolate, a tremendous treat. There are boxes and boxes of
dark-coated delights—chocolate-covered marzipan, rum and raisin
marzipan, nougat, coffee and brandy cream, raspberry,
strawberry and tangerine creams, peppermints, bittermints,
noisettes, caramels, rose and violet creams, chocolate ginger and
pineapple pieces, glossy hazelnuts and brazils, and delicious *bonne
bouches*. On high days and holidays, the windows of Prestat rival
those of the finest French *chocolatiers*—there are Easter figures
made from antique moulds, hand-decorated chocolate Easter eggs
with names written in chocolate, eggs filled with chocolate creams
or truffles, Valentine Day hearts with names or *bon mots*, special
pieces for Mother's Day or Christmas—or at any time of the
year—the most splendid sumptuous gift boxes. Prestat's
specialities are so well-loved that there are queues outside the
shop at Easter and at Christmas, and you would be wise to place
your orders early. The service is impeccable—and among the Jet
Set it's quite the thing to have Prestat chocolates flown in from
halfway round the world. Few establishments have given so much
pleasure to so many people—so come to Prestat, and taste the
sweet life!

Sample range and prices:
**Napoleon truffles:** flavoured with
rum, coffee or vanilla, from £3.60
a pound when packed in cartons,
from £3.90 a pound when packed
in fancy red boxes. **Brandy
Cherries:** made with Morello
cherries matured in brandy for

97

over 18 months, £6.50 a pound; quarter pound boxes, £1.65. Handmade chocolate Chocolate Mints from £2.60 for three-quarter pound. **Coffee Mints** and **Double Mints**, from £2.60 for three-quarter pound. **Marrons glaces**, from £3.50 for a half pound box. **Handmade Chocolates**, soft or chewy centres, £3.90 a pound. **Gift boxes** from £4.50 for a beautifully done up three-quarter pound box. Speciality charges and postal service particulars available on request.

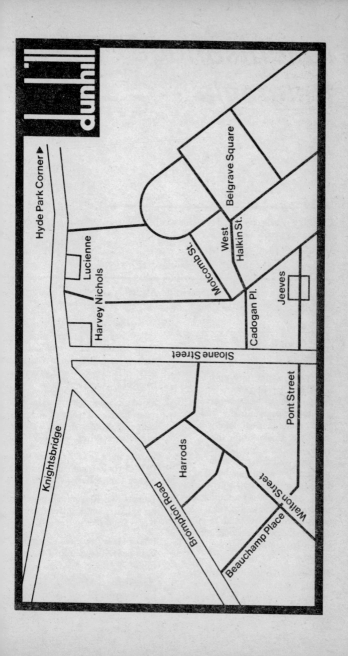

# Knightsbridge
# Belgravia

**Hardy Amies** 42 Hans Crescent, SW1
01-584 2115
Mon.-Sat. 10-6, Wed. 10-7
(Access, American Express, Barclaycard)

Winner of the 1976 Fashion Guide Award, this charming shop is
the place to see Hardy Amies' easy classics at their best.

## The Sportswear Collection

'Sport with style' sums up his
collection of young-look
designs—lots of knits, separates,
jackets and coats in a mix and
match range that will take you
anywhere. Look out for the
'two-piece dress' long an Amies
speciality and a wise fashion
investment—worn together they
make up into a classic shirtwaister
dress, and if you get a toning skirt
and top you'll have a perfect
switch—around weekender
wardrobe. Sportswear collection in
sizes 8-16, sample range and
prices:

**Knitwear:** co-ordinated knitwear
making up into matching or
contrast sets, all sold separately so
you can put together your own

look. Sweaters and cardigans in
plain colours and tweedy-look
yarn, all matching up to skirts. In
acrylic, lambswool, and cashmere,
from £18.49.

**Skirts:** in solid colours and softly
smart checks, a range of styles
including slender A-line, wrapover
and pleated skirts, from £39.

**Shirts:** *crêpe de Chine* shirts from
£45, shirts in manmade fibre
fabrics from £22.

**Jackets and Blazers:** all matching
up to skirts and knitwear. Camel
blazer from £69.

**Ensembles:** two-piece ensembles
from £60; dresses from £49; coats
from £79.

**Accessories:** *crêpe de Chine*
scarves from £14.50. A selection
of belts, bags and hats.

## Arabesque   12 Motcomb Street, SW1
01-235 7334
Mon.-Fri. 10-5.30

**Come here for the chic of Araby!** The excitement of the bazaar
and the elegance of Belgravia blend in this boutique full of exotic
contemporary designs and superb Eastern clothes and accessories.
Pride of place goes to an exclusive switcharound collection
inspired by traditional Eastern costumes—pure classic shapes that
transcend the 'ethnic look', adapted in the manner of the top
French couturiers at *a fraction of the cost.* For day, start with a
shirt-collared silk tunic with *rouleaux* ties at the neck—add
culottes in silk, cotton or wool *crêpe*, a mid-calf skirt or harem
pants, all with drawstring waists, in rich complimentary shades of
burnt orange, chocolate, scarlet, cream, green or black. For
cocktails, team the tunic with long culottes, or choose a slender
long silk shirt-dress with high side slits—just £42—to wear on its
own with high-laced gold sandals, or with silk harem pants in the
same or a contrast colour. The long shirtdess and harem pants *can
also be made to order* in the colour of your choice. This summer,
when natural textures and candystripe tints are making fashion
news, you can come to Arabesque for stripy djellabas in satinised
Egyptian cotton, field caftans in textured natural cotton,
handwoven linen robes and long village dresses in
seersucker-textured silk—very *à la mode*, at less than modish
prices. Part of the fun of Arabesque is the splendid variety of
stock—everything from antique Palestinian wedding dresses and
modified Lebanese shirts by Spaghetti to medieval Berber
necklaces and jodphur-like Egyptian trousers. Arabesque has
London's best selection of *abayas*—flowing bias-cut robes in silk
and silk chiffon—graceful, flattering, completely comfortable and
dressy enough for dinner or theatre parties. If you want to be the
star of the evening, come here for sequin-trimmed *abayas* to wear
with harem pants, Lebanese caftans in chiffon to wear with long
*hashemi* over-robes, gold-embroidered wool cloaks and velvet
waistcoats from Syria and elegant *thaoubs*—elaborate chiffon
gowns with graceful sleeves and a train—from Bahrein. Informal
lounging and at-home robes are another speciality—don't miss the
black cotton caftans with large panels of colourful cross-stitch
embroidery down the front for £25, or the *excellent selection of
caftans for men from £15.* You can finish off your outfit with silk
tassels, gold tassel girdles, glass bead neclaces, soft suede caps,

sashes and scarves galore. And there's *a year-round bargain rail at the back of the shop full of sale-price clothes from the previous season, all in the £9-£15 range*—a better buy than you'd find in any souk!

Clothes in sizes S, M and L. Sample range, all prices approximate:

**Special collections:** Drawstring wool crepe skirt, £30; drawstring mid-calf culottes and drawstring harem pants, both £28; scoop-necked *crêpe de Chine* caftan dress in stone, peacock or black, £58; all by Caroline Phipps. Tunic shirt in silk, £25; long silk harem trousers, £26. Long silk 'Marrakesh' shirtdress, £42. Long culottes in textured cotton or pure wool, £32. For Spring: switcharound collection of jodhpurs, trousers, overshirts and waistcoats in handwoven wool from Fez.

**Abayas:** Classic long wool abayas, from £32. Handwoven wool abayas, mid-calf length, perfect over boots and legwarmers, £52; in handwoven linen, £74. Multi-coloured patterned silk abayas from £52; plain raw silk abayas from £42. Syrian open-front abayas in fine wool, to wear as a cloak, £86; in stripy cotton laced with gold thread, £55. Flowing Saudi Arabian *higazis*, in chiffon, from about £98-£136; *thaoubs* from Bahrein, about £225.

**Caftans:** Field caftans in textured natural cotton, very popular with men, £15. Stripy djellabas in satinised Egyptian cotton, £28. Stripy boat-necked cotton caftans with pockets, £25. Natural silk caftans from Upper Egypt, from £28; black cotton caftans with cross-stitched front, £25. Cotton caftans, from Egypt, Turkey and Morocco, from £20.

**Dresses**—Sweeping village dresses from Upper Egypt, in bright flower prints, excellent for lounging, £18. Village dresses in seersucker-textured silk, cut like an abaya, £36. Rare antique Palestinian wedding dresses from £58; modern Palestinian wedding dresses in handembroidered silk, about £165.

**Also:** Argentinian wool **ponchos** in natural colours, £45; in wool and cotton, £28. Cotton jersey **legwarmer trousers** with drawstring waist, £18; jodphur-like **Egyptian trousers**, £35; **Turkish trousers**, £32. **Scarves** from £2.50; long **silk tassels** from £7.50; bead necklaces from £5. Gold-embroidered Syrian **waistcoats**, £48; gold-embroidered wool **cloaks**, £86. Also, antique Chinese and Eastern robes and antique Eastern jewellery, including gold Somali wedding necklaces, from £68 and antique Berber necklaces in amber and coral, from £80.

*By Linda Kee Scott for Laura Ashley*

## Laura Ashley 7-9 Harriet Street, SW1

01-235 9797

Mon. 12.30-6; Tues.-Fri. 9.30-6; Sat. 10-5.30

Like Gigi, Laura Ashley has suddenly grown up—and *vive la différence*! The Edwardian frocks, prim collars and prints as fussy as Nanny have finally been left behind—only the romantic pure whites remain, as wedding dresses, blouses and nightgowns. Instead, Laura Ashley's looks for this Spring and Summer are full of the delights of a young woman finding out about life—and *enjoying* it. There are low-cut camisoles, frilly bandeau bras and matching skirts, easy drawstring blouses, frothy petticoats, nonchalant off-the-shoulder dresses, gypsy dresses with crossover *décolletage* you can adjust to suit your mood. And though she's still a country girl at heart, Laura Ashley shows a new grown up pastoral prettiness—dungaree dresses worn with gardeners hats, smocked country tops and flounced skirts, lots of rich full-blown flower prints on cambric and voile. Last autumn's easy dresses, big shirts and full skirts turn up for summer in plain cotton and drill, and there are strappy jumpsuits with harem bottoms, sporty blousons and trousers tied at the ankle! Lynda Kee Scott's designs for Laura Ashley will be one of the treats of the season, at prices that give wonderful value for money. Thank Heaven for little girls—when they grow up in the most delightful way.

Sample range—all prices approximate:

Clothes in sizes 10-14, or S, M and L. Midcalf dresses from £8.25-£14.75; long dresses, £11.75-£14.75. Midcalf skirts, from £6.50-£10.50; blouses and camisole tops from £3.50-£7. Smocks from £5-£12.75; nightgowns from £8-£11.75; long skirts from £8-£9.25; aprons from £4.25 to £10.50.

## Browns 6c Sloane Street, SW1   01-235 7973

Mon.-Fri. 10-6, Wed. 10-7, Sat. 10-5

The pick of international high fashion, see separate listing under 'South Molton Street' section.

**Carolyn Brunn**  211 Brompton Road, SW3   01-584 9065
Mon.-Sat. 10-6
(Access, American Express, Barclaycard, Mastercharge)

Well-priced designer knitwear, see listing under 'South Molton Street' section.

**Don Cooper**  40 Beauchamp Place, SW3   01-584 2656
Mon.-Sat. 9-5
(American Express, Diners)

As one of the few remaining jewellers with workshops on his premises, Don Cooper can avoid the usual middleman mark-ups, and his shop is the place to find classic and contemporary jewellery at excellent prices. One of the best-kept secrets in Knightsbridge, he has lots of little luxuries like 9ct love knot rings for under £10, and interchangeable flower earrings in lapis, coral, cornelian, tiger's eye, rock crystal, green agate from £8 a pair. There are some excellent buys in the £300-£700 bracket, rings and necklaces that look like they cost twice as much—and would if you bought them elsewhere.

Sample range and prices:

**Rings:** single love knot gold 9ct ring, plain or twist, from £9; double love knot gold 9ct ring, plain or twist, from £15; 9ct Mother and Child ring from £42; 9-wire Russian wedding ring, 9ct gold, plain or twist and plain/twist, from £49.50; chain ring with heart set in diamonds, from £63; twist love knot ring, 18ct gold, with ruby and diamond or turquoise and diamond, from £140; eternity ring, centre band of diamonds, with two bands of twist and plain on either side, from £975; four ¼ct diamonds set in diamond shape form with twist surround, from £730.

**Earrings:** interchangeable flower earrings in lapis, coral, cornelian, tiger's eye, rock crystal, green agate, from £8 a pair or with little gold studs from £4 a pair or with tiny diamonds from £100 a pair; little gold circle earrings with tiny diamonds from £40; superb ½ct diamonds with twist gold surround, from £800 a pair.

**Necklaces:** fine gold choker chains from £12; fine gold choker chains with apples, flowers, hearts from £19; tiny choker chain in 18ct, 'Prince of Wales' design from £30; delicate gold chain, sprinkled with small diamonds six from £285; Twist bars gold choker with ¼ct diamond set in knot, from £195 in 9ct and from £260 in 18ct.

**Pendants:** diamond and enamel butterfly pendant on chain from £105; small butterfly with ruby eyes in amethyst, malachite or lapis on a fine chain from £45; rock crystal flowers with diamond centres from £90; Allah pendant, 18ct gold, on green agate with Allah sign set with diamonds, from £365; pavé set diamond heart from £695. **Matching sets:**

necklaces and earrings in twist circles of gold set with ¼ct diamonds, from £325 for the earrings and necklace from £225; clover shaped earrings and pendant set with ¼ct diamonds from £775; 18ct gold and tortoishell butterfly with four diamonds set into tortoishell wings and body, earrings to match from £460 set. **Bracelets:** plain hook bracelets from £26: 9ct gold wire 'elephant hair' type bracelet from £137.

# Emeline  45 Beauchamp Place, SW3   01-589 0552
Mon.-Fri. 10-6, Sat. 10-5

Emeline is the French accessories boutique that put the natural look into London fashion, and this is the place to come for chains, rings, bangles and beads that are the indispensible part of the smart set look. If you want to put together one of those necklaces with a hundred different pendants you can do it here in one go, or if you prefer a more subdued look you can choose a fine French gold chain that circles the neck with tiny sparkly hearts or stars. The collection includes pieces in coral, rosewood, agate, amberlite, shells, lapis, crystal and *pâté de verre*, and new shipments are always arriving from the continent and the Far East.

Sample range and prices:

**Rings:** slender 9ct gold rings for wearing several to a finger, from £6.50; twisted gold bands from £7 and in larger sizes from £17; agate bands from £3.50; 18ct gold plate ring set with a red coral rose, £8.50.

**Necklaces:** fine gold chains from £11.50; fine gold choker chains with tiny hearts or stars, £24, wear with matching bracelets, £13 and tiny 9ct gold heart or star

stud earrings, £12, gold choker chains with coral, jade, onyx, gold, lapis or rose quartz beads, £35; sporty link necklaces in gold plate, several lengths from £13.75 and real thirties *pâté de verre* necklaces from £18. Also, ankle chains to order, from £15—allow ten days for delivery.

**Pendants:** malachite and lapis hearts from £6. Pendant crosses in jade or malachite with gold from

£75. Sapphire pendants from £50.

**Earrings:** coloured stud earrings, £5 and slender 9ct hoop earrings in all sizes from £6; also lapis, tiger's eye, jade, onyx, rose quartz, gold and pearl studs, all for pierced ears from £12.50.

**Specialities:** coral jewellery necklaces and choker beads from £47; large Victorian multi-strand necklaces from £180; bracelets from £37; all types of pendants from £6; plain ear studs for pierced ears from £14.50.

# **Harrods** Knightsbridge, SW1

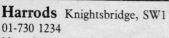

01-730 1234

Mon.-Sat. 9-5, Wed. 9-7

Telegrams: *Harrods Everything*, London SW1

(Access, American Express, Barclaycard, Diners, Eurocard)

By appointment to Her Majesty the Queen, suppliers of provisions

By appointment to H.R.H. the Duke of Edinburgh, outfitters

By appointment to Her Majesty Queen Elizabeth the Queen Mother, suppliers of glass, china and fancy goods

Harrods is the most famous store in the world, amply living up to its motto of *Omnia Omnibus Ubique*—'Everything, for everyone, everywhere'. There are thirteen and a half acres of selling space on five floors, a Customer's Advisory Bureau with interpreters for a host of languages including Arabic and Iranian, five restaurants, a fruit juice bar, an ice-cream parlour, an in-store pub—"The Green Man"—downstairs from the Man's Shop, more than thirty fashion departments for men, women and children, a children's hairdressing salon on the fourth floor, a men's hairdressing salon adjoining the Man's Shop, and the largest hair and beauty salon in the world. These items are of particular interest:

## Special Services

Winner of The Fashion Guide's 1977 Award for Service, Harrods offer their customers a splendid array of very special services. There's a Theatre ticket office where you can book for the theatre, ballet, opera and sporting events, a Travel Bureau where you can make arrangements for travel by air, rail or sea all over the world, an Export Bureau where expert advice is freely given

*Windsmoor at Harrods*

to visitors from abroad and those who wish to send gifts overseas, and a bank open *six* days a week from 9.30 a.m. until *an hour before closing time*—jolly useful if you suddenly have to *buy traveller's cheques on a Saturday, or after regular banks are closed.* Harrod's library provides readers with a constant supply of the latest titles. Biographies and books on history and travel are a speciality: books can be personally exchanged or *sent through the post*, and a years subscription costs £16. *Harrods gift vouchers can be exchanged* in any House of Fraser store in Britain, and there are Gift vouchers in Australian dollars for use in stores of the David Jones or Georges groups. Gift tokens are also available in the Hair and Beauty salon, and the tokens can be used for any of a range of treatments that include hairstyling, facials and manicures. Harrods's account customers receive copies of the Christmas and Linen catalogues free of charge, and Harrods welcome mail order requests for merchandise throughout the store. The Harrods delivery service operates within a radius of about thirty miles from London, and there's a *special all-night answering service* that takes messages and orders for the Food Halls.

## The Harrods Sales

Held twice a year, in mid-July and early January, the sales offer regular stock and high quality special purchase goods at vastly reduced prices. Bargains available on the first day are legendary—as are the crowds and queues that begin to gather well before dawn. If you're coming for the ladies fashion buys, join the queues at the Hans Crescent entrace—that way you can nip straight up to the first floor on the stairs or escalators, without having to wait for lifts.

## The Harrods Fashion Shows

Shows of international ready-to-wear held annually, in September. Shows are held twice a day for a week, at 11 a.m. and 2.30 p.m. No bookings are accepted, and all the items in the show can be purchased immediately on the fashion floors—including specially designed millinery from the first floor Hat Room. For the dates of this year's fashion shows and sales, ring Harrods.

## The Giftwrap Boutique

This boutique has every imaginable paper, ribbon and trim, and a talented staff who use them to create the most splendid and imaginative gift packages in London. There are oval and round boxes in several sizes, handmade ribbon rosettes and roses, and they excel at special orders. If you're giving a birthday present, they can make you a box that looks like a cake. A racing driver was delighted with a golden box decorated with a huge ribbon pompom in his racing colours, and they've even gift-wrapped a go-kart. At Christmas there's a special giftwrap service where you can leave your presents to be wrapped and kept under lock and key until you collect them. Minimum charge, 50p.

## Fashion

Harrods have the largest selection of clothes and accessories under one roof, with something for every taste and budget, size and shape. Every department is worth a visit.

### On the ground floor you'll find:

**The Man's Shop:** a complete men's shop with suits, shirts, overcoats, casual wear and the largest selection of ties anywhere.

**Leisure Man:** come here for the complete leisure look; pure relaxation clothes for town and country, at home or abroad, by top international names like Pancaldi, Valentino, Yves St. Laurent and Hom. The collection includes leisure suits and shirts, knitwear, underwear, beach and swim wear, shoes, bags, belts and jewellery. Leisure Man **even has its own Leisure Circle wine bar**, serving fine vintages, *pâtes* and cheeses!

**Junior Man:** a new downstairs area full of the latest in leisure clothes for boys and young men, aged 8-18.

**House and Around:** inexpensive dresses and lounging wear.

**Ladies Hats:** a comprehensive selection of inexpensive hats in all styles.

**Fine jewellery and Silver:** jewellery and silver department, including clocks and watches, the David Morris boutique and the splendid Collingwood showroom at Harrods, beautifully appointed in blue suede, grey flannel and cream leather, a suitable setting for their fine collection (see separate listing under 'Mayfair' section).

**Perfumery Hall:** the largest perfumery department in Europe, with scents from 26 perfume houses and cosmetics from 28 cosmetic houses. This is the only place in England apart from the Gucci shops, where you can buy Gucci perfume.

**Tote Bags:** useful stylish totes in a wide range of fabrics and colours.

**Haberdashery:** excellent trims, braids and tassles, and a fine collection of fabric flowers.

**Fashion Jewellery:** an extremely popular department, with a comprehensive selection of finishing touches for every look.

**Scarves:** in every size and colour, printed and plain, with a particularly good selection of silk scarves.

**Clansman Tartan Shop:** real *Highland high fashion*, the smartest tartans in town! The collection includes **tartan culottes**, sweeping capes and jabot blouses with detachable tiers of lace, so you can wear one, two or full-dress three to suit the occasion. Coloured shirts tone with every tartan—in a fine knit fabric that makes the ensembles look particularly chic. There are lots of long and day length skirts, and you have the option of a kilted style, or a real traditional kilt. More lovely things—tartan viyella blouses, knee rugs in wool or wool with cashmere, mohair tartan scarves, luxurious stoles and shawls, toning knitwear in lambswood, shetland and cashmere. Also, a fine collection of tartan everythings for children, ages 2-14.

**Fabrics:** fashion fabrics for all occasions.

**The Rainbow Shop:** a comprehensive selection of weathercoats in the medium price range.

**The first floor** is devoted entirely to women's and children's fashions—four and a half acres of the finest ready-to-wear from all over the world. Here you'll find:
**The International Room:** a salon lit up with the star names in *prêt-à-porter*. New Courrèges and Givenchy boutiques, both exclusive to Harrods. Superb Zandra Rhodes boutique with clothes from her 'Works of Art', 'Z' and luxury *lingerie* collection. The John Bates couture collection, and designs by Hanae Mori, Tiktiner, Janice Wainwright, Anna Beltrao and Ungaro.

**International Coats and Suits:** including dresses and co-ordinated knit collections by Cojana, Christian Dior London, Tricosa, Sora and others. In the same area: **Figure 18**, elegant clothes in sizes 18-26.

**The Designer Room;** an exciting collection of designer names, including Jean Muir, Gordon Luke Clarke, Gina Fratini, Jane Cattlin, Christian Aujard, Benny Ong, Jean Varon, Louis Feraud by Rembrandt and Baccarat. New Bill Gibb designer boutique.

**Evening Separates:** a whole new look with a young, easy feeling just right for the times. There are silky blouses, harem pants, quilted satin jackets, sporty striped velvet evening blousons, lots of black and white sprinkled with silver. Wear them to dinner parties, openings, anything under the moon. It's a new way of evening dressing, and the staff are expert at showing you how to make the most of it, beautifully.

**Evening and After Six:** medium price evening wear by Yuki at Rembrandt, Roland Klein at Marcel Fenez, Frank Usher, Juliet Dunn and others.

**Fur Room:** the largest selection of fine furs in Europe, mostly by Grosvenor of Canada, exclusive to Harrods.

**Suede and Leather:** a fabulous department with the exclusive Miura collection, the Roberto

111

Cavalli boutique, designs by Caroline Charles and Patti Searle, the largest collection of Beged-Or in Europe and sensational up-to-the-minute designs by Leone. The classic looks are exceptionally supple and stylish, elegant clothes of distinction. In another vein, look out for the masterful Miura casuals and Cavalli's splendid printed denim trimmed with suede, or velvets used with printed suede—a new collection every season. Top

**Coat Room and Weathercoats:** everything from mink-lined cashmere coats to snappy young styles. Names include Aquascutum, Burberry, Weatherall, Jaegar and Stephen Marks.

**Suit Room:** tailored classics and snappy young styles, labels include Mansfield's new Cache d'Or range.

**The Jaegar Shop:** top contemporary classics, see separate listing in this section.

**The Dress Room:** a huge selection of the best in medium priced dresses. Exeptionally attractive, wide choice of styles from all over the world.

**Calypso Room:** elegant swimwear and cruisewear in stock all year round, including smart coordinated wraps, coverups and accessories.

**Shirts and Skirts:** an international selection of coordinated looks and switcharound separates, including the largest selection of Cacharel in London.

**Windsmoor:** model collection of fine coats, dresses, jackets, suits, ensembles and separates.

**Younger Set Boutique:** a fine collection of young-style clothes by French Connection, Louis Caring, John Marks, Ivar Wahl, Daniel Hechter and many others—and music to help you choose by.

**The Hat Room:** a wonderful selection for every occasion, also hats to order.

**The Bridal Room:** everything for the bride and her attendants. Over a hundred styles by fifteen top designers, some exclusive to Harrods. The selection includes gowns in handpainted silk.

**Gaston Jaunet Boutique & Separates Room**

**Knitwear:** London's largest selection of cashmere, shetland and lambswool knits, complemented by fashion knits from Europe.

**Lingerie:** pyjamas, night shirts, nightgowns, *peignoirs*—everything from sweet sprigged, smocked cottons to floaty chiffons and slender satiny gowns trimmed with lace. Stylish designs by Charles Grahame.

**Younger Set Lingerie:** up-to-the-minute underthings, including slinky strappy nightdresses and matching sets of French knickers and suspender belts.

**Housecoats:** a fine and comprehensive selection, with lots of designs from America. Range includes long hooded towelling robes in super colours at a very good price, quilted housecoats, dressy velvet housecoats, light Indian cotton caftans.

**Loungewear:** everything for

relaxing and entertaining at home, to fit today's more casual mood.

**Bras and Corsets:** a vast selection of foundations, with specialist fitting and advice.

**Shoes:** Harrods' own collection of shoes from Britain, Spain and Italy. Also, the Rayne Boutique and the Kurt Geiger Boutique.

On the fourth floor you'll find:

## Olympic Way

Harrods fabulous new sport and leisure complex, with sports gear galore. The department caters for skiing, golf, tennis, squash, sailing—active sports of every sort. There are shooting-fishing-and-riding gear, backpacking and camping equipment, keep-fit kits—and fashion sportswear and accessories to go with everything.

## Way In

A one-stop world of young, with-it ready-to-wear, complete with a restaurant, record bar and Trimmers, the unisex hairdressers. The Way In selection includes: shoes boots by The Chelsea Cobbler (see separate listing under 'Chelsea' section), Chi-Cha, a jewellery boutique specialising in silver, gold and semi-precious stones, the Silver Bar, with a wide range of silver jewellery, and *the Jousse boutique for women, full of stylish separates by Jousse of France.* Also at Way In:

## For Women

In sizes 8-16, 32"-38" chest: separates and coordinates by Outlander, Dranella of Denmark, Just Gordon. Knitwear by Crochette and La Squadra. Jeans by Levi Strauss, New Man, Marshall Lester, Inega. Clothes by Stirling Cooper, Jeff Banks, Radley, Strawberry Studio. T-shirts by Emesse, swimwear by Nelbarden and Tweka, lingerie by Martin Emprex. Also, costume jewellery by Adrien Mann and

**Children's Wear:** clothes for fashion-conscious children by Gina Fratini, Daniel Hechter, Cacharel, Barbara Farber, Viyella House. Also, the Ladybird boutique and London's only Du Jardin boutique.

**Children's Shoes:** with shoes by Buster Brown.

Corocraft, make-up by Mary Quant and Biba, handbags by Burberry, sunglasses, hosiery and accessories.

## For Men

In sizes 36-44: Suits, separates and jackets by Daniel Hechter, New Man, Cacharel and Jupiter of France. Underwear by Hom, top-to-toe accessories, fine beachwear and leisurewear from the outstanding Sabre collection.

113

**Harvey Nichols** Knightsbridge, SW1

01-235 5000

Mon.-Sat. 9.30-6, Wed. 9.30-7

Telegrams: *Harveys*, London SW1

(Access, American Express, Barclaycard, Diners, Eurocard)

By appointment to Her Majesty Queen Elizabeth the Queen Mother, drapers

THE FASHION GUIDE
The Best Store Presentation 1977

Harvey Nichols is the greatest show on earth, a dazzling display of style and glamour, where shopping is an exciting adventure, a happening—and where the most wonderful things will happen to *you*. Forget categories, age and departments—think, like Harvey Nichols, in terms of *fashion*, *lifestyle* and *freedom of expression*. Do away with the barriers that hold you back, dare to see yourself in a beautiful new light. This is *total fashion* with all the flair and fancy of today—fashion on every floor—a feast that will broaden your horizons and show you, perhaps for the first time, the limitations of the small boutiques who trade more on snobbery than style. You'll find all the boutique names, like Callaghan and Krizia—but here you have the entire collections, all the clothes and accessories from each house, shown together for a total fashion image, the way they are in Paris or on the Côte d'Azur. Harvey Nichols know that every woman is special, so instead of a few Krizia 'outfits' they give you Krizia as it really is—a host of beautiful possibilities and permutations, different pieces that you can combine into the nuance that's just right for *you*, complete with all the exquisite Krizia trimmings—rose chokers, necklaces, bracelets and brooches, silk roses and scarves galore. And you can have anything you like, even a single silk rose, because Harvey Nichols believe in giving you exactly what you want, in offering you the best of everything and letting you discover yourself in your *own* way. Start on any floor, and drift from image to image, look to look—it's a *scintillating* experience. There are pieces *à point* in every corner, designs that capture all of fashion's moods, that set off the instant *snap* of recognition that style is all about. And the feeling doesn't stop at the clothes! Harvey Nichols is where you'll learn the little things that matter—how to splash scent *lavishly*, how to wear large scarves draped over one shoulder. Like all the best men, Harvey Nichols love women with glamour and mystery—and women with glamour and mystery are

114

the ones who love to discover new things about themselves and new looks that suit them, who delight in doing their own thinking. When Harvey Nichols won the Fashion Guide's 1977 Award for Presentation, it wasn't just for the windows, although they're the best in town. It was also for meeting a challenge superbly, and for presenting you with the chance to live life as it should be lived. Beautifully, and with style.

## Sales

Sales are held twice a year, in early January and mid-July. Doors usually open at 9.30 a.m.—for this year's dates, ring Harvey Nichols.

## Fashion Shows

Very special Fashion Shows are held twice a year, for a week each time, to show you the season's best looks. Shows are held twice daily; for this year's dates, ring Harvey Nichols.

And look out for the **new Harvey's Cellar**, offering superb wines and open sandwiches!

## Ground Floor

**Perfumery:** luxurious selection of top fragrances and cosmetics, subtle lighting to put you in the right mood. Look out for First, Van Clef & Arpels new perfume, and for Torrente perfume and the Stendahl skin care and cosmetic collection, both exclusive to Harvey Nichols.

**Men in Harvey Nichols:** well-groomed good looks and smashing casuals by New Man, Corneliani, Conte di Bi, Valentino, Yves Saint Laurent, Baccarat, Jaeger, Balenciaga, Burberry and Hom.

**Tappin & Webb:** fine antique and modern silver and jewellery.

**The Rayne Salon:** shoes for smart ladies.

**Les Must de Cartier Boutique:** jewellery, watches and clocks from the new collections.

**Paperchase:** pretty papers for wrapping up your presents. Also, a special gift wrapping service at Christmas, and cards by Millimetre.

**Also:** handbags, luggage, accessories, gifts and fabrics.

## First Floor

**Designer Room:** a dazzling display of all the finest designer collections from Italy, France and Britain; the Beene Bag collection

*By Jacques D'Ars at Harvey Nichols*

by Geoffrey Beene, designs by Michele Domerq, wife of Christian Aujard, by Viviane Viterbo, daughter of Tiktiner, by Bruce Oldfield, Jean Muir, Complice, Jennifer Hocking, Marina Ferrari, Callaghan, Cherry Frizzell, the complete Krizia collection, the special Guy Laroche collection and a new Charles Jourdan boutique with beautiful shoes and all the accessories to match.

**Also:** Designer boutiques for Bill Gibb, John Bates, Jean Varon, Roland Klein at Marcel Fenez, Hardy Amies, Alexon, Weatherall, Windsmoor, Frank Usher, Coats and suits by Diorling, Cojana and Valentino, exceptionally smart tailored suits by J. H. Farnel. Ravishing new look coats by Jacques D'Ars, superb French rainwear by Anne Marie Beretta for Ramosport, by Blizzard and by Byblos of Italy. Dresses by Diane von Furstenberg, Samuel Sherman, Richard Nott at Peter Barron, Hildebrand, Louis Feraud, many others. Glamorous new salon full of Bradley International Furs, exclusive to Harvey Nichols.

## Second Floor

**Tiktiner:** the complete Tiktiner collection, with all the accessories to match.

**Young Designers:** smashing selection of all the most exciting names—Gordon L. Clarke, Juliet Dunn, Jeff Banks, Gaston Jaunet.

**Knitwear:** in Shetland, lambswool and cashmere, by Ballantyne, Valentino, Mariuccia Mandelli, Helyett, Valerie Louthan, Yves Saint Laurent, La Squadra, Pringle, Rosalind Yehuda.

**Lingerie:** classic and high fashion *lingerie*, fine designs by Charles Grahame, Tuttabankem and Tricia Kerr-Cross for Rifkin.

**Young Sensations:** and they are! Clothes for children, from babyhood to age fourteen, by New Man, Little Saints, Cacharel, Paula Lee, many more.

**Also:** Tartan Bar, cruise and resort wear in stock all year round, the Baccarat collection, the Jaeger collection, shirts, skirts and pants by Reldan, Mary Quant, Synonyme and others. Pancaldi shirts.

## Third Floor

Lovely linens in the traditional style, and new high fashion collections by Yves Saint Laurent, Bill Blass and others.

## Top Floor

A ravishing discovery—*the best selection of bright young fashion in London*! Fine designs by French Connection, Hardware Clothing Company, Jeffrey Rogers, Mulberry, Marc O'Polo, Suzuya, Ketch, Amaraggi, Glyn Manson, Pret-a-Porter, Archimode, Cacharel. After seeing this, you won't want to go anywhere else for top of the pop good looks. Also:

**Inside Out Shop:** baskets, flower pots, cachepots and lots of cane furniture.

**Hair and Beauty salons:** hair by Glemby, beauty treatments by Helena Rubinstein, new ladies sauna.

**Harveys Restaurant:** relaxing garden style restaurant for coffee, lunch or tea. Coffee served from 9.30 to noon; tea from 2.30 to 5.30; lunch from noon to 2.30.

---

# Jaeger 96-98 Brompton Road, SW3   01-584 2814
Mon.-Sat. 9-5, Wed. 9-7
(Access, American Express, Barclaycard, Diners)

It's **'Jaeger—Where Else'** for the great contemporary classics, and this Spring the emphasis is on simple shapes, easy silhouettes and uncomplicated layered looks in interesting combinations of colours, textures and prints. Many of the fabrics have a slub or ribbed surface and there are lots of corduroys, rustic cottons, cotton gabardines and printed cotton *crêpes*. Skirts are longer and fuller, blouses more feminine, the country look more refined. The fashion colours for early Spring are vicuna, camel and blonde, lightening into neutral biscuit, grey and green as summer draws on. The knitwear collection has an active sportswear theme, and there are sporty Norfolk jackets, casual anoraks and jungle jackets. The classic knitwear is always good, and there are lots of new items in Jaeger's accessory range of hold-alls, wallets, purses and satchels in leather-trimmed canvas printed with the JJ motif. There are two ranges to choose from, the classic 'Jaeger' range in **very generously cut** sizes 8-18, and the 'Younger' range in standard sizes 6-14; prices are similar. The Jaeger sales, very good value, are held twice a year, in early January and mid-June. For this year's dates, ring Jaeger.

Sample range and prices:

**Blouses:** in cotton from £12.00, in silk from £39. **Skirts** in rustic cottons, satinised cottons, silk-wool-linen mixtures, cotton gabardine, classic and full skirted styles. Classic skirts from £17.50 in hopsack; gabardine from £23; full country look skirts from £19.50. **Dresses** from £33. **Trousers** from £19 in cotton gabardine. **Suits** from £79 for flannel and from £65 for light-weight wool. **Jackets** from £57 for classic jackets in gabardine; sporty blazers from £65; anorak style jackets from £45. **Coats** from £89 for camelhair/wool and cashmere from £195.

# Jeeves

8-10 Pont Street, SW1   01-235 1101
Mon.-Fri. 8.30-5.30, Sat. 8.30-1

Did your fiancé spill pink gin down his shirt front when you told him you didn't want to get married after all, because you couldn't face packing for the honeymoon? Did your brother's dog chew the handles off your Vuitton holdall while you were out looking for a place to get his hunting boots boned? Did you doze off with a box of bittermints and wake to find your Porthault sheets awash in melted menthe? Not to worry—it's *Jeeves to the rescue*, with a range of services that include dry-cleaning, shirt laundering, shoe and handbag repairs, fur and leather restoration, alterations and valeting. All of life's little problems—and quite a few of the large ones—disappear when you put yourself in the hands of these specialists in the art of caring for you in style. Jeeves are particularly well-known for their 'after-care' of bespoke tailored clothes and high fashion evening dresses, but you can send them anything from hunting-coats to hand-embroidered linens in perfect confidence. All dry cleaning and laundry are hand-finished and individually inspected, the shoes are polished by hand, experts are always on hand to advise on tricky fabrics and trims, there's a 24-hour answering service—and a night hatch, terribly useful if your *out-out-damned-spot* moods strike after midnight. And that's not all—Jeeves will arrange for fur and clothing storage, remove your curtains to be cleaned and rehang them, collect your clothes and transfer them on hangers if you are moving house, and collect all the clothes you want to take on holiday or honeymoon and return them in your own suitcase, cleaned and beautifully packed in tissue. Best news of all for transatlantic travellers—Jeeves are opening in New York! Life is so much simpler when you leave everything to Jeeves. The service is impeccable—and if the prices are out of the ordinary, so are the people and clothes who come here.

## Dry cleaning

8-10 Pont Street, SW1

A sample range and prices:

**Ladies:** day dresses from £2.30, silk dresses from £2.75, evening dresses from £5.90, beaded evening dresses from £7.95.

Jackets from £1.70, skirts, trousers and blouses from £1.40. Knitwear from £1.05. **Gentlemen:** two-piece suits from £3.10, two-piece evening suits from £3.55. Jackets from £1.70, trousers from £1.40, ties from 95p. Raincoats from £3.25, overcoats from £2.85. **Suede,**

**leather and fur:** suede coats from
£13.95, suede jackets from £11.15,
fur coats from £16.75.

## Alterations

**Dresses:** to shorten or lengthen
from £4.75. Trousers: to shorten
or lengthen from £3.55

## Laundry
9 Pont Street, SW1   01-235 1101

**Wearables:** stiff collars from 45p;
cotton shirts from 80p; silk shirts
from £1.40; stiff front shirts from
£2.40; pyjamas from £1.20; bath
robes from £2.70; other prices on
application.

**Jeeves' special services:** these
include reweaving in special cases,
curtain cleaning and hanging, a
postal service, storage, holiday
packing service and the restoration
of clothes damaged by fire. Also
delivery and collection in the
following areas: Belgravia,
Chelsea, Kensington,
Knightsbridge, Fulham, Mayfair,
Hyde Park, Victoria,
Westminster, Bloomsbury, The
City, Regent's Park, Bayswater,
Maida Vale, St John's Wood,
Swiss Cottage, Hampstead,
Finchley, Hampstead Garden
Suburb, Highgate, Hendon.

## Jeeves Snob Shop
7 Pont Street, SW1   01-235 1101

'Snob' is a colloquial term for a
cobbler and here you'll find a
quality shoe mending service with
all the special Jeeves touches.
Shoes sent in for new soles and
heels are fitted with a new leather
inner sock and new laces, *hand
polished* with Woly of Switzerland
polish and returned wrapped up
in tissue and boxed with a
package of Jeeves shoe shiner
cloths. Jeeves can mend anything
from delicate evening pumps to
golf shoes, climbing boots, ski
boots and sandals—*and you can
even send in your hunting boots to be
boned up!*

Sample range and prices:

**Ladies:** long soles and heels in
leather, from £10.85; in resin or
rubber from £9.35; in Micro from
£9.90; in crepe from £11.55. Half
soles in leather from £5.25; in
resin or rubber from £4.35; in
Micro from £4.95 and in crepe
from £5.45. **Gentlemen:** long
soles and heels in leather from
£12.65; in plain rubber from
£10.75; in Micro from £11.95; in
crepe from £13.75; **riding boots**
from £15.50. Half soles in leather
from £7.15; in *crêpe* from £7.70;
in rubber from £5.45 and in
Micro from £6.85.

**Special attentions:** waterproofing
for shoes from £1.95 and boots
from £2.75. Shine and polish for
shoes from £1.20 and for boots
from £1.95. Boning for riding
boots, from £6.75. Also handbag
grooming and luggage repairs.

## Charles Jourdan  47-49 Brompton Road, SW3

01-589 0114
Mon.-Sat. 9.30-6, Wed. 9.30-7
(American Express, Diners)

'Fashion' and 'shoes' are exactly the same thing at Charles Jourdan—so much so that if you get one of Jourdan's up to the minute styles and do a bit of accessory dressing, you won't have to buy any clothes at all to get the season's best looks. Jourdan invented the modern fashion shoe back in the Fifties when they brought out the new-look Louis Quinze pump—and they've led fashion rather than followed it ever since. At the start of the Sixties they brought out a whole *prêt-à-porter* range almost before there was a *prêt-à-porter*. The fashion boot, the first fashion espadrilles and the first polyurethane wedges were all Jourdan innovations. *They're the only shoe house that actually launches whole new fashion looks*—and after twenty years at the top, they're more exciting now than ever before. Today, Jourdan do a two-tiered collection every season, so you can have the pick of classic styles or the latest young looks, and they also make shoes for Christian Dior under license. Last autumn when evening wear was a luxurious *mélange* of *moiré* satin, *panné* velvet, taffeta and lace, Jourdan were ready with glittering golden high-heeled sandals and low heeled shoes in soft pastel suedes with gold ribbon ankle straps. There were moccasins to wear with tweeds and flannels ankle strap shoes for tartans, mid-calf boots to wear with full peasant skirts, fine high riding style boots for hacking jackets and knickerbockers. This season the look is bare and beautiful, lots of tiny gilt chains and slender straps on high lacquer heels bronzed in amber, blue, deep green, gunmetal, ruby and black. Mid-calf boots in natural toile fabric trimmed with leather accent the colours and textures of soft jackets in natural linen, and flat sandalettes in soft matte leather with closed toe and sling backs take over from the espadrille as **the** shoe for summer. Jourdan take the superb quality of their shoes for granted. It's their fashion panache they're particularly proud of, and their expertise goes a long way beyond legs. Twice a year they publish a glossy Charles Jourdan magazine showing you how to make the most of the season's looks from top to toe—*the best fashion reading in town*, mailed to account customers and available free at the Charles Jourdan salon. You can find handbags to match every sandal and shoe in Jourdan's superb accessories collection—along

121

with scarves in cotton and *crêpe de Chine*, luggage, small leather goods, watches, lighters, umbrellas and splendid 'expression' sunglasses that will put a whole new face on summer. *Jourdan shoes are one of the best fashion investments you can make*, so put your best foot forward here!

Special note: Don't miss the Charles Jourdan sales, held twice a year around Christmas and July-August. For this year's dates, ring Charles Jourdan.

Sample range—all prices approximate:

**Shoes:** in American sizes 4-9½, Continental sizes 2½-8: AA, A and B fittings. Flat sandalettes in soft matte leather, natural and pastel colours, from £31-£33; look out for the smart Odeon, Orleans and Ombrine styles. Mid-calf boot with stacked heel in natural toile fabric trimmed with leather, about £60. Little patent sandals on a medium heel with open toe and ankle straps, about £34. Elegant sandals with high lacquer heels, from £43. Boot prices last autumn: sporty pull-on boots from about £99; classic boots from £115.

---

**Medina**  10 West Halkin Street, SW1
01-235 7179
Mon.-Fri. 10-6, Sat. 10-4
(Barclaycard)

---

**One of the brightest, best, most exciting shops in London, Medina have always had an unbeatable sense of style.** They went in for the effortless 'new look' seasons before anyone else, had tiered skirts and tucked up petticoats ages ago, and launched Gordon L. Clarke's collections of silky pleated separates that have become one of the success stories of the Seventies. There's nothing quite like it anywhere else in London, a shop full of real life style clothes that work for you in scores of different ways. The silky pleat collection has pride of place—easy separates splashed with gay carnival colours, worn in layers over cotton and lace in outfits that mix checks, prints and plains with happy abandon. There are long skirts to pull up and wear as strapless dresses, scoop neck dresses to wear off one shoulder as a sarong or off both shoulders as a *decolleté* style, mid-length skirts that are worn under the dresses to turn them into cocktail frocks, halter swimsuits that double as tops, full skirts that wrap around you like a shawl. A few pieces can be worn in a dozen different ways, and when you start mixing the colours and prints, the possibilities are endless. The staff at Medina are expert at showing you how to make the most of it—how to loop skirts and tie scarves to achieve a completely new look without changing your clothes. The fabric doesn't crease or wrinkle, all the combinations are flattering, feminine and beautifully comfortable—and the prices give you excellent value for money. You'll also find the pick of the new look Continental collections—designs by Jean Claude de Luca, Chacock, Ventilo, Ter et Bantine and Claude Montana, classic evening cottons by Ninevah Khomo, hats by Brosseau, bags by Group SA, suedes by Giorgio Armani, and all the delicious Dona Alda scents and preparations. **If you only have time to visit one shop in London, make sure it's Medina.**

Sample range—all prices approximate:

**The Gordon L. Clarke collections:** in pleats! from £55 for a T-shirt dress to £130 for a long three tiered skirt; most two piece outfits £90. In cotton: trousers from £30, long easy shirts from £39, dresses about £55.

# Lucienne Phillips
89 Knightsbridge, SW1   01-235 2134
Mon.-Fri 9-5.30, Sat. 9-6
(American Express, Barclaycard,
Carte Blanche, Diners)

★

'French chic and no chi-chi, she puts us into slinky Jean Muirs . . . she understands fashion with a sense of humour . . . and I am happy to have a chance to thank her for all she has done for British Fashion.' So said Ann Price, Fashion Editor of Country Life, when Lucienne was presented with The Fashion Guide's 1977 Award for the **Best Woman's Shop.** Of all of London's fashion personalities, no one sparkles like Lucienne—and no one understands British Fashion better. When shows are to be arranged, when journalists and designers seek advice, when clients require special assistance or suggestions, every one rushes to seek her out—**and no one is ever**

By *Jean Muir at Lucienne Phillips*

**disappointed.** Even Nureyev, who came to Lucienne for two hundred and fifty organza roses to trim the ballerinas costumes for the Coliseum performances of Les Sylphides. 'I wanted to organise my days with people and lights and beautiful things,' she says. And from this wish she has created one of the finest salons anywhere—a green and white retreat, refreshing as a corner of a garden, where jaded spirits lift again and fashions fascinate, scintillate, bloom at their best. There are lovely designs by Bill Gibb, Gordon Luke Clarke, Yuki, Gina Fratini, Hanae Mori, Benny Ong, Salvador, Shuji Tojo, Ann Buck, Pauline Wynne-Jones, Caroline Charles, Virginia, Clutch Cargo, new names like Les Lansdown, Charmian and Cherry Frizzell. This is the place to come for real fashion dimension in depth as well as breadth—the complete collections of Jean and Martin Pallant and **Jean Muir,** of whom she says, '. . . **for me, Jean Muir is the only leader of fashion on a par with Saint Laurent.**' For some she was their first customer in the early days, and to all she has become a close and respected colleague, keenly interested in their work and development. As she says, 'I want to be excited and surprised by each collection, always to see something new. It is the duty to the public that the designers and I share.' And what contagious delight there is over a **tour de force,** like Jean Muir's collection for this spring and summer—**quelle merveille!** The collection she assembles for her boutique is no less individual than the designer collection from which she selects. 'To me, it is an artistic pursuit and I do it for enjoyment. I need the stimulation of many designers and many dimensions—from that I create one collection from many, and that is the core of my work!' And what a collection it is, **crème de la crème**—Bill Gibb's exotic panné velvet, Gina Fratini's romantic long dresses, Gordon L. Clarke's silky pleats in carnival colours, Cherry Frizzell's Victorian pretties, grand evening dresses by Tan Guidicelli, coloured Cardin tights to go with everything, hats by Sarah Freason, bags by Nigel Lofthouse, glass flower jewellery by Done Syen and polos in every shade of the rainbow. And so at Lucienne's, you find quite simply, **the best of British Fashion**, spiced with very special international looks—selected with her marvellous taste and charged with the excitement that should always be part of fine design. And the icing on the cake is Lucienne's uncanny feeling for clothes that make you look lively, young, and interesting—all at once. If you want to see yourself at your best, you need only look through Lucienne's eyes, for she has the gift for bringing out the best in everyone and everything.

Her **salon** is the favourite of many of London's top fashion editors, celebrities and socialites—the atmosphere is pure champagne, the clothes delightful, and the best thing of all is Lucienne.

All clothes in sizes 8-16. Knits by Clutch Cargo, Virginia and Brigid Foley, ultra modern steel sculpture jewellery by Bucchanan, designs by Caroline Charles, Les Lansdown, Bill Gibb, Jean and Martin Pallant, Salvador, Cherry Frizzell, Shuji Toji, Pauline Wynne-Jones, Ann Buck, Gordon L. Clarke, Gina Fratini, Hanae Mori, Loris Azzaro-Ville, John Bates and lots and lots of pieces from the new Jean Muir collection.

---

**Janet Reger** 2 Beauchamp Place, SW3   01-584 9360
Mon.-Fri. 10-6, Sat. 10-5
(Access, American Express, Barclaycard, Diners)

Designer *lingerie* and nightwear in silk, satin *crêpe* and lace. For description and prices, see separate listing in Mayfair section. **Note:** satin sheets to match the lingerie and handpainted silk sheets made to order are *not* available in this shop.

---

# The Patricia Roberts Knitting Shop
60 Kinnerton Street, SW1   01-235 4742
Mon.-Sat. 10-6

---

Patricia Roberts is the bright new name in high fashion knitwear, and her wool shop gives do-it-yourselfers a chance to make high fashion looks at home, for a considerable saving compared to boutique prices. The designer's four very successful knitting books are on sale in the shop, along with needles and a rainbow of yarns in lots of different weights and colours. The smart knits on display—unfortunately for show only—will give you some idea of what can be achieved. Look out for lots of distinctive bobbles, cables and amusing patterns.

Sample range and approximate prices:

All the yarns are Woollybear. Shetland 4-ply 36p/oz; thick/thin wool slub 48p/oz twisted wool slub 48p/oz; boucle wool slub

48p/oz; brushed alpaca, 79%
alpaca and 30% wool, £1.15/25
grams; mohair, in 20 colours,
80p/25 grams; cotton, 40p/oz;

cashmere, 4-ply, £1.50/25 grams;
Teddy fleece, chunky Shetland,
£1.15/4oz; Icelandic Lopi wool,
£1.40/100 grams.

---

# The Scotch House  Knightsbridge, SW1   01-581 2151
Mon.-Sat. 9-5.30, Wed. 9-7
(American Express, Diners, Eurocard, Mas+ercharge)

If your heart's in the Highlands, take the high road round Hyde
Park to this shop full of Scottish specialities. *O Caledonia!* Tartan
tams, tartan ties, tartan kilts in every size and even tartan carpets
underfoot. There are tartan trews for the fairways, tartan
deerstalkers for the glens, wee tartans for bairns, tartan luggage
for playing the Flying Scotsman and tartan slippers for sitting by
the fireside with a glass of Scotland's best. But tartan is more
than a pretty plaid—*'the fair have sighed for it and the brave have
died for it'*—and Pipe Major Iain MacDonald-Murray is on hand
to tell visitors the stirring tales that are woven into every sett.
The pride of the Scotch House is the *unique Tartan Room* with
bolts of over a hundred authentic tartans—from Anderson to
Weymms—with MacBeth and MacDuff in between. Look out for
the tartan of Prince Charles Edward Stewart, Bonnie Prince
Charlie, and for the superb Hunting Stewart—the most elegant of
the tartans from a feminine point of view—that sports a
bewitching shade of misty blue brought to Scotland by Mary of
Guise, mother of Mary Queen of Scots. Woven in pure Scottish
wool, the tartans are available by the metre, and *wall charts and
booklets are provided to help you trace the roots of your family tree.*
Upstairs in the men's Highland Dress department, the Pipe Major
will explain the fine points of the romantic traditional regalia. The
men's jackets are short and loose so as not to impede the swing of
shield and broadsword, the deep gauntlet cuffs are there to guard
the wrists in hand to hand combat—you can almost hear cries of
*A Douglas! A Gordon!* For lassies there are long tartan kilts in
scores of shades, to dress up with a lacy white jabot blouse, velvet
waistcoat and jacket, or to wear informally with a toning sweater.
You'll find cashmere, lambswool and Shetland knits, berets
knitted in the Fair Isle, blue bonnets, tartan bonnets, tartan plus
fours for men, Cairngorm jewellery, *skean dhus*, rugs and stoles in
cashmere and mohair and all the great Caledonian classics, but

the canny Scotch House have a surprise in store. This Spring, look out for an *exciting new fashion collection*—flounced dresses, unconstructed jackets, flounced and softly gathered skirts—*tartan à la mode*. Go and check out the new Scotch House looks!

Sample range—all prices approximate:

## For Ladies

Kilted skirts: knee lenght, £27; mid-calf, £29; long, £37. Highland dress kilts, with deeper pleats and more fabric, £35 and £44. Velvet jackets, £74; velvet waistcoats, £22. Knitwear: in cashmere from £26.50; in lambswool from £15; in shetland from £11. Knits by Valerie Louthan. Cashmere stoles,

19″ × 56″, £26; 24″ × 72″, £50.50; travel rug 54″ square, £99.

## For men

Tartan trousers from £26.

## For children

Kilts from £13 for an eight inch length. Party dresses: short, for a three-year old, from £19; full length, for a three-year old, £24.75. Cashmere stoles, 19″ ×

**Sylvia's** 25 Beauchamp Place, SW3    01-589 5284
Mon.-Sat. 10-5.30
(Access, American Express, Carte Blanche, Diners, Mastercharge)

It's all such fun at Sylvia's, where you'll find jewellery, accessories and an enthralling selection of Sylvia's special things. There's the Passion Apple, a sterling silver roundel shaped like an apple with two lovers standing beneath a tree on one side and the Greek inscription ΕΙΜΑΙ ΤΟ-ΔΙΚΟ ΣΟΥ ΜΙΣΟ —'I am your other half'—on the reverse. The apple is meant to be broken down the centre so special friends can each have half as a keepsake. And because each apple breaks in a different way, a half can only fit together with its true mate. Then there's the Pegasus pendant, a delightful winged horse. Pegasus is the symbol of poetic inspiration and he's also the emblem of the Inner Temple—so it's a splendid present for anyone connected with writing or writs. There's a pendant of the Ram of the Golden Fleece, a graceful Sagittarius, and an exquisite Tudor Rose—all beautifully detailed on **both** sides. Your fey friends will love the magical unicorn pendant, symbol of Spring in the heart. And if your city friends are having trouble keeping their sense of humour in the market place, give them a tiny bear and bull, in sterling silver or 9ct gold. For a new perspective on the people you know, get Sylvia's Star Scope—a circular chart where you can enter names under the appropriate zodiac sign. You'll be amazed at how neatly friends and foes fall into separate astrological areas, and it will also keep you from forgetting birthdays! Sylvia has an exceptional collection of costume jewellery, and there are lots of hard-to-find fashion basics like really large pierced loop gilt earrings with concealed ear-wires, smart stirrup bracelets and cufflinks and more than twenty styles of chain necklaces—all at tremendously reasonable prices. The range includes rings, pendants, chokers, bangles, twenty-one kinds of cross from Ethiopia and Greece, ivory and gilt jewellery from Tibet and unusual bracelets, necklaces and belts made of woven copper wire dipped in silver and gold. There are perspex earrings that pack up flat for travelling and a grand selection of elaborate clip-on costume earrings that come with advice on how to wear them—'Bring the lobe **well** out and clip them **high**'. On request: jewellery alterations and assistance with personal export scheme.

Sample range and prices:

**Rings:** a selection including jade and agate band rings, £3.50; signet style rings and twisted band rings from £1.50. Adjustable rings for children, with tiny turtles, butterflies and ballet dancers, 75p. **Necklaces:** lots of chain necklaces, including chains made of linked 'D's and 'S's, from £9. Keyhole chains, £4.50; stirrup chains, £12; woven copper necklaces from £9.50; silverplated Art Nouveau style necklace with three winged fairies, £4.50; loveletter—gilt envelope with 'I love you' note inside, on a chain, £1.50; Egyptian chains hung with tiny fish, £12; plain fine chains from 50p. **Pendants:** a selection including Greek and Ethiopian crosses, from £7.50; Greek crosses in solid silver, from £19; Ethiopian crosses in gold-plated silver, from £30. **Also:** stirrup bracelet, £2.50 cufflinks, £14; evening bags in moiré and velvet, with frogging, from £9-£11; Biomate, £5.50; woven copper wire bracelets, from £15; collector's item handmade Cumbrian dolls, from £33.

**Janet Wilson** 11 Beauchamp Place, SW3  01-584 6402
Mon.-Sat. 9.30-6, Wed. 9.30-7
(Access, American Express)

Everything at Janet Wilson's boutique is up-to-the-minute and sophisticated with it. This is the place to come for stylish clothes that will appeal to everyone who knows that looking elegant doesn't mean looking old. You certainly won't fall behind the times here, because Janet Wilson buys every two months instead of the usual six, and there are lots of special orders and exclusive designs coming in all the time to supplement the basic collection. The shop runs on the 'total look' with all the special touches—Janet Wilson chooses five or six colours per season, and builds a wardrobe of skirts, trousers, tops and knitwear around them, giving you infinite possibilities for a really individual look. Separates match in style as well as colour and all the belts are dyed to match. There's a superb collection of exclusive knitwear, lovely one-off clothes made from antique fabrics and patchwork, hand-embroidered blouses from Rumania, antique Bedouin robes and caftans, and an exclusive collection of silky muslin dresses and separates by Spanish designer Juanjo Rocafort.

All clothes in sizes 8-14. Sample range and prices:

**Trousers:** a very specialized line of jeans and trousers, some flaring, others with the new straight look, all well cut. Jeans from £20, trousers from £28.

**Skirts:** many styles and fabrics, for summer and winter, from £27.

**Blouses:** in crepe, cotton and pure silk, from £33.

**Knitwear:** all designs are exclusive and everything is made up in pure wool only. A large range of styles in lovely colours, including cardigans, jumpers and luxurious wrapover kimono coats in wool and mohair mix.

**Coats:** a small but choice range, including smart raincoats.

**Specialities:** knitwear and coats or dresses and blouses in antique fabric made to order.

# *Chelsea*
# *Fulham*
# *Pimlico*

---

**Ace**  185 Kings Road, SW3   01-351 1917
Mon.-Sat. 10-6.30

If you want to play the fashion game with a pack of aces up your
sleeve, wear a glittery pair of Peter Golding jeans and you'll be in
with the very best company. Ace is the place to find the *new
Seventies glamour*, and if you pop in on a Saturday you're likely to
find models, pop stars, party people, the livelier sorts of Hons,
Lords and Princesses, the occasional bottle of champagne, names
and faces from the gossip columns, designer Peter Golding and
his partner Desmond O'Power, and Teddy Edwards, Ace's
beautiful black super-manager, with his entourage of stylish staff.
Peter Golding's special kind of glamour means glorious glittery
*diamanté deluxe*—a sparkly six-to-midnight collection of velvets
and satins ablaze with sequins and style. There are velvet jeans
with *diamanté* trim, velvet waistcoats sprinkled with sparkle,
plunging *piqué* waistcoats with *diamanté* buttons and no back at
all, diamante hair clips, diamante ties—even sweatshirts and
T-shirts sparkling like the Ritz. Best of all, there are strapless
ombre-shaded sequin bustiers, to wear with three-tiered
ombré-shaded petticoats in pleated satin, or with flashing sequin
shorts—very Hollywood femme fatale. And there's a new
leopardskin collection—slinky leotards, scoop neck tops and
provocative draped front dresses—that will drive dangerous ladies
wild. There were feathers, fringes and beadwork at Ace long
before anyone else hit on the Red Indian look, and you can have
a lovely Indian summer in Peter Golding's sophisticated squaw
suits in soft pastel suede with delicate fringing and feathers, or in
the very special handpainted leather jackets with traditional
Kwakiutl designs on front and back yoke. Peter Golding's designs
have a tremendous *identity* and a unique feeling for *image*, and

131

*Peter Golding for Ace*

you can be sure the looks you find here will soon catch on in a big way in L.A. and Saint Tropez. This season there will be lots of smashing leather jeans, hand-dyed ombré summer dresses trimmed with cutwork and embroidered flowers, shorts, jeans and swimsuits *appliqué* with so many palm trees, sunsets, flamingos, flowers and tropical plants that they look like a Rousseau jungle. You can have anything made to order, and clients have included Liza Minelli, Rod Stewart, Sylvia Kristel of *Emmanuelle* and Mrs. Gunther Sachs. You'll hold all the trumps if you dress yourself at Ace—and if you're not quite ready to take the plunge, you can come in for the best selection of jeans in London, cords and velvets in every colour, by Peter Golding and Daily Blue.

Sample range—all prices approximate:

**Glitter collection:** glitter velvet jeans, £59 and £79; velvet glitter waistcoats, £59 and £79; *piqué* waistcoats, about £45; *diamanté* bow tie, Exotic glitter Chinese jackets with sparkly dragons everywhere, about £200. Smart crossover slacks in rich white satin, about £35. Three tier ombré satin skirts, £85; sequin bustiers, £29.50; *diamanté* sweatshirts, £45; *diamanté* T-shirts, from £25-£40. **Leopard collection:** leopard leotards, £29; V-neck tops, £35; scoop neck tops, £27. **Indian collection:** pastel fringed waistcoats, £35; jackets, £75; skirts, £45; dress, £95. Handpainted leather jackets with Kwakiutl designs, £250; also, plain trapper jackets for men. **Jeans:** for men and women, in sizes 25″ to 33″. Jeans by Peter Golding, from £13.95; velvet jeans by Daily Blue from £29.

---

**Antiquarius** 135 & 139 Kings Road, and 15 Flood Street, SW3   01-351 1145
(Access, American Express, Barclaycard)

---

Chelsea's world-famous covered antique market, a rambling barn with over 150 stalls selling everything from Deco tea sets and Georgian walking sticks to Twenties copies of Vogue. A special attraction is the *antique clothing* section, in a room with a stained glass ceiling—the largest collection of Victorian, Edwardian, 'Speciality', and Twenties-to-Fifties clothes in London. In the rear you'll find the new Antiquarius restaurant—*the best inexpensive good eats in the Kings Road*—serving fresh orange juice and *plat du jour* specialities like cauliflower cheese for 60p, avocado salad for 65p, spinach quiche for 60p, bean and bacon stew for 65p and steak and kidney pie for £1. There's a *bureau de change* near the entrance at 139 Kings Road, but as this is a convenience service, don't expect the same rates you'd find in a proper bank during normal hours. Some shops have names, but it's easier to find them by stall numbers. All are worth a visit, but the following shops are particularly recommended. Watch the stars for style.

## The Pipe Shop Antiquarius (entrance at 139 King's Road), SW3. 01-352 3315

Brian Tipping of The Pipe Shop specializes in antique pipes and smokiana—anything and everything to do with smoking. There are character-head tobacco jars, lovely tobacco tampers in brass, treen or horn from £12, and a tasteful selection of exotica: *cloisonné*-cased and silver opium pipes, a bamboo opium pipe studded with rubes, and a miniature solid silver hookah. At least 300 pipes are in stock at all times: many date from the 1700's, none are later than 1915 and although they have been fully cleaned and are fit for smoking, their beauty and rarity make them collectors' items. Stock includes handblown cranberry and Bristol glass pipes from £25; French clay Gambier pipes, from £15; Bavarian porcelain pipes from £25; and Meerschaum.

**Speciality:** a vast collection of fantastically carved Meerschaum pipes dating from 1750-1900. Originally white, the pipes acquire a patina over time, taking at least 70 years to acquire the deep ochre colour prized and cultivated by connoisseurs. Small Meerschaum pipes are about £45, and you can spend over £100 for a large and elaborate one. The Meerschaum collection includes: **Gamblers' pipes**: a traditional design with the bowl in the form of a skull supported by a hand of crossbones. **Egg and hand or claw:** designs with the bowl in the form of an egg, supported by a carved hand or claw. **Blackamoor head pipes:** particularly prized for the way the ochre colour complements the design. **Ladies' head pipes:** with bowls disguised as pretty ladies in picture hats, mostly carved 1850-1910. These were often specially commissioned, and the face is that of the owner's wife or mistress. **Hunting pipes:** with *sportif* decoration, such as a reclining hunter and his hounds carved on the stem. **Animal head pipes:** with bowls in the form of leopard, lion, bird, elephant or monkey heads. **Ladies' pipes:** small elaborately carved pipes for lady smokers, some only three inches long; bearing reclining ladies, spaniels, horses, birds. **Saucy pipes:** with erotic carvings.

---

# Vignettes (adjacent to entrance at 135 Kings Road)
01-352 4221

---

Maria Carvalho at Vignettes makes no allowances for age, and although her collection of day and evening dresses date from the Twenties to the Forties, you won't find anything that isn't beautifully clean; pressed and perfect. Speciality: designs from the Twenties and Thirties, when feminine fashions were exceptionally colourful and varied; lots of silks, chiffons, sequinned and beaded evening clothes, with scarves and accessories to add a dash of period *ton*. For those who like entertaining in style, Vignettes have a collection of fine table linens—everything from tray cloths to cloths for banquet tables—and antique lace collars, handkerchiefs, runners, throws and spreads, in excellent condition.

Sample range—all prices
approximate:

Day dresses from £15; beaded dresses from £60. Evening dresses in silk, chiffon and tooled net, velvet and satin, from £30. Table cloths from £15; antique embroideries from £15; lace collars and handkerchiefs, from £10.

---

# Edina and Lena 141 Kings Road, SW3   01-352 1085

---

Children who fancy the Fauntleroy look will find lappets, lace and lush velvets galore at these romantic nostalgia specialists. The children's collection includes Victorian pinafores and velvet dresses made from original Thirties patterns trimmed with lavish Victorian lace collars. If frills aren't quite your style, you can opt for the International Velvet look instead, in Harris tweed and cord hacking jackets dating from the Forties onwards. There are hacking jackets for grown-ups too, lots of Twenties to Forties day

135

*From David Fielden, Night and Day*

and evening dresses, Chinese robes and embroidered hangings, lace tablecloths and bedspreads, new cardigans and jumpers knitted from original Twenties to Forties patterns, and a collection of satin dresses by Willy van Rooy.

Sample range—all prices approximate:

**For children:** hacking jackets from £8-£10, Victorian dresses, from £12-£30.

**For grown-ups:** hacking jackets from £12-£15, Twenties evening dresses, £29-£179, period day dresses, from £10-£30. Tablecloths from £8-£55; scarves, £2.50; Chinese robes from £120; dresses by Willy van Rooy from £56.

---

# David Fielden—Night and Day

Downstairs at Antiquarius, don't miss this arched and alcoved salon where dancer and choreographer David Fielden has a stunning collection of antique fashions that will sweep you off your feet. All the beauty and drama of the dance have been carried over into a repertoire of exceptionally lovely pieces reminiscent of the days of sables, diamonds, Grand Dukes and champagne. There are shimmering beaded dresses in Ballets Russes colours, lacy cavalier shirts for romantic *pas de deux*, exquisite lingerie in silk, satin and *crêpe de Chine*, wraps and kimonos, rich brocade waistcoats, rows of Victorian nightgowns, camisoles and petticoats—as pale and perfect as the cygnets in Swan Lake. Everything has been chosen as carefully as a special present, and each piece has a charmed life of its own—a magic that goes far beyond simple nostalgia.

Sample range—all prices approximate:

Wrap in *eau-de-Nil* silk trimmed with coffee lace, £45; peach silk and satin wrap with smocked sleeves, £27. White cotton cavalier shirts with lace trimmed bodice, collar and cuffs, from about £28. Twenties flapper dress in white *rèpe*, with crystal bugle bead bodice, tiny fluted silver beads in centre panel shading from waist to hem, £90. Deep cream *moiré* blouse, with pintucking, lace-trimmed collar and sleeves, Alexandra collar, £36. Silk lace-trimmed camisoles, in peach, pink, celeste blue and almond green, trimmed with lace, from £15. Light blue silk nightgown with tiny straps and shirred bodice trimmed with lace, £24. Twenties summer frock in white cotton lawn with white embroidery, short sleeves and square neck, £15. White lawn camisoles with crochet and lace trim, from £10. Black *crêpe* Twenties flapper dress with gold *diamanté* and silver bugle beads worked in the pattern of a spider web stretched between *fleurs du mal*, £130.

---

# Acushla Hicks (Stall P-10), near entrance at 15 Flood Street
01-352 9025

Come here for superb jewellery and *objets* from the Art Deco days of the Twenties and Thirties, when fashion was a real way of life and accessories much more than an afterthought. There are collector's items like early Lalique and George Jensen pieces, Twenties Cartier watches and boxes by Van Cleef & Arpels, amusing novelties like telescopic cigarette lighters and enamelled compacts that will make you want to freshen your makeup in public, occasional pieces of period Vuitton luggage. Everything is original, intact, irresistibly lovely!

Sample range—all prices approximate:

Cigarette lighters from £20 to £265; cigarette cases from £15-£120; boxes from £15-£2,500, watches from £40-£1,150; cufflinks from £15-£260. Note: Acushla Hicks also at Stall 333 in Gray's Antique Market, 58 Davies Street, W1.

---

# Michael Pruskin (Stall P-10) near entrance at
15 Flood Street, SW3

Fashion is as fashion does—and if you want to know how fashion was, visit this wonderful stall. It's the only place in Paris, London or New York that specialises in Nineteenth and Twentieth century fashion art, and Michael Pruskin's superb selection includes everything from Twenties Vogue covers in perfect condition to Mucha posters and *objets* by Lalique. Most of the examples come from the French, who never distinguished between what the English call the Fine and Applied Arts, and consequently paved the way for a unique collaboration between

138

artists, writers and *couturiers*. One of the results were the rare and marvellous fashion gazettes, produced in limited editions using the *pouchoir* techniques of stencilling and hand-colouring. Every one of these issues is nothing less than a treasure. A single edition of the *Gazette du Bon Temps* contains designs by Lanvin, Poiret, Vionnet, Max-Leroy, Roger Chastel and Worth, sketched by Lepape, Marty, Thayat, Martin and Barbier, with texts by Astruc, Van Moppes, Vaudreuil and George Cecil. All of the coloured plates are suitable for framing, and what pictures they paint! Ladies arch along the Promenade des Anglais looking as smart and predatory as an Arlen heroine, pout prettily as they pet a pair of borzois or slink off into the night with a tophatted gentleman friend, bound for cocktails at midnight and all the things they lead to. No costume film or period snap can ever evoke the style and mood of the times as these illustrations do, and you'll only need one look to realise how much fashion and art have lost to the photographer's flash. Textile designs are another speciality, and there are books of *tissues* by Sorokin, Sonia Delaunay, Seguy, Benedictus, Mucha and Klinger, books of handpainted Japanese textile designs dated 1906, and rare finds like the portfolio of fifty samples of Twenties French silk and cut velvet. Rare books are another important feature of the collection—*Les Robes de Paul Poiret* illustrated by Paul Iribe, *Tamara Karsavina* illustrated by Barbier, *Parfums et Parfumeurs* illustrated by Lepape and a complete collection of the 1925 Paris Exhibition '*Les Arts Décoratifs et Industriel Modernes*', in eleven volumes bound in vellum and board. There are copies of the luxurious *Art, Goût et Beauté* magazine of the Twenties, copies of *Femina* from 1919 to the late Thirties, copies of *Vogue* from the Twenties to the Fifties and copies of *Art et Décoration*—the best applied art magazine ever produced, full of details on art, jewellery, furniture, interior decoration and fashion during the years 1898-1940. People who really care about fashion will love the mounted showroom sketches from the Thirties, limited edition pouchoir prints by Barbier, Martin, Van Dongen, Sacchetti and Benito, and there are lots of amusing novelties like Forties *Vogue* pattern books and Twenties *Folies Bergères* programmes. A word of warning—this long neglected field is rapidly coming into its own, and prices and stock are moving very quickly. Customers have included leading museums, collectors and designers like the Missonis. They know what they're doing—so hurry!

Sample range—all prices approximate:

**Gazettes and magazines.** *Gazette du Bon Temps:* complete editions, £45. Single plates for framing, from £5. *Art, Goût et Beauté*, complete Twenties editions, £25. *Femina*, prices £10-£15. *Le Miroir de Modes*, prices from £4. *Vogue*; from £1 for Fifties to £25 for Twenties. **Limited Edition prints and watercolours.** Beautiful Barbier *pouchoirs* from *'le Gout du Jour'*, *'Modes et Manniers'*, *'Nijinsky'* and others, from £15-£90. Martin *pouchoir* plates from 1919, from £20-£25. Colour plates from the *Gazette du Bon Temps* and other publications, sold separately and unframed, from £5. Twenties *Vogue* covers by Lepape, Helen Dryden and George Plank, in perfect condition: framed from £29.50; mounted only, from £15. Superb original watercolour by Degas, £950; posters by Muchas Mucha from £200; a small 'affiche' by Privat-Livement, £25; original watercolours by Herouard, from £80. **Textile books and rare books.** Books of handpainted Japanese textile designs, £85. Portfolio of fifty samples of Twenties silk and cut velvet, £280. *'La Ligne Grotesque'*, forty-five samples of Art Nouveau designs and motifs, by J. Klinger and H. Anker, £300. *'Combinaisons Ornamentales'* by Mucha, Verneuil and Auriol, £280. *'Documents de Bijoux'*, twenty plates if Art Nouveau jewellery design, £180. Eleven volume set of *'Arts Decoratifs et Industriels Modernes'*, £550. **Also:** choice objets by Lalique, Hageman, Joseph Hoffman, Liberty, Wedgewood, Daum, George Jensen and many others, from £50. **Speciality:** you can make arrangements to view Michael Pruskin's private collection of Art Deco pieces, furniture and other examples of the applied arts. The collection includes figurines and sculpture, extremely rare handmade signed carpets by McKnight Kauffer and Marion Dorn, and an exceptional fabric collection. Rugs from £50, carpets from £300. Fabric pieces, suitable for bedcovers and cushion covers, from £1 to £150.

---

# Bellamy (Stalls N8 & N9) near entrance at 15 Flood Street, SW3   01-352 3334

---

Bellamy specialise in fine Art Nouveau jewellery, particularly in beautiful silver pieces with the Liberty look and feeling, by the English Arts and Crafts school. All the English pieces are unique, handmade and superbly executed—less commercial and far more artistic than their Continental counterparts. Enamel and silver buckles in the Liberty style are as wearable now as they were during the *Belle Epoque*, and an Arts and Crafts brooch will give exactly the right touch to a Liberty shawl worn over the shoulders, so look out for pieces by Sybil Dunlop, Murrle Bennet, Liberty and George Hunt. Bellamy also have turn-of-the-century French horn pendants carved in the shape of butterflies, dragonflies and flowers, and a lovely collection of Edwardian pendants and necklaces set with pink sapphires, diamonds, rubies, amethysts, tourmalines, peridots and lapis.

Sample range—all prices approximate:

**Art Nouveau jewellery,** circa 1895-1910: Arts and Crafts jewellery by Sybil Dunlop and others, from £60; Liberty silver and enamel belt buckle, £150; gold penant set with jade by Murrle Bennett, £350. *Plique à jour* enamel butterfly pendant, circa 1900, £260. Large selection of Victorian and Edwardian rings from £40-£300; Art Deco enamel cufflinks from £10-£30. French carved horn pendants, from £70; carved brooches from £20. Edwardian pendants and necklaces, from £70.

---

## Carolyn Brunn  287 Brompton Road, SW3   01-584 1966
Mon.-Sat. 10-6
(Access, American Express, Barclaycard, Mastercharge)

Well-priced designer knitwear, see listing under 'South Molton Street' section.

---

## The Chelsea Cobbler  54 Kings Road, SW3
01-584 2602
Mon.-Sat. 9-6, Wed. 9-7
(Access, American Express, Barclaycard, Diners)

Boots used to be for riding and walking in the rain—but that was before The Chelsea Cobbler. Their first shop in Draycott Avenue created the colourful boots that led the Sixties fashion revolution. As demand grew, so did Chelsea Cobbler. Retaining the quality and style that distinguished their made to measure work, they went on to create collections of ready-made boots and shoes that took London by storm. Today they are one of London's most exciting shoe shops, full of footwear with the unmistakeable

141

Chelsea Cobbler look—stylish, up-to-the minute and always well made. This Summer, look out for pinholing and punched flower detail on shoes in pastel colours and natural shades. Boots are in paler colours, kept in stock all year round. Chelsea Cobbler's men's range has been specially created to co-ordinate men's footwear with trends in fashion, whilst not forgetting the customer who requires classic styling. A collection of luggage, acessories and leather goods for both men and women available at main branches.

## For women

Sizes 3-8.
Strappy high heeled sandals—lots of colours, styles and materials—from £19.99 to £45.00; new 'Californian' sandals in delicate pastels from £13.99; this year's flat look—satin pumps at £9.99, Roman sandals in canvas and leather at £9.99 and £19.99, chunky sport shoes in Nubuck and canvas from £12.99; also, classic shoes and boots at all prices.

## For men

Sizes 6-11.
Wide range of men's shoes including classic woven shoes—around £70.00; new burnished leather shoes at £38.00; comprehensive range of casual/sport shoes in a wide selection of colours, materials and styles, from £24.99.

**Bombacha**  104-106 Fulham Road, SW3  01-584 5381
Mon.-Sat. 10-7
(Access, American Express, Barclaycard, Diners)

Come to Bombacha for new wave fashion in the style of the Cafe Flore—casual classics, relaxed but very definite, **everyday** good looks that really make you think for yourself. The overall lines are clean and classic—lots of button-down shirts, loose trousers, waistcoats, easy skirts and big blazers to wear in layers, accessorized with flat loafers or bar shoes, pastel or white short socks and Bombacha's own *moire* satin bow ties. Everything blends in colour and texture, and these are collections you have to **work** with, mixing cotton and linen, pleats with piecrust frills, linen with needlecord, prints with stripes and plaids until you achieve that perfectly effortless style that makes people-watching such a pleasure at the Flore. The pick of the new wave collections are here—shirts from Island in Paris, Ventilo's linen jackets printed in Prince of Wales check, Ecriture's white flared skirts and little box jackets, France Andrevie's plain needlecord dresses and ribbed beige slipovers, Claude Montana's printed linen smock dresses, Daily Blue's slinky knit cardigans and gilets to wear with baggy trews, beige and khaki linens by Ferrer y Sentis, blouses, waistcoats, skirts and jackets by 11342, all in contrast checks. Bombacha put a lot of effort into showing you how to get the details just right—how to wear your belt tightly or knotted, how to wear shoulder bags slung across the chest. They want you to look good, and they want you to be able to work and play in style without having to change your clothes. You'll also find evening dresses by Sheridan Barnett and Shelagh Brown, Wendy Dagworthy's lemon and white summer collection, velvet and cotton jeans by Daily Blue, pure silk stockings and Bombacha's own Eau de B perfume. This is one of the best-considered collections in London—don't miss it.

Sample range—all prices approximate:

**Skirts:** from £30-£70 for skirts by Claude Montana. Shirts from about £20-£30; blazers from about £40-£70. Shoes in sizes 34-36-38, loafers and bar shoes, about £20. Big needlecord smock dresses, from £50. Daily Blue cotton jeans, £20; matching blazer, about £20.

Little waistcoats, from £15. Pure silk stockings, £6. White linen blazer with matching scoop neck top, £25 the set—**superb value for money.** Also, lots of lovely Mulberry belts. Bombacha's Eau de B perfume, in two sizes, £2.50 and £4.50.

---

**Brother Sun**   171 Fulham Road, SW3   01-589 6180
Mon.-Fri. 10-6, Sat. 10-5.30
(American Express, Barclaycard, Diners)

---

Brother Sun shines with the magical light and warmth of Provençe, captured in gay **Souleiado** cottons printed by the Demery family of Tarascon, available here by the metre, or made up into a delightful array of pretty things. The traditional peasant patterns glow in rich shades of blue, ochre, terracotta, saffron, red and green splashed onto pure white cotton—so powerfully Provençal that you can almost smell the lavender and garlic. Fabrics are available in two widths, with separate border prints, giving tremendous scope for do-it-yourself fashion, crafts and interior decoration; for those who'd rather not, Brother Sun accept decorating commissions, and offer everything you need to dress yourself and your house, ready-made. This summer Brother Sun will have Gina Fratini's new designs in Provençal prints, a new collection of printed quilted jackets, silk shirts and skirts, and dresses in fine wool and cotton by Evelyn Reifen, printed espadrilles with plain or open toe, printed scarves and shawls and bright bikinis—one of the best buys in town at £7.50. Bags are a Brother Sun speciality—soft handbags, totes, pochettes, weekenders, make-up bags, toilet bags, drawstring bags and super drum-shaped bags with long shoulder straps—very popular with models. If winter gets you down, you can turn your house into a summer garden with the new bedsheets and bedspreads, printed pillows, tea cosies, tissue holders, tiles, tablecloths and trays. Although the fabrics are not inexpensive, Brother sun have lots of little items like chequebook holders and address books that makes very special presents at under £5.

Sample range—all prices approximate:

**Clothes:** in sizes S, M, L. Quilted jackets, £38; silk shirts, £75; fine wool wrap skirt, £39; dresses with full collar and cuff, in wool, £81. **Scarves:** in cotton, 40 × 40cm, £2.20; 60cm × 60cm, £4.50; 80cm × 80cm, £5.60 in silk: 80cm × 80cm, £34. **Shawls,** in fine wool, 130cm square, £32.50. **Bags:** open quilted totes, zipped handbags and button tab bags, from £12.40-£21. Weekender grip bag, £31.80. Drum shaped shoulder bags, £13.70 and £27. Toilet bags, £10.95; makeup bags, £5; little drawstring bags, £5.65. **For the house:** new bed sets, one printed sheet and two matching pillowcases, £39.50. Quilted bedspreads, from £120 for single, from £250 for double. Round 72″ tablecloths, £35.78. Quilted place mats, set of six, £28.50. Quilted cushion covers, £117.50. Tiles: border print tiles, £11.35 per linear metre; pattern tiles, £61.50 per square metre. Trays, £9.75 rectangular, £5.75 round. Tea cosies, £15.35. Little sewing cases, £6.50. **Fabrics** in cotton: border prints, £1.65-£2.10 per metre. Printed cotton 90cm wide, £5.25 per metre; in 130cm width, £7.90 per metre; toning plain cotton fabric, 130cm wide, £4.05 per metre. **Also:** credit card holders, £2.70; pretty lace-trimmed showercaps, £5; telephone book, £4.50; address book, £3.15; espadrilles, about £11; padded hangers, £2.25; birthday books, £1.60; tissue holders, £4.25; bikinis, £7.50; little strappy sundresses for girls aged 2-3, £7.50. Long printed cotton aprons with quilted pocket, £11.50.

Do you wear a dress with your jewels, or jewels with your dress? The best looks happen when you think about your accessories *at least* as much as you do about your clothes, and the very best looks start here. Butler and Wilson are the finest of London's 'accessories boutiques', with a fabulous collection of jewellery and *objets* displayed in an evocative Art Deco setting. These are *real* accessories, not hairline gold chains or plain wire chokers but pieces with tremendous style that really *add* something to the total look—which is what accessory dressing is all about. You'll find everything from stylised Art Nouveau butterflies and flowers to distinctive Art Deco geometrics, handpainted Twenties bangles and rich Egyptian-style ornaments inspired by the discovery of Tutankhamen's tomb. There are flapper necklaces, Victorian pendants, brooches, rings, earrings, scarves, cigarette holders, Twenties beaded evening bags, bangle holders and enamelled Art Deco and Art Nouveau belt buckles—add fabric or leather and you have on a piece you can build any number of outfits around. You can even go on to accessorize your house with Deco decanter sets, Robj figurines and heads, standing dumbwaitrs and Butler & Wilson's own delightful Thirties-style ceramic scarab plant holders. Best of all, you can treat yourself to something from *Butler and Wilson's new collection of fashion jewellery* in the tradition of Schiaparelli and Chanel, thoroughly contemporary but using the same techniques and materials that were used in the Twenties, the last high point of craftsmanship and style. Look out for galalite Pierrot bangles to go with this summer's Pierrot collars—hand-cut, carved and tinted with Pierrot playing the mandolin or holding a rose. There are Pierrot brooches and brass handmirrors, ceramic heads, silver enamel brooches with golf and tennis motifs, brooches and pendants with smiling crescent moons, exquisite glass flower chokers, lots more lovely things. Women's Wear Daily gave the collection a rave review when Butler & Wilson opened their new boutique in Henri Bendel—and so will you, as soon as you see it. Butler & Wilson's accessories brighten up the glossy fashion pages frequently, and they have provided accessories for a number of films including *The Big Sleep* and *Death On the Nile*. People who care about fashion love the challenge to the imagination they find here. Stock

145

*By Gordon Clarke at Draycott*

is always changing, so you'll want to come back again and again.

Sample range—all prices approximate:

**Necklaces:** a selection of beads, chains and chokers from £8-£40. Antique ivory necklaces from £20-£50; ropes of reconstituted amber beads, from £12-£30. Rare Victorian muff chains, from £15-£30. **Bangles:** colourful lacquered bone bangles, 1910-1930, from £10-£20. Twenties galalite bangles, from £4. **Enamel:** Art Deco belt buckles, enamel on gilt, £4-£12; Art Nouveau enamel belt buckles, £12-£25; enamelled poppy and pansy pendants and brooches, from £10-£14. Enamel and silver Egyptian style pendants in the shape of a mummy or **ushabti**, £16-£24. Enamel on chrome Art Deco compacts, £10-£20. Art

Nouveau pendants in carved tinted horn; birds, butterflies and flowers, from £20-£70. **Also:** rings from £15-£40, evening bags from £10-£20; cigarette cases from £10-£20; Twenties silk scarves from £4; Art Deco pendants in bakelite and chrome, from £10-£30. **Butler & Wilson collection:** ceramic wall plant holders in the shape of scarab, glazed in opalescent colours, several sizes, from £4-£20. Silver crescent moon brooch, £12.50; silver crescent moon and stars pendant, £10; smiling silver full moon brooch, £16.50. Handcut Pierrot bangles in galalite, £12.50; Pierrot silver brooch, £18.50; brass Pierrot handmirror, £45. Glass flower chokers, £25. Gold and tennis silver brooches, £12.50.

---

# Draycott  102 Draycott Avenue, SW3   01-584 2289
Mon.-Fri. 9.30-6, Sat. 10-4

---

Just open, Medina's exciting new shop, full of the young free and easy fashions that they understand better than anyone else in town. This is the place to splash out on the brightest new looks from England and the Continent; at prices that give smashing value for money. This season at Draycott: Ninevah Khomo's cotton evening classics, cotton knits by Vera Finbert, printed cottons and linens by Robin Rother, Ferri jeans, suedes by Giorgio Armani, designs by Claude Montana, Ventilo, Gianfranco Ruffini, Camelot and La Maison Bleue, Gordon Clarke's cotton collection, lots more lovely things. **Don't miss it!**

Sample range—all prices approximate:

By Robin Rother, embroidered shirts from £12, and dresses from £22. Cote d'Azur pastel cheesecloth dresses trimmed with lace, from £24-£40. Linen blazers, skirts and trousers by Camelot,

from £18-£35. By Gentry Portofino, linens and knit linens, from £12-£60. By Gordon Clarke, long cotton shirts from £39; loose cotton trousers, £50; cotton dresses from £55.

**Essenses** 410 Kings Road, SW10   01-352 0192
Mon.-Sat. 10.30-6

*Take a tip from top designers, and turn to the past for your best looks.*
Suki Wraight of Essenses was the first to show antique clothes as
fashion, and she still has London's largest collection of wearables
dating from 1895 to 1940. Her World's End shop is a delightfully
*browseable* place, overflowing with Twenties and Thirties dresses,
blouses, kimonos, evening gowns and wraps, fox furs and antique
fans, shawls galore and a flurry of white Victorian nightdresses,
petticoats and camisoles. You can count on finding quality, cuts
and colours far superior to those of today, at prices that put the
fun back into fashion. Essenses's unique flair can be seen in the
*special theme collections* that are assembled with great care and
shown in the shop at regular intervals. Every year there's a pure
black collection, a pure white collection to start off summer, and
a sparkly evening collection just before Christmas, with lots of
sequins, velvets and beaded dresses. Because of their large stock
and quick turn-over, Essenses can afford to sell at very good
prices, and there are lots of useful and amusing items starting
from about £3.50—*look out for old Hermes scarves for just £5*!
Better still, you can now come to Essenses for the best of both
worlds, old and new—*made-to-order* skirts, tops and dresses in
antique fabric and lace. 'Confection' is the only word for these
cascading flamenco flounces of pillow lace, *broderie Anglaise*, silk
and fine cotton lawn. Each piece is unique, and they're as lovely
as extravagant designer evening gowns—at about half the price.
For *soigné* sophisticates, Essenses make pure silk pyjamas in
shades of peach and cream and exotic catsuits in pure silk chiffon,
with abaya sleeves and harem pants. Romantics musn't miss the
floaty filmy blouses in Thirties printed *crêpe*, or the white cavalier
shirts with fine lace trim and swashbuckler sleeves. Not on
display, but available to view by arrangement, are a selection of
embroidered antique Chinese robes and Suki Wraight's superb
*couture* collection. Her treasures include ensembles by Lelong,
Worth, Schiaparelli, Caillot Soeurs and a long beaded dress by
Poiret that shades from black at the hem to grey and back to
black at the shoulders—just like three layers of caviar in a dish!

Essenses hire period *lingerie*, hats, gloves, clothes and accessories
for photographic work, but not for personal wear. Terms: for
models and photographers, 15% of total value of the items per
week, plus deposit. For magazines: no charge, but photocredit.

Sample range—all prices approximate:

**Victorian lingerie:** in white cotton trimmed with lace and *broderie Anglaise*; camisoles, £6.50-£25. Underskirts, £18-£65 and nightdresses, £12-£54.50. Camiknickers, £8-£15. **Knitwear:** a selection, including knitted silk sweaters and cardigans from £6.50-£18, and Thirties Fair Isle slipovers from £3.50. **Dresses and wraps:** *crêpe* day dresses, from £7.50-£14. Long chiffon dresses, from £17-£45. Cut velvet dresses from £35-£55. Cut velvet jackets from £18-£45. Velvet coats from £35-£85. Capes from £30-£45. **Lounging Wear:** Thirties pyjama sets and kimonos, from £18-£45. **Shawls:** an excellent selection in a kaleidoscope of colours, textures and sizes—embroidered Chinese and Spanish shawls, woven Paisleys and Kashmiris, French and English shawls in silk and fine wool, luxurious shawls in *faconné* velvet and Benares silver shawls, which are made by pounding tiny studs of solid silver onto net. Embroidered shawls from £14-£200, Paisley and Kashmiri shawls from £16-£200,

plain silk shawls from about £10, *faconné* velvet wraps from £30, and Benares silver shawls from £7—depending on the weight of silver. **Also:** Long Thirties silk and *crêpe* scarves, from £3.50-£9.50. Twenties perfume bottles from £4.50. Beaded handbags from £6.50. **Pierrot heads**-Essenses's logo—to give a nostalgic touch to your home: wall plaques, £10.50; head to put on your dressing table, £9.50. Lots of furs, feather boas, hats, blouses, skirts and accessories. **Speciality:** made-to-order mid-calf or long skirts, with matching tops in camisole, off-the-shoulder, sarong or Edwardian styles; each unique. In antique lace and satin with satin ribbon trim; two piece ensembles from £145. **Luxurious lounging pyjamas,** three piece set with camisole top, in pure silk. In shades of peach and cream, other colours to order, from £125. Scheherazade style **catsuit** in pure silk chiffon, from about £38. **Cavalier shirts** for men or women; in white cotton with pintucks and antique lace trim, flowing sleeves; from £18.50-£45.

---

# The Frock Exchange 450 Fulham Road, SW6
01-381 2937
Mon.-Sat. 10-5.30

---

The first and still the best of the stylish second-hand frock shops, the Frock Exchange gives you a crack at some of the best fashion buys in town. Samples by Wendy Dagworthy and Jeff Banks are sold here and through Sign of The Times at a third of their original price or less. Fancy a loose Dagworthy jumpsuit in stripy

149

silk at £24 instead of the original £84, a long openweave mesh waistcoat in beige for £10 instead of £25, a Dagworthy printed shirt for £10 instead of £26.95? You could find them here along with Ossie Clark dresses at £3, a long Jean Muir for £20, a Jane Cattlin three piece for £18, a Sally Tuffin smock for £3 and an Anne Klein blazer for £15. If you prefer a Continental look there are velvet New Man jeans at £8, a Ferrer y Sentis two-piece in silk jersey for £10; a silky knit Kenzo top at £5 and a Saint Laurent blazer at £17. Occasional period pieces turn up, like silk kimonos at £12 and Victorian petticoat dresses at £15, and there are lots of good sound classics like a Jaeger printed velvet suit at £14. Stock turns over every day, so it's worth coming in often and taking the time to have a thorough look around. The Frock Exchange is always happy to consider anything you'd like to put on sale yourself, and if you're looking for a particular style and designer and haven't had any success, they'll take the details down in a book and phone you directly something suitable comes in.

**Janet Ibbotson**   7 Pond Place, SW3   01-584 2856
Mon.-Fri. 10-6, Sat. 10-4
(Access, Barclaycard)

You won't believe how colourful, imaginative and stylish fine suedes and leathers can be until you see Janet Ibbotson's superb collection. This exciting shop is one of the brightest spots on the London fashion map, and it gets better every season. This Spring the look is soft and feminine, with a pretty peasant feeling—summed up in the superb country smock in soft goat suede embroidered in the traditional Sussex ploughman pattern. The country look goes on into gently gathered suede skirts with printed border and toning trim, to wear with a matching suede-trimmed printed wool shawl draped lightly over one shoulder. Other peasant styles have a hint of the cossack—overshirt dresses with bands of printed suede on neck, sleeves and hem, long-sleeved peasant shirts with drawstring waist and printed suede trim worn with a printed suede skirt. There are lovely combinations of fabric and suede—suede gilets bound in subtle **Soieries Nouveautés** prints by Sarah Campbell, to wear with matching fabric skirts or shirts. And Janet Ibbotson's delightful *appliqué* designs feature patterns taken from old kelims,

150

scattered on the front and back yokes of slender jackets with high tulip collars, or along the shoulders, wrists and hem of the simplest of cardigan style tops. Colours are soft and natural—pale mushroom, rust, duck egg blue, thyme, slate and dusty rose. All the skins are of superb quality, and Janet Ibbotson specialises in using silky hardwearing pig suede and soft African suede and goatskin that require little seaming. You can have handframed knits to match the clothes, from £28, skirts in plain or printed fabrics that tone perfectly with the suedes, silk shirts and silk scarves dyed up in all the suede colours. As this is the designer's own shop, there are no middleman markups to contend with, and you get truly outstanding value for money. These days it pays to buy fewer things of finer quality, so start your investment dressing here. Without a doubt, *these are the loveliest suedes in London*, with a rare originality and a special kind of elegance that can take you anywhere in the world.

Sample range—all prices approximate:

Suede skirts from £75; suede jackets from about £115; country smock jacket with Sussex ploughman embroidery, £136; cardigan jacket with kelim *appliqué*, £146. Suede skirt with border print and matching printed wool shawl, £136.50. Peasant shirt dresses with printed suede band trim, from £133; peasant shirt with drawstring waist and printed suede skirt, £216. All to order.

---

**Inca** 45 Elizabeth Street, SW1   01-730 7941
Mon.-Fri. 10-6, Sat. 10-1

---

You can find everything from straw hats to *huichi-huichis* in this shop full of handmade garments and crafts from Peru. Summer wear includes embroidered blouses and long cotton skirts, but Inca is best known for its knitwear which is *available all year round*. The popular sheepwool knits come in electric colours—bright yellows, hot pinks, strong blues and greens—worked into frieze-like patterns with stripes, geometrics, animals and birds. Inca specialize in soft Alpaca knits in natural creams, browns and beiges, and one of the most popular items is the fringed Alpaca poncho that can be worn as a skirt. For the total Inca look there are gloves, caps, mitts, scarves and astonishing socks that match the knitwear. Don't miss the Peruvian ethnic art section on the first floor where you will find a

*Norfolk Jacket and Knickerbockers by Ladies Habits.*
*Sketched by Angela Landels*

wide range of handwoven rugs, *primitive* pottery, handpainted mirrors, tin ware, toys and naive paintings. There are shopping baskets of all kinds from £3.75, woven belts from £1.50 and *huichi-huichis* (long pompom tassels in bright wool) to hang from them, 95p.

Sample range and prices:

**Multi-colour knits:** in adult and children's sizes. Adult size V-neck pullovers are £9.80, sleeveless waistcoats from £4.95. Wear them with matching ear-flap hats from £1.75 and scarves from £6.60. Gloves and mittens are £2.50. Socks and leggings are £4.20 and children's socks, £1.50. **Alpaca knits:** in adult and some children's sizes. Adult-size pullovers and cardigans from £13.95, waistcoats from £6.95. Ponchos that double as skirts from £13.95. Socks with animal patterns, £4.25 **Also:** mats from £6.50, rugs from £21, mirrors from £3.25-£28, baskets from £3 and thick sheepswool socks in natural colours for wearing with gumboots, £1.90.

---

# Ladies Habits  5 Cale Street, SW3   01-351 3281
Mon.-Fri. 9.30-6

Here at Ladies Habits the superb techniques of English tailoring are used to create ladies of made-to measure of classic, dateless style—and a sophisticated chic that gentlemen's tailors rarely achieve. The tweeds, worsteds and flannels have been chosen in weights and colours more suitable for ladies, and it is only here that you'll find the exquisite feminine line and glove-like fit that Edwardian beauties wore to such advantage. There are knickerbockers and Norfolk jackets for shooting parties, silk mohair smoking jackets with smart cummerbund trousers, evening skirts with matching capes and jackets and stunning specialities like the long Ascot suit—slender as a champagne glass and worthy of a thousand toasts. Blazers sport hand-made buttonholes and antique brass buttons, trousers have raised side-seams top-stitched by hand, skirts have pleats which never lose their edge. Don't miss the new shirt and safari style dresses, or casual skirts, tops and boleros—so right for lazy summer days. Everything is beautifully made and finished in the best tradition, and there are several fittings to ensure a perfect silhouette. Practical as well as elegant, these fine clothes can be worn again and again—so come along and pick up some good habits!

Sample range and prices;

**Blazers:** single and double-breasted styles in a range of fabrics including gabardine, serge and twill from £160; velvet and mohair jackets from £190.

**Trousers:** many styles and fabrics from £80; velvet and mohair from £90. **Day skirts:** wrapovers, four panel skirts, pleated skirts and classic A-lines, from £80. **Suits:** jackets with matching skirts or trousers, in a range of styles that include knickerbockers and Norfolk jackets from £245. **Coats:** overcoats from £250, capes with or without hoods from £240 and cashmere coats from £350. Also proofed gabardine coats, trench coats and coats in Ultrasuede.

## Liberty Prints  340a Kings Road, SW3
Mon.-Fri. 9.30-5.30, Sat. 9.30-1
(American Express, Barclaycard, Diners, Mastercharge) ★

Liberty's new shop, full of Liberty prints and nothing but. Start out by looking at Liberty's furnishing fabrics in printed cotton union, a cotton-linen blend. As designer Susan Collier explains, cotton union is very hardwearing, the *only suitable fabric for upholstery*. It's meant for family life, for *real living* and all the things that light cotton simply can't stand up to. New designs in the furnishing fabric range—**Esfahan**, Klimt-like squares of colour in an abstract basketweave pattern; **Tambourine**, a strong ethnic stripe with a handwoven look; **Titania**, a huge floral print with gigantic hyacinths and peonies melting into each other, and **Pharaoh**, inspired by an antique Egyptian tapestry. The cotton union furnishing fabrics all come with curtain fabric to match. Go on to look at the season's new dress fabrics—paisleys, abstracts, geometrics and swirling florals in Tana Lawn and Nimbus Voile, peasant prints in Country Cotton, and a new collection of Tyrian Silks—pretty pastels at sensible prices. The shop also has Liberty scarves and ties, and a choice selection of delightful small gifts in Liberty prints.

Sample range—all prices approximate:

**Furnishing fabrics:** in Liberty cotton union, 48″ wide, £4.75 a metre; matching curtain fabric, £3.45 a metre. **Dress fabrics:** Tana Lawn, £3.15 per metre; Country Cotton, £2.25 per metre, Plain Dyed Tana Lawn, £2.45 per metre, Nimbus Voile, £3.15 per metre; Tyrian Silk, £4.50 per metre.

## Mexicana 89 Lower Sloane Street, SW1 01-730 3871

Mon.-Fri. 9.30-5.30, Sat. 10-1
(Access, Barclaycard)

Traditional Mexican costumes are the great romantic classics of the folklore genre—and Mexicana is full of charmers from south of the border that will sweep you off your feet. Everything has been specially designed for the shop, and you can choose between the aristocratic *patrone* look—lacy Castilian elegance transplanted to the tropics—or the simpler peasant styles of the Mexican *péon*. The *patrone* designs are lavish confections of frills, pintucking, lawn and lace, and there are graceful long dresses perfect for Glyndebourne, Edwardian-style lace blouses, extravagant grandee dress shirts for men and *a special collection of snowy white frocks that make lovely wedding gowns*. The *péon* look means cotton smocks, shirts and tiered skirts in gay fiesta colours like bougainvillea pink, turquoise, lemon yellow and guacamole green. This is the place to find those stunning San Antonio dresses—slender long frocks with a rich yoke of hand embroidered flowers, no two exactly alike—that go so well with chignons, suntans and holidays at Las Hadas. And for real fashion value, don't miss the wedding shirts in natural cotton with colourful filigree embroidery, to wear with blazer and trousers or loosely belted over a skirt, for just £9.50. Accessories include belts, paper flowers, stoles, beads, baskets and hammocks to hang in your *hacienda*. You can have hammocks for one, two or *three* people—*olé*!

## For women

**Wedding shirts:** £9.50; Tiered skirts in handwoven cotton, mid-calf length, £40; long skirts, £50. Lace blouses, about £33. Long evening dresses with pintucking and lace, in white or colours, from £85-£115. San Antonio dresses, hand-embroidered in cotton from about £39.

## For men

**Wedding shirts:** £9.50; white dress shirts with pintucking and lace from £30.

**Also:** Stoles from £7.50, beads from 25p. woven shopping baskets from £1.75, hammocks in three sizes from £15.

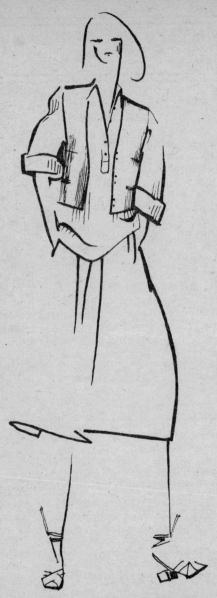

*By Cerruti at Piero di Monzi's Cerruti Shop*

## Piero de Monzi 68-70 Fulham Road, SW3
01-589 8765
Mon.-Sat. 10.30-7

No one can top the Italians for pure elegance—for subtlety, perfect shapes, sheer luxury. And when it comes to taste in the Italian manner, no one rivals Piero de Monzi. His shop has always had the cream of the Italian collections—cool and classic—but **the collection he has assembled for this season surpasses any that have gone before.** Designs by Krizia, Tan Guidicelli, Caumont, Geoffrey Beene and Claude Montana introduce you to the exciting **new elegance**—fresh, free, completely relaxed. Sweaters are turned back at the cuff, shoulder bags are worn slung across the chest, the look is easy, natural, assured—and young. Skirts and shirts are looser, more interesting, always simple enough to show **you** off—the secret of style. There are lovely things for day, cocktails and evenings, jeans by New Man and Jacques Pernet, superb shoes, dresses, suits, skirts, shirts and coats specially made for Piero de Monzi. This is **the** Italian shop; if you care about the very best, there can be no question of going anywhere else.

## Piero de Monzi's Cerruti Shop 66 Fulham Road, SW3   01-589 8765
Mon.-Sat. 10.30-7

Next door, Piero de Monzi's exclusive collection of Cerruti designs for women.

### Themes from this season's Cerruti collection

Blazers are masculine, unlined, double-breasted, straight-backed and tight on the hip. Jackets are unconstructed, supple as a cardigan, with kimono sleeves that can be rolled up to the elbow. Shirts come in every length, to be worn from morning to evening, long over trousers or short with a skirt, in cotton or *crêpe de Chine*. Skirts are 10cm below the knee, with softly gathered waists. The season's evening colour is black, to wear with very high heeled evening shoes and beaten gold pendants in the shape of moons and stars.

157

**Night Owls**  78 Fulham Road, SW3   01-584 2451
Mon.-Fri. 10-6, Sat. 10-4.30
(Access, American Express, Barclaycard)

A favourite with early birds, night owls and all those who like
time to fly by in style, this is the place to find the stuff that
dreams are made of—nightgowns, wraps, dressing gowns,
négligées and lounging gowns—delightful flights of fancy to see
you to your rest. You can satisfy every taste from fun to frilly,
pick from a garden of flower prints, choose simple T-shirt
nighties in snappy stripes and colours, be swept off your feet by
Zandra Rhodes' spectacular night sets or plump for pure white
Victorian style nightgowns with prim pintucks and proper *broderie
Anglaise* trim. There's something for every age and every
size—lots of 6's and 8's, with a number of XL's at the other end
of the scale—and there are always plenty of *exceptionally pretty
front-opening gowns for maternity wear.* The clothes are of excellent
quality, and cottons are a speciality—fine lawns and voiles from
the Continent, warm brushed cotton from America, Liberty
prints, comfortable cotton jersey, quilted cotton, soft towelling
robes in appetising colours and lots of those hard-to-find
lightweight cotton dressing gowns, available all year round. *Soigné*
sleepers can choose from a collection of lace-trimmed satin
nightgowns and *négligées* by Tuttabankem, Charles Grahame and
Finewear—look out for imaginative styling details, like long
gowns with little lacy bolero tops instead of the conventional long
wrap. *Romantics will love Sara Fermi's collection of classic
charmers*—long lawn shifts modelled on traditional smocks with
handsmocking and embroidery, warm Clydella gowns cut like a
chorister's robe, long Liberty print smocks with handsmocking at
neck and cuffs, pure wool kimono wraps trimmed with Liberty
print, fine nightgowns and bedjackets in silk. And for the country
fresh look, don't miss the flower print nightgowns designed by
Julia Smith for the Night Owls label, or the casual long Liberty
print dresses she designs exclusively for the shop. These and
many more of the things are pretty enough to wear to a
dance—and lots of Night Owls customers do just that.

Clothes in sizes 6-18, some XL's.
Sample range and approximate
prices:

**Nightgowns:** fine satin
nightgowns with deep lace bodice

and tiny straps, all washable, from
£40. Satin nightgowns with
matching dressing gowns in
bittersweat brown, honey, white,
dove grey, pale blue and *eau de*

158

*By Sara Fermi at Night Owls*

*Nil*, from £80. Finest, frilliest Swiss cotton nightdresses, exclusive to Night Owls, in a range of styles and colours, in stock all year round, from £30. Large selection of pure cotton and cotton-polyester nightdresses from America, lots of styles and colours, printed and plain, from £12. Long granny nightdresses by Lanz, in brushed cotton trimmed with *broderie Anglaise*, £16.50. Night Owls label flower print nightgowns, from £15; exclusive Liberty print casual long dresses by Julia Smith, from £50. By Sara Fermi: long lawn shift with smocking and embroidery, £37.80; long Liberty print smocks, £34.60; cream Clydella choristers style gown, £33.50. By Vandy: T-shirt dresses with long or short sleeves or sleeveless, from £21; matching wrap, about £30.

**Robes and wraps:** towelling robes in a range of styles and colours,

from £30. Long shirt style button through towelling robe with pockets, by John Kloss for Cira, £34.90. Lightweight cotton dressing gowns, from £15. Long quilted cotton dressing gowns from America and Belgium, from about £30. Pure wool kimono wraps trimmed with Liberty print, by Sara Fermi, £43.20.

**Also:** exclusive accessories in Liberty print. Rubber soled espadrilles on rope-trimmed wedge heel, open toe, ankle strap or lace up styles. In sizes 4-8, £14. Padded clothes hangers, £2.10; mackintosh-lined mob caps for bath or shower, £3; exceptionally pretty Kleenex box covers, £7. Also, shoebags, *lingerie* bags, cosmetic bags in three sizes, towelling slippers, herb-scented pillows and a remarkable large soft bag with a mackintosh lining, eighteen pockets and an infinite capacity.

---

**Maxfield Parrish**  4 Woodfall Court, Smith Street, SW3
01-730 4867
Mon.-Fri. 10-6, Sat. 2-5
(American Express, Barclaycard)

---

The dashing aviatrix in the Virginia Slims advert got her blonde leather flying jacket and jodphurs from Maxfield Parrish, and if you fancy high-flying styles in suede and leather, this is the place for you. The look is sporty, casual, free and easy—band-neck blouson dresses and jumpsuits, big loose shirts, knickerbockers, hacking jackets—all the clothes that sum up the new relaxed chic. The emphasis is on 'fashion' rather than on 'leather', and the fine supple skins simply enhance the effortless style of Nigel Preston's designs. There's a small stock of ready-to-wear, but *most of the clothes are made to measure* so you can be sure of getting a perfect fit. Look out for the long leather motoring duster coat, the leather riding breeches with suede insert on the inner legs and the saucy suede shorts to wear with soft suede T-shirts. The collection includes jeans, shirt jackets, trousers suits, skirts, coats, boxy blazers and waistcoats in suede or leather, and there's a small choice selection of designs in natural slub silk. The leathers come in black, bittersweat brown and brick, the suedes in subtle shades of sage, smoky biscuit, tan, taupe, natural and brown—*allow one week to ten days* for made to order delivery.

Sample range—all prices approximate:

Leather motoring coat, £250. Unconstructed shirt with blouson detail at back, two flap pockets, £85. Jeans in suede and leather, about £80-£85. Blousons in leather, £110 and in suede from £95. Loose casual jacket with wide smock yoke, gathered front and back, lined with quilting or Viyella, in two lengths: hip length, £110; long, £140. Leather and suede waistcoats, £35. Band-neck blouson dresses with dropped shoulders and drawstring waist, £120 in suede; £50 in silk. Long sleeved button through blouson dress in washable suede, four patch pockets, £120. Blonde leather flying jacket with deep sheetskin revers, £135; matching jodphurs or knickerbockers, about £85. Suede hacking jacket about £125: suede and leather riding breeches, about £75. Suede skirts from £65; shorts about £35: T-shirts £65. Three-piece casual trouser suit in natural slub silk, £95.

---

**Retro**  229 Kings Road, SW3   01-352 2095
Mon.-Fri. 10.30-6.30, Wed. 10.30-7

---

If you like old Hollywood movies, you'll love Retro's lively collection of nostalgic clothes from the great days of the Judy Garland generation. There are lots of tightly-fitted tailored jackets like Betty Grable used to wear, clinging draped dresses in the Maureen O'Sullivan style, silver stilettos for the Ginger Rogers look, swingback swagger jackets, sorority sweaters straight out of *Andy Hardy goes to College*, circular Mexican skirts and a riot of silky flowered Forties afternoon frocks in bright California colours. The clothes come from America, and their frankly extrovert style will delight anyone who adores really individual looks and bright red lipstick. The buttons are as elaborate as costume jewellery, eye-catching trims are splashed everywhere, and the pockets come in a staggering array of shapes, styles and sizes. Retro is a very sympathetic shop—snappy big band music sets the mood, and they pay a lot of attention to detail. The tags often carry helpful comments like—'This dress is almost an exact copy of a 1938 Balenciaga dress'. Accessories include hats, scarves and Forties *lingerie*, and there's a *fabulous collection of Fifties perspex purses and handbags*, clear or tinted silver-grey or amber. Retro's premises are the oldest shop in the Kings Road, and there's a charming inner plaza under a glass roof, with the original tiled roof up one side, hanging baskets of lush greenery, and plenty of space for trying on their sweeping evening gowns. The clothes may be old, but there's nothing tired or tawdry about them—everything has been cleaned, and mended if necessary, and the fabrics have a very fresh look and feel. The day and evening dresses are particularly good, and now that pencil skirts are back in style, the jackets are just the thing to wear with them. Best news of all for the fashion-conscious—there are lots of clothes in smaller sizes.

Sample range and prices:

**Jackets:** tailored jackets from £8.50; V-necked five-buttoned black jacket with bead clusters on lapels and pockets, £8.50. Flecked brown and natural fitted jacket with loop fastenings and clear round amber-coloured buttons all the way up to the neck, £8.50; swingback jackets with dropped shoulders and up to six panels in the back from £9. **Evening Dresses:** good selection, lots of draped *crêpe* dresses, from £15-£40; black cut velvet sleeveless evening culottes, with band of rich colours around the bodice and matching tie-belt, £48; lilac *crêpe* bias-cut gown with *diamanté* trim, £28; scarlet *crêpe* dress with diamante trim, dead ringer for Balenciaga, £15.

**Dresses:** plenty of pretty frocks from £10-£30; red velvet cheongsam, £30; tie-neck dress in tipsy plaid print, £10.50; illusion dress in red and black, made up to look like suit, £10; cap sleeved navy dress in flowered primrose chiffon, £30; lots of flowered rayon dresses, from £10.50
**Perspex handbags:** Fifties bags in mint condition—fluted amber bag with flowers pattern cut into the lid, £25; clear handbag with crystal-cut lid and three-ball gilt clasp, £30. **Also:** pure silk blouses and £6 and printed rayon blouses from £4.50; Knitwear from £7; skirts from £6; a selection of furs including full beaver coat, £45; racoon coat, £160, Kimonos from £15-£75 and a selection of scarves from £6.

Clothes by Vivienne Westwood at Seditionaries

## Seditionaries—Clothes for Heroes
430 Kings Road, SW3   01-351 0764
Mon.-Fri. 11-6, Sat. 11-4                    ★

**The ties that bind aren't quite what you think**! The straps, zips, rings and rips that make up the Punk look may not be easy on the eyes, but they're not easy on the mind either—which is the whole point of these costumes of provocation. Although her punk designs have been the most definite fashion statement of the Seventies, designer Vivienne Westwood prefers to think of them in political terms. They are uniforms for urban guerillas, clothes of commitment to anarchy, and they aim to seduce you into revolt. Sex and shock in equal measure are used to stir the murky depths beneath society's bland surface. As she explains—'If you want to find out how much freedom you *really* have, try making an extreme sexual statement in public.' Punk costumes are hung with all the trappings of bondage, assessorized with safety pins, razor blades and little silver phalluses, finished off with lurid makeup, hairstyles and Sex Pistol T-shirts. It all adds up to what onlookers have called 'the cult of ugliness'—and the reactions it provokes are even uglier. The clothes call out for confrontation and get it in spades. Punks are screamed and spat at, chased and battered—it's not hard to see what they're revolting against. And as soon as you do, you're halfway to being seduced. As Vivienne Westwood says, 'You dress to attract other people, and if you look like you lead an exciting life, you'll attract exciting people. What could be more exciting than confronting apathy? It's very romantic to be in a minority, and anti-Establishment. We're not for "pretty" ladies out to attract male chauvinist pigs.'

**Jackets:** Bondage jackets in black cotton or tartan, £35; parachute harness jacket with six straps meeting at a central ring on the chest, £25. **Trousers:** bondage trousers with straps everywhere, in black cotton, £30, including kilt or loincloth to wear over them. **Tops:** mohair sweaters, £15; long-sleeved string tops interwoven with mohair, £15. **Shoes,** a selection including peep toe, snap side and thick soled styles, from £25-£30. **T-shirts:** Sex Pistol, Destroy, Cambridge Rapist designs, broken flags, other motifs, from £4.

## Sign of The Times   17 Elystan Street, SW3   01-589 4774
Mon.-Sat. 10-5.30

High fashion second-hand frocks for ladies; for description and prices, see separate listing in this section for The Frock Exchange. Also, top second-hand clothes for men and children, see separate listing in 'Menswear' and 'Children' sections.

# Uniquity   170 Old Brompton Road, SW5   01-373 8956
Mon.-Sat. 10-6.30, Wed. 10-7.30

British fashion is like Hollywood—a kind of star system with a few big names in lights, a sprinkling of character parts, extras' roles galore in the cast-of-thousands mass manufacturing industry—and starving, struggling fashion starlets waiting for the Big Break. Goodness has nothing to do with it—Britain has the best young designers in the world, and the end-of-term Dress Shows at the fashion colleges often outshine the top designer collections in sheer exuberance, originality and style. But after that, the iniquities of the system take over and without backers, government support or small retail outlets, young talents often get stifled and wasted. *So three cheers for Uniquity—where starlets get the chance to twinkle, and you get the chance to shine!* This unique shop specialises in the work of young free-lance designers, and one look at the collection will knock the stars right out of your eyes—the looks are great and so are the prices. Some of the designs were made for the Dress Shows, original one-offs that took a whole year to make. The lavish trim, beautiful finish and details like handpainted leather and handprinted fabrics are exceptional—and the styles have a tremendous vitality and flair that rival the best *prêt-à-porter*. Don't miss it!

Sample range and prices:

By **Coupé**, plaid hacking jackets, £48.50; to wear with waistcoats, £12.95; culottes, £24.50 or skirts, £26, in black, brown or camel, all in wool. By **Clem Aubury**, elaborate designs inspired by old costumes. Velvet skirts with frilly petticoats, £25.95; velvet corselette jackets with lace trim, and matching long skirt, £77. By **Karen Ashton**, bridal outfits trimmed with quilting, *plissé*, pintucks and lace, usually two-piece outfits that you can wear later as evening separates. Blouse only, from £50. Wedding outfits and dresses from £150. By **Yvanka Bates**: slinky sophisticated evening dresses in black or white silk jersey, from £45. Evening ensemble in black silk jersey, tight trousers, wrapover skirt and blouse, about £60. By **Lisa Lawrence**: pure wool knitwear, including

*By Coupé at Uniquity*

three-piece outfit of zebra-striped skirt, matching top, and black polo neck sweater, £125. By **Irene Benn:** large chunky mohair blouson sweaters in subtle pale colours, £29.50. By **Carolyn Agius:** skirts, tops and jackets in Viyella or in Liberty print wool and cotton. Liberty print skirt and overshirt, £41.50 together, to wear with Liberty print jacket, £44, and Viyella shirt, £21.60. Caftans and harem outfits by **Ray Tanva**, from £15 for caftans and harem suits in plain cotton to £150 for very special beaded hand-embroidered caftan dresses with chokers and skullcaps to match. Also at Uniquity, a selection of corduroy trousers by Simon Chapman of Frog's Legs: each size comes in three fittings so you can be sure of finding something that's just right. Trousers from £19, matching jackets, about £38.

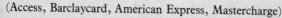

# Zapata Shoe Co. Ltd.

49-51 Old Church Street, SW3
01-352 8622/3863
Mon.-Sat. 10.30-6
(Access, Barclaycard, American Express, Mastercharge)

Since the best clothes in the world can be ruined by the wrong shoes, the easiest way of finding the best in high fashion footwear is to follow the experts Zapata. This is the place for superb handcrafted shoes for men and women, all designed by Manolo Blahnik and showing the style and attention to detail that have gained him an international reputation and clientele. The look is classic with panache, and there are shoes for every occasion—doing the Grand Tour, dancing the night away at Las Hadas or teasing the accelerator as you speed up the Moyenne Corniche. If you follow the world's best dressed feet, they'll soon lead you to this door.

## Women's shoes

Continental sizes 32-42, in leather, suede, fabric and lizard. Many styles, including some trimmed with luxuriant cut-suede flowers, others with exclusive 'needle-point' heel. Women's silver and gold sandals from £30, flat sandals for day and evening wear, from £28; high-heeled court and evening shoes from £35; country-style walking shoes from £45; boots from £120.

## Men's shoes

Continental sizes 40-48. Styles include leather boots in range of colours from £75; wide selection of loafers, several colours, from £48; knee-high riding style boots from £120; sandals, both leather and suede, from £35.

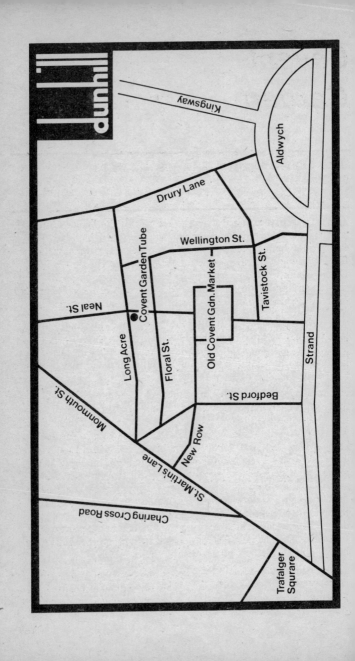

# Covent Garden

## The Dance Centre  12 Floral Street, WC2
01-836 6544
Mon.-Fri. 9-10, Sat. 9-6

The largest private dance school in the world, the Dance Centre
is where the Beautiful People make sure they stay that way. You
can trip the light fantastic through a repertoire that includes
Intense Mime, Modern Dance for the Stage and Pas de
Deux—about forty different classes every day. You can join a
class at any time, and for about £1 a lesson you can keep yourself
in step, in shape and on top. Classes with special *cachet* include
Ray Collins' Jazz General, Sylvester Sylvester's Modern Jazz
and—very popular with models—*Arlene Phillips' Rock Jazz classes
in the sizzling Hot Gossip style*. On the ground floor you'll find a
marvellous dance bar stocked with the Dance Centre's own
leotards, tights, legwarmers and dance shoes at *the best prices in
town*. The leotards fit like a glove and come in twenty-two exotic
colours like *eau-de-Nil*, fondant pink, celeste blue, gunmetal,
hyacinth, burnt orange and canary. There are halter neck styles
that look great with harem pants, crossovers, V-necks, boat- and
scoop-necks, polo necks with collars that come right up to the
chin—for just £2.50 to £3.60. There are lots of useful things for
everyday wear—French-cut leotards, cut high on the legs, that
make *perfect swimsuits*; all-wool catsuits with sweater-cuff sleeves
and V-neck for only £8, *panné* velvet T-shirts with an airbrushed
dancer design, new towelling tracksuits in the leotard colours,
jingle taps to let people know you're there. Stock up so you can
dance, dance, dance in style—and try to come in at least three
times a week. The best fashion looks start with a lithe and lovely
body—and all the best bodies turn up here.

Sample range—all prices
approximate:

**Leotards:** in twenty-two colours,
sizes 1-6 (very small to size 14/16):

£2.50-£3.60. Also available
abroad, see Out-of-London
Addresses section. Pure wool
*legwarmers*, twenty-three colours,

*By Roy Peach for Howie*

£3.90. Striped tights, £1.75. Ballet **tights** with or without feet, in the leotard colours, £1.90. Ballet ankle socks in peach, pink or white, 50p. Dance Centre **sweatshirts**, £6; Dance Centre *panné* velvet T-shirt, £9.50. Pure wool footless tights in black or peach, sizes S, M and L, £5.70. Leather **ballet slippers** in peach, white, red, blue and black, £2.75; satin ballet slippers, £2.30. Leather **tap shoes** in black, white and red, with lace tie and toe plate, £6.95; men's tap shoes, £9.90.

---

SPECIAL NOTE: After all that exercise, treat yourself to a gorgeous plant from **Once Upon An Orchid**, at 11 Floral Street (01-240 2744): the only shop in Britain that deals in orchids and nothing but. Choose a cane orchid, vanda, catteleya or dendrobium—flowers last for one and a half to two months, and bloom again the next year. Prices from £4.50, most plants in the £5 to £15 range. Afterwards, relax in the new **Hairim** downstairs at number 11: cutting, tinting and perming in an orchid-decked Moorish salon.

---

# Howie  138 Longacre, WC2   01-240 1541
Mon.-Fri. 10-7, Sat. 10-6

Top P. R. Lynne Franks—Mrs. Paul Howie—is one of London's most ebullient fashion personalities, all go, with a non-stop instinct for the fashion mood of the moment. Always a shop to take London's fashion pulse by, Howie reflects the new feeling for quality and quiet—for clothes that make a definite statement but don't shout. The looks are clean, without gimmicks, but with plenty of interest and style—clothes you won't tire of, clothes that don't date; classics for the Seventies. Paul Howie sets the tone of the shop with a collection he calls 'prim and pretty'—pastel separates that you can mix like a cocktail into prim **or** pretty combinations, and every look inbetween. The same originality shows in the shop's selection of special clothes by exciting young designers like Jaime Ortega, Fred Spurr, Sarah Dallas and Roy Peach. Sarah Dallas's creamy knits for summer have pinked edges on every seam and pleat, a completely new classic look, and Roy Peach mixes summer sorbet colours like lemon, lime and orange

171

in swirly floral gathered skirts to wear with lace-trimmed cap sleeved tops. Look out for more unusual designs by Reet Petite, Sharon Lewis, Sandra Dodd and George Hostler, handbags by Mulberry and Christopher Trill, knits by Altona and Island, designs by Ferrer y Sentis and Peppermint. Howie is linked up with lots of the young new look shops on the Continent, and special things come in all the time. Whatever you buy, you can match up to Walkers shoes—brogues, courts, stacked heels and school girl sandals—and you can finish with tiny pots of Village lipgloss, flavoured in peach, green apple, strawberry and lemon. Howie has always been the place to find good looks with a difference, so if you really want to put on the style, this is the place for you.

**Paul Howie collection:** Jackets in linen and poly/silk; double-breasted, about £57; single breasted, about £57; in cotton, single and double, about £47. Blouses: ruffle blouses in voile, about £32; in print, about £29. Collarless shirt in satin, about £38. Ruffle front shirt in gauze, about £22. Dresses: blouson sundress in gauze about £30; in print, about £39; flared sundress in gauze, about £30; square neck dress in print, about £40. Skirts: ruffle waist skirt in print, about £32; pleated print skirt about £32; wrap skirt in gauze, about £21.

**Trousers:** narrow trousers in print, about £27; ruffled Indian trouser in gauze, about £36; in jersey, about £44. Wide shorts in gauze, £20. Also, bandeau tops from £5, halter tops from £12, camisoles from £15, pure silk hand-knits from about £40. **Walker shoes** in sizes 3½-7, from £17.

---

## The Neal Street Shops 23 and 29 Neal Street,
WC2  01-240 0135/6
Mon.-Fri. 11-5.30, Sat. 11-3 (longer opening at Christmas)

---

Now expanded into two premises, the Neal Street Shops are lucky dips on a lavish scale—full to bursting with a headspinning selection that includes antique Mandarin fingernail guards, English kitchen kitch ceramics, potted palms, colourful Chinese kites, peacock and ostrich feathers, fabric flowers, wicker chaise lounges and the **best collection of basketware in town.** Many of the items have been specially imported from the People's Republic of China, and there are antique embroideries to inset into clothes or use as wall hangings, intricate antique boxes and a **magnificent collection of antique Chinese jewellery at stunningly low prices**. Look out for antique jade and silver rings from just £7.60, carved jade earrings from £4.50 and superb silver hair ornaments—**perfect for slipping into evening chignons**—plain or set with jade, seed pearls, agate or rose quartz, from £3.50. And don't miss the modern jewellery collection, because it boasts loose **cloisonné** enamel beads in exquisite colours to string yourself, loose carved cinnabar beads and buttons and wonderful glass bead necklaces in rose quartz, jade and lapis lazuli colours. You can pack your jewels up in a wicker vanity case, part of a selection that includes small wicker dolls furniture, large wicker peacock chairs, wicker suitcases and a charming wicker picnic hamper with two side holders for thermos jugs so you won't have to fret over coffee or tea, red or white wine. There are hundreds of baskets in every shape and size, raffia carriers, sisal bags and corduroy pochettes—and this is the place to come for those unusual baskets that make such smart handbags. You can even dress up your house at the Neal Street shops—start with the silk pictures and colourful cut paper medallions for lampshades and wall friezes, and go on to the patterned bead curtains, bamboo bookshelves and brass trimmed black lacquer chests. Set your table with pieces from the shop's collection of amusing ceramics—pretty Portmeiron, teapots shaped like cottages, bowls masquerading as cabbage leaves and hyacinths and irresistable celery jugs that look good enough to eat. You can feed the inner man here too, with Culpeper spices, Welsh chutneys and jams, Scottish mustard, colourful sweets from France, Chinese tea and Jacobs Cream Crackers in those hard to find large tins. Something for every reason, and every season too—Chinese oiled paper umbrellas for the monsoons, and paper and feather fans to soothe sultry summers away. Prices start at just 1p, for old enamelled copper letters and numbers to mount on a wall. The selection of British ceramics, mugs and nibbles make perfect presents for visitors from abroad, and at Christmas the splendid array of stocking presents has queues forming in the street well before opening time. If you're looking for something really different, at exceptionally good prices, this is the place for you.

## At No. 23

Still the best collection of baskets in London, lots of interesting well-priced jewellery in Hunan jade, horn, agate and rose quartz, colourful Chinese kites and greatly expanded collections of toys and houseware.

**Glassware:** good basic range, including Guinness goblets, 59p; Pepsi and Coke glasses, 66p and lovely apothecary jars for kitchen or bath, in several sizes, from £1.95-£6.70. Also, Le Parfait & Kilner.

**Ceramics:** colourful mugs with period facsimile adverts for Cadbury, Cinzano, Guinness, Gitanes, Sunlight Soap, Pears, and many more, about 90p; charming cottage wear, each piece shaped like a cottage in mellow Cotswold stone, teapots, jampot, sugar, mug and plates, butter dish with cow, £2.20; teapot, £5.60. For children, charming china with storybook bears; a range including plates, £1.16 and bowls, 82p.

**Basketware:** in every size and shape, from 25p. Woven wicker vanity case, £4.50; suitcases in two sizes, lined with small flower print cotton, £5.90 and £7.60. Spacious woven raffia carriers in two sizes, 55p and 65p; floppy woven raffia hats, 60p. Bamboo shelves in several sizes, from £6.90 for a perfect bedtime reading size to £32 for a tall model with four shelves. Two tiered lacquer workbasket 2 feet high with inner trays, in red, £18; smaller version in natural, £14; all from China.

**Fabric:** splendid selection of cottage-shaped tea cosies, several styles including Tudor and Cotswold, range of sizes from £3.25.

**Toys:** colourful Chinese kites in two sizes, £1.50 and £1.80.

Wicker dolls furniture: table and chairs, 70p each; wooden cottage chair with woven rush seat, £1.38. Hand puppets from 70p; wonderful hand or string puppets from Fukien, figures from Chinese traditional opera, £2.95 and £3.15.

**Also: Fans** from 10p; feather fans, 35p; enamel on **copper letters and numbers,** several sizes, colours and scrips, from 1p to 20p each. Little brass boxes from £1.50; colourful wheat straw boxes, from £1.50; Hide schoolboy **satchel,** in black, £16; silk scarves in a rainbow of colours, several sizes, from 99p for small plain to £3.60 for large print.

## At No. 29

Potted plants from 55p, and an enormous selection of attractive **sika**—hanging cords—to go with them, from 50p-£17; lots of baskets and ceramic pots.

**Beauty:** preparations and spices from the Culpeper range, the Molton Brown collection of hair preparations, Taylor of London's foaming bath seeds, Scottish honey and oatmeal soap, 27p. Potpourri from 75p, sachets from 34p, and a good selection of herb pillows including Kitty Little's fabulous large pillows, the only herb pillows with removable covers, £10.20.

**Food:** in colourful octagonal tins, Chinese black tea, mint, orange and jasmine tea, £1.10; tins of Droste cocoa, £1.25. Excellent scotch mustard from the Isle of Mull, £1.62; Welsh Lady lemon cheese, chutney and jam.

**Glass:** selection including smart, useful plain glass cylinders, several sizes, £1.85-£8.70; small yard-of-ale glasses, £1.12; Dartington cider glasses, £2.21 and lager glass, £2.52.

**Wicker:** wicker briefcase with fabric lining, £8.20; wicker picnic hamper with holders for two thermoses, £6.80.

**Lacquer:** black lacquer trunk boxes with brass fittings, three sizes, £42-£62.

**China:** irresistible celery jug that looks like celery, good enough to eat, £3.40, spring onion jug, £1.50; cottage riverside motif piece, rushes and a swan, vases and dishes, also hyacinth, from £1.90.

**Embroideries:** antique embroideries in unusual shapes, to use as wall hanging or inset on a dress, from £8; embroidered soft hat, £12.50; embroidered waist purse, £7.50. Modern silk prints from £1.10.

## Antique Jewellery

**Necklaces:** long rare Mandarin necklaces in coral, jade and glass, £90. Carved jade earrings, from £4.50. Victorian Chinese cufflinks in jet and agate, £3.50. Cabochon amethyst earrings, £38; delicately carved jade leaves on chains, rose quartz stud, £39; good selection of Chinese Victorian rings, set with jade from £7.50 including simple small jade oval with 4 claw setting, £7.60 and large cabochon white jade with leaf and flower mount, £14.50. **Hair ornaments:** raised cloud of flowers in jade, ruby, rose quartz and seed pearls, £30. Simple silver hair ornament, plain ball on a spike, £1. Large agate ornament, £9.10; rose quartz ball ornament, £12. Silver ornaments in shape of stylised lucky bat, £3.50. **Mandarin nail sheaths:** from £2.95 ungilded, from £4.95 gilded. **Antique bangles:** twisted silver rope bangle, £28.85; in silver and coral, £27; in plain silver, £10,50; rattan and silver bangles, £16. Agate archer's rings, £7.50.

## Modern Jewellery

Stone bangles, very like jade, from £6. **Cinnabar:** carved cinnabar beads, from 77p each in small size to £2.75 each for large. Carved cinnabar buttons, £1.55 each. Carved cinnabar necklaces: £26 for small size, £49 for large. **Cloisonné beads:** from 85p for small enamel on copper to £4.35 each for large enamel on silver. Necklaces of agate and cloisonné beads, £43.

---

**Penhaligon's** 41 Wellington Street, WC2   01-836 2150
Mon.-Fri.10-6, Sat. 10-1
By appointment to His Royal Highness the Duke of Edinburgh, manufacturers of toilet requisites

---

A red door in the shadow of the old Flower Market leads into the special world of Penhaligon—makers of toiletries for the most elegant men in the world. The famous Penhaligon preparations are made to the original formulae created a century ago, and each has an impeccable pedigree—Blenheim Bouquet was created for the Duke of Marlborough, and Bayolea dressing for Lord Lee. The perfumes are made of the finest essential oils, delicately blended by hand at the back of the shop. The labels are engraved with graceful script and Edwardian flourishes, the bottles have stoppers instead of tops, tied on with pretty bows, and all purchases are gift-wrapped in turkey-red paper with personalised labels or parcelled up in brown paper, tied with string and sealed with sealing wax. There's no better place to discover the heady delights of scented self-indulgence, the private pleasures of the great British bath. Start with exotic **Hammam** or fresh **English Fern—green and woody like a garden after rain**—and splash out on soap, bath oil or essence and shampoo in the same fragrance—as indispensible as loofas, sponges and Turkish towels. Finish off with lashings of matching eau de toilette and talc—you can even take a bath by candlelight with **candles perfumed in the same fragrance**. There are superb toilet waters in an unrivalled array of romantic scents—Eau de Primrose, Gardenia, Lily of the Valley, Night Scented Stock, dashing Violetta and Esprit de Lavande—considered by many to be the best in the world. Although Penhaligon caters primarily for gentlemen, sophisticated ladies like Gertrude Lawrence have always come here for scents. The Orange Blossom toilet water is the perfect fragrance for a bride to wear at her wedding, and Penhaligon celebrated the Jubilee with their first perfume for ladies only—a delicious woody scent with hints of jasmine, sandalwood and oak moss. Penhaligon pride themselves on personal service—they'll make gift boxes of their preparations and they have a superb collection of antique scent bottles, travelling cases and brushes and reproductions of Victorian scent bottle cases in wood or leather that make charming presents. Connoisseurs expect the best from Penhaligon—and they are never disappointed.

Penhaligon's catalogue and price list available on request.

Sample range—all prices approximate:

**Bouquets:** Hammam from £10 for 1oz, Jubilee £15 for ½oz. **Eau de Toilette:** Hammam from £7.50 for 4oz, English Fern and Blenheim Bouquet from £6 for 4oz. Eau de Cologne, Eau de Verveine, Extract of Limes from £4.25 for 4oz. Eau de Primrose, Esprit de Lavande, Gardenia, Lily of the Valley, Night Scented Stock, Orange Blossom, Violetta from £5 for 4oz. **Bath Oil** in

Hammam, £5.50 for 4oz; in Blenheim or English Fern, £4.50 for 4oz. **Talcum powder** in Hammam, £3.50; in English Fern, £3.25. **Soap:** bath soap in Hammam, £2.75; in English Fern, £2.50. **Hair Dressings** in Aleimma, Bayolea, Florimelle, Honey and Flowers, £3.25 for 8oz. **Scented candles** in Hammam or English Fern, £12.50. Travelling cases in wood from £10, in leather from £18.50. Antique cases and bottle prices on request. **Gift boxes** made up to order from £15.

---

## Clive Shilton  58 Neal Street, WC2   01-836 0809

Mon.-Fri. 10-6, Sat. 11-4
(American Express)

---

**Clive Shilton is a fashion designer who doesn't design clothes**, and his delightful shop is the place to learn a whole new way of putting on the style. Slip into a satin tent salon, settle yourself on ethereal grey satin cushions, and feast your eyes on irresistible shoes, sandals, handbags, boots, belts and necklaces nestling in the hearts of huge satin flowers. This is *couture* with a difference—accessories *made to order*, with such style and finesse that clothes become a mere afterthought. The designs are grouped in themes—everything matches up like the pieces in a diamond *parure*, and you can wear one piece or five, depending on the occasion. For this Spring and Summer, start with the pearlised scallop series—fine leather clutches with scalloped sides matching up to high-heeled sandals or flat sandals, scalloped tote bags with shoes or flat sandals, and scallop shell clutchbags with high heeled sandals to match, in pearlised pink, white or *eau-de-Nil* kid or satin. For evening, there's the exquisite rose collection—a luxurious *thirty-six* petal rose in finest gold or silver leather, set on to smart flare frame clutch bags, neck bags, chokers, brooches, belts, and over the toes of strappy high evening sandals in black or brown suede. You can also have the rose collection in pastel leather, for long summer nights or high summer days. For scintillating soirées, there's a whole collection in plain or handscreened swirly waterprint satin—svelte pleated bags and frilly frivolous purses, with peep toe, frill-trimmed, high-heeled ankle strap sandals to match— in *fifteen colours of satin*! For Autumn, don't miss Clive Shilton's topping designs for the tailor-made look—drawstring, clutch and shoulder bags in cape or suede with smart topstitched pinstripe detail. Then go on to his classic collection of scallop-edged clutch, Deco-motif clutch and smashing shoulder-style music bag—**the smartest briefcase in town**—with high pull-on boots, plain or trimmed with scallop, shell, or Deco piping. And that's not all! There are small leather goods to go with the handbags, a suede and snakeskin series, sporty satchels in suede and leather, leather weekenders and duffles, amusing leather necklaces and smart bangles, and very special *limited edition* handbags and shoes in ruched leather. **This is where top models, pop stars and personalities come to get the most fascinating portfolios in the world.** You can have anything you like—double-sided cases with special compartments to carry photographs or artwork on one side, and papers on the other; plain photographic cases, cases with company logos or personal initials *appliqué* on either side, cases made up in any shape, leather-trimmed portfolios with jute or woven leather sides. And getting back to basics, you can order a scallop-shell *monokini*, with matching scalloped-edge shawl scarf, if you'd like to dress yourself at Clive Shilton from top to toe. There's nothing quite like it anywhere in the world, a new kind of accessory-dressing with all the sophistication of the Twenties in a completely contemporary mood. With mystery, glamour and panache coming back in a big way, this is where you'll find everything you need for the new femininity.

Large selection of necklaces, belts and bangles *ready to wear*: also, choice selection of bags. For shoes and bags made to order, allow three weeks. For portfolios, allow four to six weeks. Good things are worth waiting for.

**Scallop collection:** in pearlised leather or six shades or glazed kid. Clutch with scalloped edges, shell or Deco detail, in two sizes, about £68 for large. Scalloped tote, about £90. High heeled backless sandal to match, £55; flat sandal about £45; also available in styles with shell back at heel. **In satin:** scallop shell clutch, £69; matching high heeled sandal, £55. Scallop shell belt, satin appliqué on leather, £20; matching necklace, £12.50. **Evening:** scallop shell or scallop-sided clutches, from £68, in black or brown suede piped with gold or silver. **Rose**

collection: flare frame clutch, £49; belt, £22; neck purse, £18.50; choker, about £10; high-heeled sandal, £55; flat sandal with ankle tie, £50. **Satin collection:** in fifteen colours, plain or frilly styles, to go with every evening dress, bags from £20-£52; matching open-toe ankle strap frill-trimmed sandals, £42. **Tailored** pinstripe collection: drawstring bag, £39; wrist-strap or shoulder bag, £60; half-moon clutch, £65. **Suede and snakeskin** collection: bags from £39-£45; matching strappy snakeskin high heeled sandals, £55. **Classic** collection in burgundy, camel, brown, beige, tan, navy: scallop edged clutch, from £78; Deco clutch, from £69 to £78; music bag in two sizes, £92 and £115; high boots, £120. Plain portfolios: in size to take 8″ × 10″ photos or A4 sketches, about £130. In sizes to take 15″ ×12″ photographs, about £170. Special portfolios to order, prices on application.

---

## The Warehouse  39 Neal Street, WC2   01-240 0931
Mon.-Fri.10-5.30, Sat. 11-5.30

If you're going ethnic, come here for the Eastern version of **utility chic**—cotton tunics, trousers and shorts as worn by millions on the Subcontinent. There's plenty of Folk Fashion too—the real thing instead of copies made for the export market, so you get quality, style and some fabulous bargains. From Rajahstan—the only place in India where women wear skirts instead of **saris**—come completely circular skirts that sweep and swirl with every step, in handwoven cotton handprinted with tiny traditional patterns in rich jewel colours. There are **Ghatas**, reversible quilted cotton jackets and hand-crocheted vests, Afghan knits splashed with folk motifs in beige, brown and black, long tasselled belts in fine fishnet, **sari** petticoats and vials of perfumed oils. There's no limit to what you can do with a bit of imagination. Start with the traditional Indian **kurta** in pure handwoven cotton—a proper below-the-knee tunic with side slits, long sleeves, stud-fastened front and Nehru collar. Worn as is, it doubles as a night shirt and beach shift—roll up the sleeves and add a belt to turn it into a rather daring day dress. Slip on a pair of matching drawstring shorts to turn it into a stylish summer layered look. Wear with drawstring trousers instead, and it turns into lounging pyjamas. Eastern chic is cheap as well—the three pieces together come to £10, including scented sandalwood studs for the **kurta**. If you want to make your own ethnic clothes, come here for handwoven and handprinted cotton by the yard, colourful bands of border prints to run along hems and sleeves, and lacquered round buttons painted with Indian playing card designs. Look out for the lovely 'turban lengths'—voile-fine cotton tie-dyed into a rainbow-tinted lattice pattern, just the thing for floaty evening frocks. Finish off with brass anklets and grass bangles, pouch purses to hang around the neck or tie at the waist, beads that cost as little as 1p for ten, and natural fibre chaplets from Goa, woven to look like ropes of jasmine, to wear around the wrist or in the hair. And don't forget the perfect touch for your ethnic wardrobe—lacquered bamboo coathangers, 75p each. Mail order catalogue available on request, send 10p in stamps.

Sample range and prices:

**Tops:** stripy short-sleeved top in handwoven cotton, £2.20. Long tunics in cotton, £4.50. **Jackets:** reversible quilted cotton jacket, plain on one side and printed on the other, £13. Quilted coats in handloomed cotton, £22.

**Trousers:** whites **khadi** cotton trousers with drawstring waist and buttoned fly, £4.25; drawstring trousers in heavier milled cotton, in white, brown and dark blue, £5. White khadi drawstring shorts, £1.50; striped khadi shorts, £1.65. **Knits:** handcrocheted vests in natural beige cotton, £3.95. Afghan knit slipovers, £6.50 and gloves, £2.

**Waistcoats:** quilted cotton waistcoats in traditional prints, trimmed with contrast piping. V-neck or Nehru collar, £6.50. Handwoven Indian tweed waistcoats with button front, £10. Men's handwoven rough silk waistcoat, in cream, lined with handwoven cotton, £37.50. **Skirts:** long Rajahstani skirts in handprinted cotton, about six yards of fabric at the hem, £14; mid-calf skirt with even more fabric, £20; **Sari** petticoats printed patterns, to wear as a summer skirt or tied higher to wear as a strapless summer shift, in a range of colours, £5.50: silk and cotton skirts with embroidered borders, £10-£28. **Fabrics:** handloomed

white khadi cotton, 48in wide, £1.30 a metre. Handwoven printed cotton, 43in wide, £1.75 a metre. Border prints, 4in wide, 50p a metre. Turban lengths, each piece 9yds long and 36in wide, £8. Ghatas, 6ft by 9ft, to wrap around your shoulders like a cloak, tie-dyed in lovely patterns and colours, £6. **Also:** woven screwpine **pochettes** edged with blanket stitching, £2.25; lacquered wood buttons in three sizes, a half inch to an inch across, prices from 20-40p each; handpainted lacquer rings, 40p; translucent stone rings, 50p; grass rings, 12p. Vials of Indian scented oil—jasmine, sandalwood, lotus, Mogra, patchouli and musk, 25p; carved bone scent holder to wear as a pendant, 20p; boxed henna sufficient for several applications, 30p; Mysore sandalwood soap, 45p for a box of 3. **Brass anklets,** £1; grass bangles, 20p; fine fishnet belts with tassels, in a range of colours, 60p; jasmine-look chaplets from Goa, 15p; cotton pouch bags to hang around neck or tie at waist, £1.35; matching change purse, 60p. Also, a wide selection of ethnic furniture, kitchenware, lots of amusing little toys, a range of glass and bone beads, Indian silk threads, fasteners and tassels.

## Westaway & Westaway 65 Great Russell Street, WC1
01-405 4479
Mon.-Fri. 9.30-5.30, Sat. 9.30-12.45

'Bloomsbury' may mean Virginia Woolf to you, but to Continentals it means woollies—and Westaway. Better known abroad where they appreciate such things, this delightfully old-fashioned family firm is bursting with **the best knitwear and tartan bargains in London**; and when you see their staggering range and splendid prices, you'll be very cross indeed at the way certain famous London shops have pulled the wool over your eyes, played the wolf in sheep's clothing and flannelled you into the deal. *Only the finest natural yarns are used—pure wool, camelhair and cashmere.* Westaway stick to the classic, and do it with style. They can offer you Shetland knits in no less than sixty colours—heathery mixes, high fashion naturals, perennial favourites like bottle green and City blue, up-to-the-minute shades of daffodil yellow and *eau-de-Nil. The firm buys direct from makers in wholesale quantities, stagger their deliveries so new things are coming in all the time, accept special orders for anything that isn't in stock and ship anywhere in the world.* There are men's Fairisle pullovers at £11.95, Prince of Wales check flat caps in pure cashmere for £7.95, children's pure wool kilts in authentic tartans from £4.95, ladies classic ribbed cardigans in pure blonde camelhair, *very elegant*, for £17.95—and that's just for starters! At Westaway, as in Wonderland, you begin at the beginning and go on to the end, but not in meticulous order. Shelves marked with sizes and styles stretch to the ceiling, drawers labelled 'Harris tweed socks, handknit, all sizes' and 'caps, tweed, 6½' spread along the floor. There are unmarked boxes with one-off oddments, racks, rails, eager shoppers trailing everywhere; you throw yourself in the *mêlée*, and have a lovely time. The lady assistants are usually Continental, the gentlemen English—the best of both worlds—and one way or another, you'll find everything you could possibly want, at prices that make the world your oyster.

Sample range—all prices approximate:

## Ladies knitwear

In chest sizes 20"/51cm to 46"/116cm. **In Shetland:** in size 34": round neck pullovers, £7.95; V-neck and roll collar pullovers, £7.95; round neck cardigans, £8.55. **In Fairisle:** sizes 26"/66cm to 46"/116cm. In size 34": Fairisle round neck pullovers, £11.95;

Fairisle round neck cardigans, £12.95. Long scarves with Fairisle trim, £5.95; Fairisle berets: £2.95; also, Fairisle gloves. **Aran knitwear:** pullovers from £21.95, cardigans from £23.95. **In lambswool:** round neck pullovers from £9.95; V-neck and roll pullovers from £9.95; V-neck and crew neck cardigans from £10.95. **In cashmere:** Round- and polo-neck pullovers from £15.95; scoop neck slim fitting pullovers from £16.95; V-neck cardigans from £17.95; ribbed polo-neck pullovers from £19.95; classic twin sets from £27.95.

**Ladies tartans: Kilted skirts** in standard day length, 27″-30″ lengths, £11.50; long kilted skirts, lengths 37″-41″, £15: all in standard sizes. **Special orders:** £12.50 for day length, £16 for long kilts. Kilted skirts in 70% **cashmere** 30% wool, from £35. Tartan waistcoats, all sizes, £10. **Scarves:** pure wool tartan scarves, 9″ × 45″, £1.50; tartan 70% cashmere 30% wool scarves, 9″ × 45″, £5.95; pure cashmere tartan scarves, 11″ × 54″, £9.25.

# Men's knitwear

In sizes 20″/51cm to 46″/116cm. **In Shetland:** in size 36″: round neck pullovers, £7.95; V-neck and roll-neck pullovers, £8.25; V-neck cardigans, £9.95; intarsia pullovers, from £12.95. **In Fairisle:** sizes 26″/66cm to

46″/116cm only. In size 36″: Fairisle round neck pullovers, £11.95; round neck cardigans, £12.95. **In cashmere:** roll-, polo- and V-neck pullovers from £19.95; V-neck cardigans from £21.95; slipovers from £15.95. Socks, 70% cashmere: calf length, £2.95; short, £2.50. **In lambswool:** Round neck, roll neck and V-neck pullovers from £10.95; V-neck cardigans from £11.95; slipovers from £7.95. **Aran knits:** pullovers from £21.95; cardigans from £23.95.

**Men's tartans:** kilt hose, tartan leg, from £4.50; plain leg from £3.30. Tartan shirts from £11.95; tartan waistcoats from £9.95; tartan kilts from £55; tartan dressing gowns from £18.95. Tartan ties, £1.75.

**Also:** Ladies **mohair triangles**, £5.50; **mohair ponchos**, £10.95. **Travel rugs** in pure wool: 58″ × 70″ from £11.95; 32″ × 50″, from £5.95: in pure mohair, 36″ × 46″ from £16.95; in cashmere and wool from £35.95. **Blankets** in several sizes, in Merino wool from £18.95, in mohair and wool from £28.95; in mohair from £45.30. **Mohair scarves** from £1.75; **mohair stoles** from £4.95. Cashmere and wool stoles 24″ × 72″, £21.95. Pure **cashmere stoles:** £39.95 for plain, £33.95 for tartan. Welsh tapestry St. Davids capes from £31.95; Welsh tapestry tabards, from £15.95. Pure **cashmere flat caps**, £7.95. **Children's knits and tartans**, see separate listing under 'Children's' section.

## Westaway & Westaway  29 Bloomsbury Way, WC1
01-405 2128/0497
Mon.-Fri. 9.30-5.30, Sat. 9.30-12.45

Just around the corner, Westaway's fabric shop with fine cloth by the metre. Tartans from £5.10 per metre, ladies tweeds from £6 per metre, suitings from £10 per metre, coatings from £14 per metre, pure camelhair from £32 per metre, jacket weight pure cashmere from £20 per metre, pure cashmere in coat weight from £35 per metre.

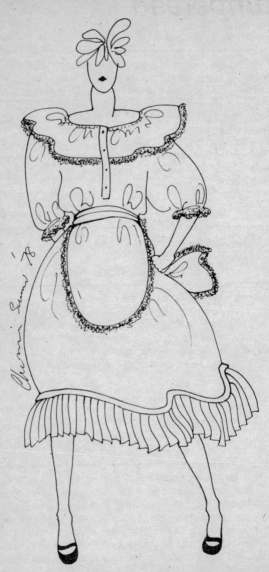

*By Charmian at Casablanca*

## At 78 Heath Street

Chic's collection of *negligées*, *peignoirs*, dressing gowns, night dresses, lounging robes, hosiery and *lingerie*. Labels include Christian Dior and Abecita of Sweden. Bras by Erys and Lejaby, and very special soft bras by Donald Brooks at Maidenform. Nightwear by Charnos, caftans and housegowns by Tracy Lowe. Designer *Lingerie* and Chic's own exclusive negliges and nightgowns in fine *satin-de-lys*.

## At 82 Heath Street

Day and evening wear by top British designers, smart separates and coats, fashion knitwear, fine leather goods and handbags. Look out for stylish tailor-mades by Jobis, in cotton; switcharound sets of skirts, jackets, dresses and trousers. Also, Marimekko cottons, pretty print dresses by Carin, soft chiffons by Kathy Manley and Meng. All clothes in sizes 8-16.

## Culpeper  9 Flask Walk, NW3   01-794 7263
Mon.-Sat. 10-6, Thurs. 10-1

Herbal delights and remedies, spices, honey, pure essential oils, natural perfumes. For description and prices, see separate listing under 'Mayfair' section. Also: a selection of potted herb plants, including rosemary, tarragon, basil and parsley.

## Jeeves of Belgravia  at Hampstead, 6 Heath Street, NW3   01-794 4100
Mon.-Fri. 8.30-5.30, Sat. 8.30-1

A one-stop shop for Jeeves' special services—dry cleaning, shirt laundering, shoe mending, and all other services featured in the Pont Street shops. For description and prices, see separate listing in Belgravia section. *Note: no night hatch.*

# Kingston
# Richmond
# Putney

**Bazaar**  6 Duke Street, Richmond, Surrey   01-948 3626
Mon.-Sat. 10-6
(Access, American Express, Barclaycard)

Stylish folk fashions; for description see separate listing under
'Mayfair' section.

**Bentalls**  Kingston Upon Thames   01-546 1001
Mon.-Fri. 9.15-5.30, Sat. 9-6
(Access, American Express, Barclaycard, Bentalls Card,
Diners, Eurocard)

Remember when departmental stores had a warm friendly
atmosphere and lots of exciting special events? When good service
was the rule rather than the exception? When parking wasn't a
problem and children were actually welcome? *When fashion was
something you could afford*? Don't waste time on a trip down
Memory Lane—just get the suburban line to Kingston and this
remarkable store where things are just what they used to be, and
much more besides. The house motto is 'to strive, to seek, to
find', and a quick look around will show you that they've found
looks as good as any in the West End, *and often better*—without
yielding to the West End temptations of high mark-ups and a
take-it-or-leave-it attitude to style. Last winter when boots
crashed the £100 barrier, Bentalls had leather boots in
up-to-the-minute styles from only £19.95, and when the
highwayman look was sweeping central London at highwayman's
prices, the shop had long flounced *moiré* skirts by Czarina for just

£12.95! Don't worry if you missed out, because the fashion departments get better every season, and you can start out with a Spring tonic in the beauty salon—a session with eyebrow tidy, full Helena Rubinstein make-up and three quarters of an hour of body massage for just £5.75. If you check with the shop on dates, you can time your visit to coincide with one of the special fashion shows compered by celebrities like Mary Quant, Lionel Blair and Katie Boyle, or the fashion fabric shows by houses like McCalls. There's been a Bentalls in Kingston since 1867, and today the complex includes over a hundred and fifty shopping departments on several floors, four restaurants and a multi storey car park. Most of the ladies fashions are on the first floor, now rearranged and redecorated, boasting dynamic new departments buzzing with excitement. Look out for the 'new ideas wardrobes' with the pick of goods from different departments so you can see how to put the season's top looks together for yourself, the *fabulous* Club 25 full of high flying fashions at prices you really can afford, and a superb selection of classic clothes that give unbeatable value for money. Fashion aside, there's something for everyone, with lots of the little touches that have largely disappeared elsewhere—special 'shoppers choice' lunches, nutritious mini-priced meals for children and babies, ramps for invalid chairs and prams, a four-hour dry-cleaning service, export bureau, bank, bureau de change, theatre ticket bureau, a branch of Thomas Cook, and a special 'At Home Evening' at Christmas, for all the family to enjoy. Bentalls really do think of everything, and in the unlikely event of your not being able to find what you want, you can fill in the details on a *Couldn't Get It* card, and they'll do everything they can to get it for you as soon as possible.

## On the ground floor you'll find

**Perfumery:** a sparkly new department with gold-plated fittings, lots of special promotions, top scents and cosmetics.

**Fabrics:** London's best selection of printed and plain needlecord, an excellent selection of cottons and poplins at very good prices, lots of fur fabrics. Look out for washable bridal lace at £1.25-£3.25 per metre.

Specialities: embroidered georgette and handpainted georgette, *couture* style and quality, no two bolts the same, £4.95 and £5.95 per 45" wide metre.

**Ladies shoes:** *wonderful value for money*, this department had last winter's best boot buys, with prices starting at only £19.95. Boots in sizes 3-8: with all leather uppers; zip up knee boot with brogue punch trim on toe and top, £19.95. Pull-on tan boot with stacked wood heel, £32.95. High

*By Jeff Banks at Bentalls*

sheepskin boots with crepe sole, £29.95. Top price £57.50 for smart all leather pull-on boot with ruched back, *very Knightsbridge*.

**Also:** Men's outfitting, men's tailoring, ladies hats, knitting shop, costume jewellery, hosiery, luggage, Ciro pearls, the **Chelsea Cobbler** shop with stylish shoes for men and women and Woly of Switzerland shoe polish, and an exellent **food hall**.

## On the first floor you'll find

**Ladies hairdressing:** bright cheery salon offering cuts, colouring, waving, henna, highlights, hair and scalp treatments by Glemby International. **Beauty salon** with *some of London's best beauty buys*. Session including make-up, eyebrow tidy and 45 minutes of body massage, just £5.75! Body massage only, £3.50; body massage with face mask, £4. Half hour cleanse and make-up, £2.80; all using Helena Rubinstein preparations. Also, skin treatments, Depilex hair removals, full range of wax treatments.

**Children's hairdressing:** rocking horse barber hairs, nursery print wallpaper and cuts from 90p. Also: **theatre ticket bureau** and **Thomas Cook**—no queues!—and a **foreign exchange** bureau.

**Wolsey Hall:** Bentall's special events room for fashion shows, exhibitions, Christmas displays, something on most weeks in the year.

**Furs. Suede and leather** including sheepskin coats. Classic suede jerkins from just £12.95. **Coats** from £19.95, range includes classic tweeds, camel wools, stylish capes and ponchos, sporty hooded coats, smart tailored coats with fur collars. Also, coats, raincoats and jackets by Aquascutum. **Jackets:** classic camel and tweed jackets, French-look blousons and ponchos, tweed hacking jackets and velvet blazers from about £38, cord blazers from about £45.

**Rainwear:** the **Dannimac** shop, Pack a Jac rain ponchos that fold up into a pouch, cagoules, zip-up hooded blousons, no dull 'mackintoshy' macs. **PM Dressing:** evening wear by Domino Dee, Monet, John Marks, John Charles, Andre Peters, Lady Charlotte, Mr. Darren. Sizes 10-16, some 18's, good medium price range. For informal evening wear, djellabas from £8.50, pretty printed caftans from £14.25. **Berketex bridal boutique** with wedding gowns from about £30. **Berketex** shop, **Jean Varon** shop, **Jersey Masters** collection.

**The Dress Department:** including the **Peasant Shop**, an imaginative boutique with special collections of clothes in the mood of the moment. Last summer it was the Patio Shop, full of summery lounge wear. This spring—go and see for yourself. **Dresses** in the main department are grouped by sizes, 10-16, some 8's. Look out for special displays of new styles, shown with matching scarves and accessories. Excellent ranges by Samuel Sherman, Monet and the Hamilton Collection. **Shorter fittings:** long on style, for those in

191

the 5'2"-5'3" bracket, by Richard Stump. **Larger Fittings:** in sizes 18-22, some 24's, lots of imaginative styles, good prints and colours. By Linda Leigh, Richard Stump, Dumarsel, Clifton Slimline.

★**Maternity:** one of the best in the country, a *young* maternity department full of up-to-the-minute styles, fabrics and colours at excellent prices. Lots of exciting *fashion* designs including long-line French style blousons, big cord shirts and trousers with tapered bottoms: clothes you'll want to go on wearing after the baby has arrived. Superb selection of trousers from £9.95; smocks in cord, velvet or tartan from about £10. Printed pinafore dresses from £14.50; cord pinafores by Pageboys about £16.95. Gigi style dresses with white collar and cuffs, by Alldae, £19.50. Always lots of pretty cheesecloths and cottons in summer, designs by Brimmell, Pia and Paula of Finland, Maria Mia.

★**Spotlite Her:** an exciting perspective on what being young in the Seventies is all about—fun instead of frenetic, no flashing lights, never vulgar, silly or little-girl frilly. Today's young looks are smarter, softer, simpler with lots of stylish swagger and a Continental flair. Come here for clothes uncannily right for the moment—silky knit evening dresses and printed *panné* velvet skirts with diamante trimmed tops, culottes and sheik's trousers, stripy pastel sweaters, flounced skirts and matching waistcoats, new things coming in all the time.

In one corner, a complete **accessory bar** with everything you'll heed to put yourself together—scarves, velvet and tweed ties, flower-trimmed combs, satchels, slides in every colour, bangles galore, Millimetre's colourful keep-forever cards printed with witty throwaway lines and bon mots. Don't miss it!

**Around the central well:** peek into Bentall's special **Wardrobes**★, fitted out with rails, shelves and hangers holding the pick of merchandise from all the fashion departments, so you can see what goes with what, and how to organize your own wardrobe. During the holiday season, this area includes a **Glitter Shop** full of sparkly cocktail and party dresses.

★**The Homespun Shop:** a superb selection of separates with the high fashion handknit look, the best traditional British designs and imaginative models with a continental flavour. Look out for Aran-look chunky knits, traditional Icelandic cardigans, fluffy big sweaters in sugared almond colours. Fairisles, big dropped shoulder blousons, sweater dresses, hats, scarves and gloves.

★**Club 25:** a fabulous department full of high-flying looks straight out of the fashion glossies—and at down-to-earth prices you really *can* afford. New stock comes in all the time, and the shop has the same kind of dash and excitement as the best weekly French fashion magazines. There's nothing quite like it anywhere else in London, and you can expect all the chic of a designer boutique at half the price or less. This season at Club 25; designs by Chatters, Jousse, Dawnbreakers, Wahl, Coopers, Mary Quant, Pamela Frances and *the complete Jeff Banks collection.*

★Lingerie and Corsetry: excellent value for money, good selection of little luxuries at bargain prices. In corsetry: very pretty suspender belts with lace, ribbon and embroidery trim, lovely colours, from £1.25; gathered lace-trimmed garters, 55p each; French knickers from about £2.75, many with matching bras. Collections of special lingerie at Christmas. Bras in sizes 28AA-44DD, skilled Berlei-trained fitters. Specialities include pre- and post-natal bras, post-surgery fittings, support corsets with back or front lacing. Next door in lingerie, exclusive lace-trimmed culotte slips, about £3; exclusive camiknickers, about £6.50. Bikini briefs from 45p, lacy tennis briefs just like Gorgeous Gussie's, £1.99. Also, pure cotton broderie Anglais petticoats by Sally Poppy, nightgowns, negligés, housecoats, pyjamas, and towelling robes.

**Also on the first floor: new fashion coordinates room ★**, top collections by **Alexon, Windsmoor ★, Eastex** and **Dereta. Bazaar,** exceptionally good selection of stylish ethnic and eastern clothes. **The Jaeger Shop. The Country Casuals Shop. Children's** shop with a range that goes from nursery to teens. **Knitwear,** the **Shirt Shop,** the **Bellino Shop** with smart colourful day and evening separates. **Skirts and Pants:** pants from £5.95. Good selection of evening skirts including, last winter, long black *moiré* look evening skirts with ruffled hems, by Czarina, £12.95 and long velvet skirts, £24.

## On the second floor

New linen department and everything you'll need to dress up your house. Emphasis on colour coordination, exceptionally tasteful selection of shades. **Young Furnishing** department with lots of imagination and style, some of the best prices in London—three-shelf bamboo bookcase, just £12. **Sportswear and Equipment**—for men and women, complete kits for every sport under the sun.

**Craftsmith** 18 George Street, Richmond, Surrey
01-940 9987
Mon.-Sat. 9-5.30

Now that prices are soaring and the handcrafted look is back in fashion, there are more good reasons than ever before to pop into this creative leisure centre. Like the W. H. Smith group of companies of which it is part, Craftsmith gets top marks for a really comprehensive approach and very dependable quality. Fun is fun, but these days it makes good sense to make your hobbies work for you—and this is where Craftsmith comes out on top. Starting from scratch, there's an excellent selection of fine British fabrics—everything from Liberty prints to subdued county tweeds—with Vogue, McCalls and Simplicity patterns to help you cut corners and still come out in style. Trims from the haberdashery department will help you bring your wardrobe up-to-date. If you want to start working on next winter's accessories, there are lots of bright yarns for handknit patterned hats, gloves, scarves, socks—and Lopi Icelandic fleece in natural colours for luxuriously warm good looks. You can turn yourself into a 'happy hooker' with a Craftsmith crochet kit, and there are bead weaving kits, shells to string into necklaces for this summer's South Seas look, kits and tools for suede and leather bags and belts, and books to tell you how to do everything. And don't feel intimidated if you've never dabbled in *do-it-yourself* before, because the staff are lavish with information, free leaflets and advice.

Sample range and prices:

**Fabrics:** each Craftsmith shop stocks several hundred rolls of fabric, representing leading fashion names such as Liberty, Epatra, Tootal and many more. Budget fabrics at less than a £1 a metre to luxurious fun fur fabrics at around £10 a metre. British fabrics play an important part in the Craftsmith range. Selection includes Golden Fleece, a washable dressweight pure new wool from Sanderson's Afgalaine range, available in 18 colours at £2.99 a metre; Liberty's Tana Lawn at £3.15 a metre; Liberty Varuna wool, £7.75 a metre; Liberty jubilee, £3.15 a metre. Stock includes lots of fashion prints, pure new wool fabrics and plain silk, and artifical flowers for trimming hats and dresses. **Yarns:** for hand or machine knitting, crochet, tapestry, embroidery and rugmaking. Yarns and patterns from Sirdar, Robin and Hayfield. **Kits and Trims:** kits for leather bags and purses, tooling leather and equipment, belt buckles from 18p; leather thongs, 16p each, to team with an excellent selection of colourful beads from India, starting from 1p and ideal for pretty chokers, necklaces and other accessories; tiny beads at 40p a pack can also be made up into simple jewellery on a bead loom at £2.35; shells from 30p; sterling silver rings from £2.30, with tumbled stones from 5p; resin at £1.99 and moulds at 60p can be put to good use by making a resin-cast pendant. Other Craftsmith kits and materials cover candle-making, painting and sketching, flowercrafts, modelling, craft finishing, doll and soft toymaking.

# MENSWEAR

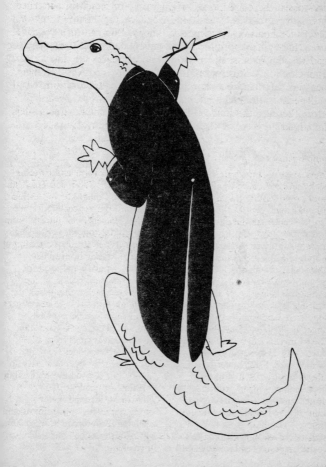

**Adam Owen**  13 Chiltern Street, W1   01-487 4864
Mon.-Fri. 10-6, Sat. 10-5
(Access, American Express, Barclaycard, Carte Blanche, Diners)

You couldn't meet a nicer shop than Adam Owen, where you'll
find an easygoing approach to fashion and a welcome that will put
you at ease. This is one of the new look designer shops for men,
but don't expect anything too extreme. Adam Owen prefer
clothes that simply look and feel good—very masculine and
casual—clothes that come to life when you put them on, but
never take you over. Putting yourself together is a piece of cake
when you choose from the shop's collection of relaxed good looks
by Paul Smith, Wendy Dagworthy and Paul Howie, Island shirts
from France, nautical sportswear by Ackel, separates by Ciao,
Renoma, Ecriture, Amariaggi, Façonnable and Giorgio Armani by
Falke, all carefully chosen in complimentary colours, textures and
cuts. Interest and individuality are very important at Adam
Owen, and they pride themselves on having lots of things you
can't find anywhere else. This summer you can come to Adam
Owen for Hilton's superb tweed and cord suits styled by Giorgio
Armani, Adam Owen's own linen-look cotton suits, big cotton
knit sweaters by Jean Claud Lewin, casual clothes and beach wear
by Equip, and blousons and trousers by Santana. You can chat
over a cup of real French coffee while you make up your mind,
and the shop's thoughtfulness extends to nice touches like the
complete collection of Floris No. 89 toiletries and shaving bowls,
delicious scents by Stanley Hall and Crabtree & Evelyn, and a
fine selection of pure wool and cotton socks. Prices give very
good value in terms of style and quality, and after the sales in
mid-January and July-August, sale goods are not marked back up
to the original price. A **very** pleasant shop indeed.

Sample range and approximate
prices:

**Knitwear:** an exceptional
collection, lots of handknits,
including heavy knit cotton
sweater, long-sleeved with long
sleeves and a racing strip straight
across the shoulders, £32.50;
boatnecked long sleeved mohair
cuddly bear, £32.50; David Farrin
mohair knits from £32. **Tops:**

pure wool blouson with braid
binding, by Amariaggi, £29;
textured cotton pullover by
Armani for Falke, with boatneck
and kangaroo pockets, £41; to
wear with natural textured blue
and white cardigan, £38. **Shirts:**
in sizes S, M, L. A casual soft
look with small collars or

collarless. Long or short sleeves. In cotton, from around £16.50-£24.50; Also, silk shirts, classic styles, £24.50, and big full overshirts, in cream and colours, from £28.50; Island shirts from £22.50; light khaki cotton overshirt, with two patch safari pockets, long sleeves to roll up and fasten with loop, £15; hessian overshirt, £14.95. **Suits:** superb suits, Hilton styled by Giorgio Armani, exclusive heathery tweed jackets in exceptionally smart patterns and toning cord trousers from £160. Own label suit in linen-look cotton or very lightweight tweed, unconstructed jacket, pleated front trousers in sizes 34-42, from £70. **Trousers:** cotton fatigues from about £23; Adam Owen tweed trousers from £22.50; cord trousers from £24; classic baratia trousers with jet pocket, from £31; in pure cotton, £22.

---

# Hardy Amies  32 Hans Crescent, SW1
01-584 7998
Mon.-Sat. 10-6, Wed. 10-7

---

Hardy Amies's menswear collection is just what mainstream dressers have been waiting for—a new version of the classic well-dressed look. As he puts it—'*My styles give authority to the appearance of youth, and give youth to those in authority!*' The best of the casual trends have been reflected and refined—jackets have soft shoulders, leisure shirts have button-down collars or contrast facings and there are lots of natural colours and textures. The silhouette is long and lean—shoes have inch and a half heels to emphasize the slightly narrowed trouser bottoms, and trousers are worn at the waist instead of the hip to accentuate the length of the legs. Classic suits have jackets in the new shorter length, while the frankly modern leisure suits have tunic length jackets with shirt-cuff sleeves. Hardy Amies has always been a superb stylist, and there are lots of little touches like the crew neckline of the tank tops—very flattering for older men, and ideal for keeping an open neck shirt from going too far. Don't miss the long Hardy Amies socks, the smart towelling robes and bath sets with the new HA lozenge logo, the elegant black Hardy Amies signature lighter and the Hardy Amies cologne—an exceptionally fine fragrance that makes you think of sun and the south of France. Hardy Amies is a consultant to leading menswear makers

all over the world, and the styles and colours you see in the
London shop will give you an idea of what the new international
looks will be in a year's time.

Sample range—all prices
approximate:

**Shirts:** in sizes 14½-17, all natural
fabrics. Cotton shirts from £14.95
to £25. Silk shirts £25 to £49.

**Trousers:** in sizes 28-38, in a
range of fabrics and colours, with
or without turnups, from £25.

**Suits:** classic and casual styles
from £95.

**Jackets:** from about £60-£120.

**Also:** a selection of classic
knitwear in Shetland, lambswool
and cashmere, and fine wool and
silk ties.

---

# Anderson & Sheppard  30 Savile Row, W1
01-734 1420/1960
Mon.-Fri. 8.30-5
Telegrams: *Andershep*, London W1

---

**Even in Hell, you'd float about showing off your Anderson and
Sheppard waistcoats**, hissed Priscilla over the strawberries in
Michael Arlen's 'Babes in the Wood'. Arlen certainly knew.
When nightingales sang in Berkeley Square, that most elegant of
authors **always** went to 'Andershep' to suit himself in style. He
introduced Rudolph Valentino to the Anderson & Sheppard
look—Diaghilev was a client, and so was Fred Astaire, who
tripped the light fantastic through the fitting rooms to check the
fit and flair of his tails. They came for Anderson & Sheppard's
unique 'soft touch'—*the original unconstructed style Anglais*; softly
tailored, beautifully textured, completely relaxed, with natural
shoulder lines and virtually no padding. A 'new look' that bridged
the gap between stiff formality and the informality of pure sport
and leisure wear. A bit *avant-garde* in the Twenties, Anderson &
Sheppard's special touch is absolutely right for today's more
casual, natural life style. And if you want to see how right it is,
look out for Ken Russell's *Valentino*; Anderson & Sheppard
provided all Nureyev's suits, adapted from Valentino's own
orders. Anderson & Sheppard rely on consummate cutting and
excellent finishing to achieve their look. Since there is no
restrictive filling or heavy padding, the jackets are so comfortable
that you're hardly aware you're wearing one—just the way a
perfect city suit *should* feel. Anderson & Sheppard will make

198

anything to order except riding breeches and military uniforms, and are delighted to create a design if you'd like something really extraordinary. The shop has the best selection of fabrics in the Row—glen checks, stripes, tweeds, herringbones and plains in a splendid array of colours and textures—fully the equal of the fabulous fabrics of the Twenties. Over three hundred bolts are stacked neatly on tables—and since the cloth is in the piece, you can drape the fabric over your shoulder to see if it suits, much more satisfactory than looking at swatches. The evening dress fabrics are particularly elegant—mohairs and baratheas with the very finest stripes or herringbones, and several fabrics in midnight blue, which often looks smarter than black. The lightweight suitings have clear, lively colours, and the tropical suits never look washed out or dull. Anderson & Sheppard are an extremely friendly and helpful establishment. They remain open all through the lunch hour, are happy to arrange to clean, repair and valet your clothing, and, through their association with Herbert Johnson the hatters, offer the unique service of caps made up in fabrics to match your suits, jackets or trews. And getting back to soft touches, their prices are extremely reasonable for the Row, with two-piece suits starting from £250, including VAT. That's within a few pounds of the most expensive off-the-peg suits. As they like to say at Anderson & Sheppard—'There are two kinds of men who can afford suits in our price range. The ones who only care about convenience buy off-the-peg. The ones who care about how they look and feel, who want to look well-dressed without wearing a uniform, come to us.'

Sample range and prices:

Allow two to three weeks and several fittings. Two-piece suits from £250; three-piece suits from £285; silk suits add another £100; dinner jacket and trousers from £325; smoking jacket from £240; sports trousers from £95; overcoats from £275; Norfolk jackets from £200; yachting blazers from £175. Others by consultation.

---

**Bally**  116 New Bond Street, W1   01-629 6501
Mon.-Sat. 9-5.30, Thurs. 9-7
(Access, American Express, Barclaycard, Diners, Mastercharge)

---

Bally are the masters of classical elegance, and their collection boasts over forty different styles of slip-ons—*not* counting the colour variations! You can have formal evening pumps, casual unconstructed moccasins, glossy kids with discreet gilt trim, hand-stitched slip-on brogues, slip-ons with lizard inserts, slip-ons *lined and trimmed with foulard silk*, luxurious designs in crocodile—and Bally's good looks don't stop there. Lace-ups are back in fashion, and Bally have a superb selection of handsome Oxford classics, beautiful brogues and two-tone correspondant shoes. Colours are light and natural—look out for stylish combinations of beige with caramel and camel, subtle texture contrasts of Nubuck or linen on leather. There are three designs in plaited leather for hot climates, and a wonderful selection of high summer sandals and backless sabots. Wear the plain-front Florida sabots with well-cut jeans and cords, the plaited-front Mentons with easy linen shorts and silk T-shirts. Whatever you choose, Bally shoes will give a lift to your walk as well as your looks—they're beautifully light, completely flexible, *with such a perfect fit that you don't have to break them in*. It's just as well that the atmosphere and service are exceptionally pleasant, because you're bound to be back. Bally shoes are so comfortable that once you've worn them, it's difficult to wear anything else.

Sample range—all prices approximate:

**Shoes:** in sizes 5½-11, D and E fittings. Summer **sabots:** Menton with woven front, £39; plain front Florida, £49.50. **Boots:** fabric and leather ankle boots, about £50; soft unlined summer boot in white, camel, beige and dark brown, zip side, £69; classic town boot with side zip, £75. Woven leather over-the-ankle pull-on, £47. Unconstructed **moccasins,** £37.50; glossy kid slip-ons around £60. **Slip-ons** lined and trimmed with foulard silk, in black, tan or light grey, £62. **Crocodile** slip-ons, £165. Classic Oxford lace-ups and correspondent lace-ups brogues in leather with Nubuck, both about £85. **Evening pumps** in grosgrain or patent, from about £49-£59.

---

**Browns** 23 South Molton Street, W1   01-491 7833
Mon.-Wed. and Fri. 10-6, Thurs. 10-7, Sat. 10-5
(American Express, Barclaycard, Diners)

---

The prettiest men's shop in London, with a special look of its own. The Browns team, headed by Simon Burstein, have their studio over the premises, and their collection has a soft English look with unconstructed shapes, muted colours and natural textures—clothes for living easy. They're go-anywhere-do-anything designs—a country look that lets you feel completely free in town. This season Browns splash out in silks, wools, cottons and linens, a larger collection than ever before. There are lots of single and double breasted jackets, soft but with a firmer set to the shoulders, in light taupes, naturals, creams and beige, to show off the weave of the cloth. Wear them with linen waistcoats and classic single pleated linen trousers, knits in Fairisle and birds eye patterns, and fine striped silk shirts. There's a second Browns collection with a completely casual theme—reversible jackets in cotton and cord, peg top farmers jeans with very wide legs and cotton and leather braces, zip-fronted fatigues with hammer pockets, scoop neck T-shirts in woven cotton, loose gusset shirts in polished cotton and coloured linen. For summer showers, Browns have side buckled rain jackets and three styles of raincoat in rubberized cotton, and to go with everything, their own collection of English bench-made shoes. You'll find the season's smartest looks from the continent too—the exclusive Giorgio Armani and Missoni collections, more elegant looks by Basile and Cerruti—and you can go on to get summer haircuts at the Molton Brown salon, summer salads at the Molton Brown restaurant, household accessories for all seasons from the Browns Living Shop. Browns have always had the pick of the classic Continental designs, and their own collections give the shop a fresh, younger feeling. Get your summer off to a promising start at Browns.

Clothes in sizes 34-44; suits, separates, coats, knitwear, shirts and trousers by Missoni, Cerruti, Basile, Giorgio Armani and Browns. **From the Browns collection:** unlined singlebreasted jackets in silk and wool blends, twills, herringbones, openweave and windowpane checks, from £90. Unlined singlebreated jackets from £70. Five-button shirt jackets, £76; completely unconstructed singlebreasted jacket in natural linen, £50; matching trousers, £80. **Trousers** in sizes 26"-36"; classic single pleat trousers with adjustable button waist, £26; plain front trousers in cotton and natural linen, £26; faitgue jeans, £19. **Shirts** in superfine silk stripes, £54; short sleeved natural linen shirts and gusset front shirts, £24. Sea Island cotton T-shirts, £14. **Knits:** button-front gilet in birdseye check, £20; plain gilets, £20; openweave T-shirts, £15; subtle spring Fairisles, from £28. Very special knits by Kaffe Fassett. **Shoes** (at 25 South Molton Street) in sizes 6-10½, by Rossetti, Cerruti and Browns. **From the Browns collection;** buckle moccasins in redwood, taupe, grey and white; £38. Canvas and

*At Cue Shop*

leather shoes in sage green with beige canvas, £30; commando *crêpe* soled canvas lace ups, £28; buckle sandal with slit sides and apron front, £36; hide sandals with apron front and commando soles, £30; canvas and leather sport shoes on crepe soles, £32.

---

# The Cue Shop at Austin Reed 103 Regent Street, W1   01-734 6789

Mon.-Sat. 9.30-6, Thurs. 9.30-7
Telegrams: *Sumitkolla*, London W1
(Access, American Express, Barcalycard, Carte Blanche, Carte Bleu, Chargex, Diners)

---

Spot on cue, the Cue shop at Austin Reed provides a fresh alternative to denim emporiums, pop boutiques and exaggeratedly sporty stores. The Cue shop is aimed at younger men, twenty-five and over, who grew up in the exciting clothes of the Sixties and are now looking for a new, interesting 'young executive look'. After a decade in jeans, they want suits that really fit. After a few years of buying in the boutiques, they're ready for *real* clothes, with durable quality and style. They want the *right* looks, the ones that can open new doors—and they want them at the right prices. The Cue shop collection falls neatly into well-groomed good looks and completely casual styles, with no grey area inbetween. Since they only cater for slender sizes 36-42, the Cue Shop can lash out on a tremendous array of merchandise—everything from dashing leather trench coats to inexpensive English-made T-shirts—but don't worry about getting confused, because Cue Shop believe in doing the thinking and hard work for you. Every three weeks or so there are 'theme collections' that spotlight a special fabric, colour, designer or look, with windows and displays that show you exactly how the shirts, knits, scarves, trousers and jackets all link up. Last summer they showed the Ketch collection of bright Italian sportswear and the full summer range from Daniel Hechter of Paris, and this summer you can look forward to easy shirts in satin-finished cotton, slender trousers in elephant cord, sporty jackets in sugar bag blue—*so much nicer than navy. Best of all, there will be a superb collection in flannel and tweed—flannel suits with the new softer lines, in five subtle colours, also available as separates with toning tweeds, knits and shirts*! Austin Reed is an established name, but there's nothing old-fashioned about Cue, and you'll find accessories like long scarves, cravats in *foulard* silk, Mulberry holdalls and smart silver jewellery that you only find in the most up-to-date shops. Cue Shop take fashion and shopping very seriously, and everything possible has been done to make your visit a pleasure. The staff are extremely helpful and there are credit facilities, music to choose by, plenty of light and space and soft couches to sit on while you make up your mind. Don't forget to pick up a complimentary copy of Austin Reed's lavish Summit Magazine with notes on the season's best fashion looks, features of interest to members of the Austin Reed Wine and Travel clubs, and a special section devoted to the Cue Shop. When it comes to reasonably priced young executive fashions, you couldn't do better to take your cue from Cue!

**Summit Magazine** is published twice a year, in Spring and Autumn. Copies are available at the door, and are mailed to all account customers. Copies will be sent on request, and all copies are free.

Sample range—all price approximate:

**Suits** from £65; velvet suits from £95, blouson suits from £50; corduroy suits from £65. **Jackets:** check tweed and plaid, from £55. **Coats:** from £40; trench coats from £30 and leather trench coats from £125. **Shirts:** half-sleeve cotton shirts from £9; T-shirts from £2. **Leather** and Suede blousons, from £75. **Trousers:** good selection from £10-£30; Hoofer jeans from £12. **Knitwear:** Shetland and lambswool sweaters from £10: high fashion knits from £15. Also at: **Cue Shop at Austin Reed**, 163/9 Brompton Road, SW3.

**Alfred Dunhill** 30 Duke Street, St James's, SW1
01-493 9161
Mon.-Fri. 9.30-5.30, Sat. 9.30-4.30
Telegrams: *Salaams*, London SW1
(American Express, Diners)
By appointment to Her Majesty the Queen, suppliers of smoker's requisites

Molière called tobacco '**the passion of all decent men**', but for those who prefer to lavish their attention on clothes, Dunhill have a whole salon full of luxurious good looks, with toiletries and accessories to match. Meant for international men who like the relaxed English style, the clothes are quietly confident, beautifully understated, equally at home in town or country. You'll find all the classics—velvet evening suits, smart blazers, Norfolk and hacking jackets—with the attention to detail that is so essential to *le style Anglais* at its best. The tweeds are of the finest quality, in elegant herringbone, dogstooth and Prince of Wales weaves, and all the jackets have real four-button cuffs. The easy English manner has been carried over into a collection of exceptionally stylish casuals—dashing cord trousers, handknit gilets, sporty blousons and fine leather shirts, accessorized with rich silk stocks and fringed scarves in silk and cashmere. You can go on to choose Dunhill watches, Dunhill pens, Dunhill 'S' lighters in the new nugget finish. Don't forget the Dunhill 'D' cufflinks in solid silver or gold, to show off your jacket cuffs, or the Dunhill Diary, printed in Dickensian flourishes—a well-dressed man never has time on his hands!

Sample range—all prices approximate:

**Jackets:** in sizes 36-44, some 46's. Tweed Norfolk jackets, £155, and hacking jackets, £138. Classic double-breasted blazers, £126, Tweed sports jackets, plain or trimmed with Alcantara, about £145. **Casual jackets:** zip-fronted cord blousons with Tattersal check lining, ribbed knit shawl collar and cuffs, in navy or cream, £94; suede-trimmed tweed battlejacket, £86; plain, £74.50. Fine antelope shirt jacket with safari pockets, £195; antilope sip-fronted blouson, £145. Smart golf jacket in biscuit gabardine, £45.

**Trousers:** in sizes 28"-40" waist, two classic styles with side or patch pockets, in cavalry twill, fine wool flannel, gabardine, cottons and linens. Winter trousers from £42; dashing elephant cord trousers, in natural shades, £49.

**Suits:** three-piece tweed suits from £185; three-piece evening suits from £175.

**Knitwear:** Argyll cashmere pullovers, about £60; sporty shawl collar knits, £39; shawl collar cashmere knits in natural colours, £71.50; handknit gilets, £42; V-neck Shetland knits from £16; very smart V-neck ribbed knits, about £35; all in sizes 36-44.

**Also:** leather trenchcoat lined with silver fox, £1,280; plain leather trenchcoats from £325; fringed cashmere scarves lined with silk, £33.50; matching cashmere ties, £12.70, handwoven rough wool scarves, £65; ribbed black cashmere scarves, £59; Dunhill silk ties, £10.50; silk stocks, £13.75; untied silk bow ties in two styles from £3.75, Dunhill 'D' cufflinks in solid silver, £18.50; Dunhill 'S' lighters in nugget finish from £65 for silver plate; Dunhill Diary in black hide cover, £20; gilt-edged refills, £6.

*At Ebony*

**Ebony** 45 South Molton Street, W1   01-629 4721
Mon.-Sat. 10-6, Thurs. 10-7
(Access, American Express, Barclaycard, Diners,
Eurocard, Mastercharge)

Being in Ebony is like being in love. *This is the most exciting men's shop in England*, and it can do everything for you that love can—possibly more. Ebony will take you out of yourself, show you how great life can be, how good you can look—turn your world upside down and leave you smiling. The Ebony studios give young English designers the chance to create *small collections of stunning originals, with a style and quality you'll never find anywhere else*—clothes with *such personality and imagination that you'll be bowled over the minute you walk in the door.* There are big handknit hand-dyed sweaters of intertwined natural wool and mohair, each one unique—swashbuckler shirts in heavy antique silk, handloomed waistcoats, big Borg coats—designs that are striking, but never outrageous. John Kaye of Ebony works closely with the designers, so you get the best of both worlds—clothes that combine art with realistic touches like pockets in big heavy sweaters, so you can wear them *instead* of a coat. Although the choice is tremendous, there's a definite 'Ebony look'—free, fascinating, completely relaxed—a look that says you think for yourself. Ebony's own label collection gives you plenty to think about, starting with the most dashing suits in town. These are suits you can really get involved with—beautiful fabrics, textures and colours that switch around into lots of different looks. Everything is made in England, handcut and handfinished, and top marks for style go to the tweed and cord combinations that you can wear in five different ways. There are textured tweed jackets and trousers, trousers in toning plain tweed and cord, handknit waffle textured waistcoats that reverse to cord, Fairisles in yarns dyed to match the tweeds; combine them at random and you'll still come up with a winner, and there's a spring collection in silk and cotton that does the same trick. Ebony have *the best casual jackets and coats in London*—30's style shirt jackets, blousons, Norfolk jackets in blackface ram tweed, completely reversible square set coats with long shawl collar, tweed on one side, proofed cotton on the other—*the* casual coat of the season. There are no shirts like Ebony's anywhere under the sun—*so romantic, sexy, imaginative and fun that you won't want to cover them up.* You have a choice of *four* kinds of silk—*crêpe de Chine,*

207

silk chiffon, Chinese slub silk and Thai raw silk—and a dazzling array of styles. Don't miss Ebony's fabulous collarless silk shirts with deep box pleats on front and back yoke, or the new stud-fastened western cut shirt with lots of flair, but no flash detail. There are Ebony's own antique silk shirts with an open seam inverted pleat running the whole length of the sleeve, small collar shirts by Jenny Phountzi with heavily gathered front and back yokes, contrast facings and Art Deco buttons, no two shirts exactly alike. Ebony has its own shoes, T-shirts specially dyed to match the clothes, shorts galore for summer, everything you could possible want to make you happy—and a new international collection that will be available abroad from this spring. The staff are delightful, their enthusiasm is contagious. You can tell a lot about a shop from its clients—and the men who walk into Ebony are the best looking men in town. Join them, and let Ebony's black magic put a spell on you.

Sample range—all prices
approximate:

**Suits** in sizes 34-44: from £75-£120. **Jackets:** single and double breasted blazers from £65. Norfolk jackets, about £67.50. Travel suit: safari jacket with passport sized pocket, £43; herringbone or gabardine waistcoat, £25; trousers, £29.50. Cord blousons, £45. Lightweight reversible blousons, £39.50. **Trousers:** in sizes 26-36, all exclusive to Ebony: in Harris tweed, £39.50. In cotton, silk and linen, £29.50-£39.50. Cord and twill jeans from £15.50.

**Knit:** superb selection including Fairisles to tone with tweed suits, £29.50; big sweater with side pockets and lattice and bobble design by Edy Lyngaas, £75; bright mohair and natural wool sweaters, about £80. **Shirts:**

Ebony's box pleated band neck silk shirt, £45; western shirts in raw silk, £42.50; antique swashbuckler shirts by Andrew Yiannakou, black or cream, £45; £24.50 in cotton. Cotton shirts by Jenny Phountzi, £19.50-£35. Box pleat shirts in Thai silk, £49.50; in antique cotton, £22.50; box pleat cotton shirt with collar, £24.50. Classic shirts in prewar cotton, from £15.50-£19.50. Ebony T-shirt, £4.50; winter T-shirts specially dyed to go with jeans and sweaters, £7.50. **Shoes:** handmade and leather lined, from £29.50-£35; boots from £45.

**Also:** long collarless shirt bath robes in brushed cotton, £18.50; long towelling robes for winter, £32.50. Reversible square set shawl collared coat, £79.

## Howie

Fun, funky fashion is a thing of the past at Howie, and although you'll still find lots of imagination and interest, the emphasis is on quality casual classics. Always the most novel of the men's shops, Howie give the classics a very special treatment. The lines are clean, without any gimmicks, but so completely relaxed that its impossible to look too dressed up. The shapes are generous and unfitted, so the linen and herringbone cotton jackets seem to drape instead of hang. Deep pleated trousers and shirts with small collars and slender yokes give an impression of overall roundness and there are soft cream pure silk handknits with stripes and stipples of camel, peach and blue to complete the look; a classic beachcomber suit for the seventies. You can go on to khaki braces, American pack-a-macs, smart sweatshirts by Ferrer y Sentis, Kruger cotton drill jeans, lots of super knits by George Hostler, Island and Altona. Howie is the only shop in London with the complete collection of Walkers shoes—very English in style, with the traditional bench-made look. There are T bar leather and canvas sandals, canvas laceups and classic white bucks, fringed tongue golf shoes, black and white spectator pumps and canvas laceups to wear with separate garters; everything you need to go with Paul Howie's gentle classics. New things come in all the time, and if you're looking for a shop with real fashion identity, this is the place for you.

Sample range—all prices approximate:

**Paul Howie collection:** Shirts in sizes S, M, L; cotton cutaway collar shirts from about £30; collarless shirts from about £29; hessian shirts from about £28. **Silk handknits:** jerseys, slipovers, waistcoats and cardigans, from about £36-£65. **Trousers:** in cotton from about £30; in poly/silk linen, from about £40. Cotton shorts, from about £20.

Double-breasted **jackets** in poly/silk and linen from about £68, in cotton from about £57; Single-breasted jackets in poly/silk linen about £65; in cotton from about £54. **Walker shoes:** in sizes 6-11; from £27 for canvas and leather sandals to £28 for canvas laceups with gaiter. Black and white spectator shoes, £31.

**Herbert Johnson** 13 Old Burlington Street, W1
01-439 7397
Mon.-Fri 9-5.30
Telegrams: *Browbound*
(Access, American Express, Barclaycard, Carte Blanche, Diners)
By appointment to Her Majesty the Queen, hatters

What would stylish men be without their hats—or without 'Herbie J.' the most dashing of hatters. The house motto is *Nunquam non Paratus*, never unprepared—you're sure to find something for every clime and occasion, and you can really let style go to your head with Herbie J.'s unique 'personality' hats. There are bush hats with *pugaree* bands for the soldier of fortune image, artistic wide-brimmed velours and panama hats for the Cecil Beaton look, harvest straw hats for playing the romantic tax exile in havens far away, and indomitable Chartwell felts modelled on Sir Winston Churchill's favourite painting hat. Herbie J's hats look just as good on the screen, and they supplied all Steed's bowlers for *The Avengers*, hats for Ken Russell's *Valentino* film, and the tweed hat worn by Peter Sellers as Inspector Clouseau. The darling of the county set, Herbie J. always take a travelling hat shop to Burleigh, Badminton, the Game Fair and the Wembley Horse Show, and their Old Burlington Street shop is the place to see the English country look at its best. There are trilbys for race meetings at Newmarket and Cheltenham, tweed caps and hats for informal meetings at Lingfield, understated 'Off Parade' and 'Sandhurst' hats for running up to London, soft tweed 'Peatmore' pull-ons for shootin', fishin' and county shows, floppy canvas cricket hats, straw boaters for Henley, riding bowlers and toppers for the hunting field—even *silk guards to keep the hunting hats on and special top hat polish*. For sporting lives of other sorts, Herbie J. have tennis hats, sailing hats, tweed motoring caps for vintage car rallys, traditional tweed golf caps and new golf caps in Oxford and Union flannels—very Ivy League. Back in town, you'll find all the right hats for officers and gentlemen—top hats, regimental caps, classic bowlers in black—or in any colour to order, for those who'd prefer to bowl the City over. Whatever you select, you're bound to come out with a topping good look, so stroll off to celebrate at the nearby Burlington Bertie pub, named after the Edwardian dandy who rose at ten-thirty and dressed to the nines.

Sample range—all prices approximate:

**Flat tweed golf caps**, the largest selection in London, from £8. **Tweed country hats**, from £13.50. **Felt hats** from £18. **Tweed motoring hats**, £8.50. **Flat caps** for summer in ticking stripes, hessian, gabardine and herringbone patterned linen, about £6. Canvas **cricket hats**, about £4. Wide brimmed canvas 'Nomad' hat, £12.50. Wide-brimmed **velours hats**, £23.50; wide brimmed **panama hats**, £21.50. **Hunting caps**, in black or dark blue velvet, from £39. **Hunting bowler hats** from £31.75. **Panama hats** from £18. **Town bowler hats** in three shapes and two finishes, from £22.50. Felt **top hats** from £40; top hats from £80. **Silk riding hat guards**, about £3; **top hat polish**, Herbie J.'s own recipe, £1.50 for a half pint bottle.

---

# H. Huntsman & Son  11 Savile Row, W1
01-734 7441
Mon.-Fri. 9-1 & 2-6, Sat. 9-12
Telegrams: *Carpack*, London W1   ★

Huntsman is the kind of tailor that gave Savile Row its reputation, and besides being a byword for superb made-to-measure day and dress wear, its name is also a happy aide-memoire for the fact that it makes some of the finest riding clothes in the world. Huntsman spare nothing in the way of craftmanship and service—all work is done on the premises and a visit will impress anyone who appreciates the very best. The individual patterns that are made up for an order are kept in a fireproof room and carefully marked over the years to correspond with alterations in customer's measurements. The fitting rooms contain saddled wooden horses to ensure a perfect fit for all riding clothes, and one room even boasts a side-saddle—for Huntsman make the elegant habits that so enhance the feminine equestrain arts. The outer room is taken up with samples and bolts of the finest quality fabrics, offering thousands of possibilities in the thousands. In addition to all the standard patterns and colours, Huntsman have a large selection of exclusive tweeds which are made to their order in limited editions, providing only enough fabric for ten garments, and they also have exclusive fabrics in their shirt and tie ranges. You can order anything from a diplomatic uniform or full evening dress to velvet jackets, pyjamas and colourful summer trousers; if it carries the

Hunstman label it will be superbly styled, masterfully executed, and will not leave their premises being anything less than perfect.

Huntsman make an annual trip to major cities in Europe and also to America and Canada, in conjunction with their sister shops, Henry Maxwell—bootmakers and spurriers, and Rowes—boy's and girl's tailors and outfitters. On these trips, customers can be measured for garments which will be made up in London and returned by post. For dates and further particulars, write to Huntsman.

All prices are exclusive of VAT

## Made-to-measure clothes for men

Made-to-measure garments take ten to twelve weeks with five fittings if possible. You can expect the highest standards of craftsmanship and all the touches of consummate tailoring—shoulders that are painstakingly moulded by hand, handmade buttonholes, velvet lapels understitched by hand to hold their shape forever.

**Three-piece suits:** from £481 for wool, £603 for silk, £520 for mohair and £457 for cotton denim. Two-piece suits about £23 less. **Sports and hacking jackets:** from £325-£360. **Overcoats:** from £538 fro tweed. **Formal wear:** dinner jacket suits in mohair, £613; dress coat and trousers in worsted, £605; morning coat in worsted, £444; Ascot type morning suit in worsted, £627. **Velvet smoking jacket:** from £480. **Pyjamas:** from £43.75 for cotton poplin to £91 for silk. **Shirts:** Huntsman have a particularly fine selection of cottons—Bermuda and Oxford cloth, denim, voile and Madras. Sea Island cotton in herringbone weave and pure cotton in many patterns including their own exclusive designs. They will replace collars and cuffs. Shirts from £23.75 in cotton poplin to £56 for silk. Dress shirts from £31.50 for cotton poplin, £68.50 for silk. **Made-to-measure clothes for women:** a selection of very classic tailored styles from £561-£591.

## Made-to-measure riding clothes for men and women

Riders all over the world treasure their Huntsman habits as much as their horses, and no wonder. Only the centre seam of the breeches is done by machinery; every other is carefully handsewn and finished to stand up to hard wear, buttons that go under boots are flat so as not to press under the leg, and all button holes and fastenings are done by hand. The tails of the coats are carefully backed to give extra protection, large pockets are fitted in both inner fronts and coats can be made of the heaviest or the lightest fabrics to suit hunts in all climates. Hunstman have the hunt buttons for the English, American, Canadian and most European hunts, a comprehensive repair and alteration service and an excellent re-dyeing service to cope with troublesome stains that result from the increased chemical content of the soil. **Breeches:** regular hunting breeches, £174 for cotton and £180 for wool; pantaloons in special stretch fabric for showjumping, and polo, £136; jodphurs, £173 for cotton and £190 for wool. **Hunting coats:** grey Melton coat, £376; scarlet coat, £396; very special scarlet dress coats for hunt balls, £469. **Ladies' riding coats:** tweed riding coats, £325-£351; formal riding coats in black or blue, £352-£386. **Side-saddle habits:** these elegant habits consist of a specially-cut shortfronted jacket with an elaborate skirt that can be looped up for comfortable wear when the lady dismounts, £506 for tweed; £557 for formal habit in wool. **Jockey's silks for racing:** the rule is satin for flat racing, jersey for National Hunt racing—and Huntsman do them both. Satin blouses are from £38-£70; wool knit jersey blouses from £29.25-£32.50; covers (caps) to go over hard riding from £14.25-£25.50; in all cases prices vary with the complexity of the design. **Hunt shirts:** with very long tails for exra protection, in three fabrics and all wool, £22.75; wool and silk, £25.75. **Stocks:** to wear with them in two styles and fabrics. Shaped—partly tied—stocks in cotton are £16; in cotton-silk blend, £22.50. Four-fold stocks are £10.50 in cotton; £16.50 in cotton-silk blend. **Stockpins:** steel-shaft pins with gold casing, sizes 1¾-3in, from £2.25. Also, solid 9ct gold stockpins. **Riding gloves:** a large selection in all sizes, including string gloves which give the best grip, and gloves with string palms and wool backs for extra warmth. **Also:** ties, hundreds to choose from in two widths, with many exclusive designs. Regular range of silk ties from £10.75; foulards in plain and printed silk for wear with jackets, £8.56; socks in wool, cotton lisle, silk and cashmere and a large selection of knitwear.

---

# Jaeger  204-206 Regent Street, W1   01-734 4050
Mon.-Sat. 9.30-5.30, Thurs. 9.30-7
Telegrams: *Purwulpiccy*, London W1
(American Express, Barclaycard, Diners)

---

'Wool' and 'Jaeger' have been synonymous since 1884, when the first Jaeger shop opened with a stock of pure wool clothes designed to fit the requirements of 'Dr. Jaeger's Sanitary Woollen System'—based on Dr. Jaeger's belief that since people were animals themselves, they would be much healthier if they dressed only in clothing made of pure animal hair. George Bernard Shaw caused a sensation when he strolled down Piccadilly in a Jaeger made-to-order knitted natural wool outfit that looked remarkably like a suit of long underwear, but although Jaeger goods went out to Africa with Stanley and into the trenches during World War I, it wasn't until the early Sixties that Jaeger entered the menswear fashion field. Natural fabrics, good traditional knitwear, complete colour coordination and classic styles have been keynotes of the Jaeger look from the very first, and recent collections have reflected the new casual mood in menswear. This Spring you can look forward to a more versatile range than ever before—everything from suits and blazers to towelling shorts and drawstring trousers. Suits have a natural silhouette with a soft shoulder line, longer narrower lapels and slightly tapered trousers. Blazers are back in a big way, single and double breasted styles in luxury lightweight lambswool that will take you all way from early Spring to Indian summer. Wear them with serge trousers, pure cotton shirts, pullovers in stripy cotton or cashmere intarsia, all colour-linked in the Spring shades of cypress green, tan hide and azure blue. The new leisure collection gives you the choice of sporty or sophisticated looks. Play the field in Jaeger's luxury cotton towelling kits—shorts, drawstring trousers and blouson jackets—all in bright paintbox colours, with cotton knits to match. Then slip into one of Jaeger's classic leisure outfits—lots of smart blacks accented with stone and beige, just like a Black Velvet cocktail.

Sample range and prices:

**Suits** in sizes 46-58, several length fittings. Two-piece lightweight suits from £79.50. **Trousers** in sizes 46-58; serge trousers from £29.50; cotton trousers from £19.95. **Blazers** in sizes 46-58 and from £65 for a single-breasted in serge. **Jackets** in polyester wool, from £59.90. **Knits** in lambswool, botany, shetland and cashmere, sizes 36-44; shetland from £11.50; cashmere from £37.50; cotton knits from £12.50. **Towelling collection:** blousons from £29.50; drawstring trousers from £17.95; shorts from £11.50. **Shirts**, in sizes 14½-17½; in cotton from £14.50; in polyester cotton from £12.50.

---

# Charles Jourdan  47-49 Brompton Road, SW3
01-589 0114
Mon-Sat. 9.30-6, Wed. 9.30-7

---

Charles Jourdan launched their first men's collection three years ago, and they've already established themselves as makers of the most *fashionable* men's shoes in the world. Certainly, men have never had such a splendid choice before—really elegant dress shoes, shoes in linen and leather, a medley of moccasins in weights for every season, the most beautiful boots in town and a wonderful range of clogs, mules, and sandals. Jourdan's are dress shoes with a difference—subtly constructed, in fine kangaroo or kid, with kid inner socks and a choice of square, oval or tapered toe, in the classic proportions or in the *new narrower style*. This Spring, there will be dress shoes in beige, grey, navy, patent, bordeaux and tan, and soft kid boots in all six shades. As the season wears on, you can slip into the lightest moccasins under the sun, soft and supple, in fine beige and natural tones, lots of two-tone natural and tan combinations to wear with easy suits in linen and cotton. Thanks to Jourdan, the summers of discontent are over, and this is the year to make waves with Jourdan's high summer looks—open-toe sandals, sandals in woven leather and the new matte leather T-bar sandalettes. Don't forget to look in on the accessories boutique in the salon, full of belts, umbrellas, luggage, travel bags, sunglasses, scarves and ties specially designed to go with the shoes in the Jourdan collection. Treat yourself to a 'J' watch in white or yellow gold, and a mother-of-pearl lighter complete with electronic transistorised circuit that lights up with a sparkling flash. Sign the cheque with a new Jourdan pen in brushed steel sprayed with gold or silver—and be sure to call back in time to pick up the first of Jourdan's fabulous boots for autumn!

Jourdan's sales give the best shoe value for money in town. Sales are held twice a year, around Christmas and July/August: for this year's dates, ring Charles Jourdan.

Sample range—all price approximate:

**Shoes** in sizes 6½-10½, some 11's. Moccasins from £33-£44; average price for dress shoes, about £68; boots from about £70.

Clogs, mules and sandalettes, from £28-£45. **Accessories:** watches from £2.50; lighters from £75; sunglasses about £18-£20.

---

**Kickers** 183a Brompton Road, SW3  01-589 2211
Mon.-Sat. 10-6
(Access, American Express, Barclaycard)

---

If you want to make a real splash, jump in feet first with Kickers!

Kickers are the hot-foots of fashion—bright canvas shoes on
bouncy kick-up-your-heel soles, with a red dot under the left
heel, a green dot under the right, and tiny Kickers labels
everywhere. If life seems a lot brighter these days, it's entirely
due to Kickers. And believe it or not, the English are the most
daring men in Europe when it comes to feet! Kickers sell more
red men's shoes here than anywhere else in the world. Kickers
are the weekend shoes that sneaked out of the wardrobe and
kicked off a new sporty look and lifestyle. Wear them all week
long with blousons, anoraks, jeans, jerseys, and big loose shirts.
Better still, wear them with Kickers caps and soft hats, T-shirts,
sweatshirts, and satchels and socks dyed to match the shoes.
Kickers are tops for quality and comfort, and now there's a whole
Kickers collection to wear all year round—sandals, boots, ski and
riding boots, casual moccasins in Nubuck, new laceups with
corrugated soles. There are lots of new colour combinations, new
shades of sage green, oxblood red and sandy beige. Kickers come
up with fun things all the time and this summer you can look
forward to the new J'aime Kickers collection of white canvas
shoes with grass round the sides and a heart under each instep. If
you want to get a real kick out of life, just get yourself some
Kickers.

For full description and prices, see separate listing in 'South
Molton Street' section.

---

**Les 2 Zebras**  38 Tavistock Street, WC2   01-836 2855
Mon.-Sat. 10-8
(Access, American Express, Barclaycard, Diners)

'*Les Deux Zebras*' is French slang for two good friends with a
slightly different—but very nice—way of doing things: a bit like
'birds of a feather' as they say in *Anglais*. If you don't *comprenez*,
come to see what these two zebras are up to, in a shop that more
than lives up to its name. This is the place to find the Continental
version of the 'new look'—less extreme than the English—
relaxed, but always *just right*. Apart from Paul Smith's
go-anywhere clothes, the designs are all from French and Italian
houses—Ventilo, Ecriture, MicMac, Scapa, Jean-Franco
Ruffini—favourites with all those who want to be dressed nicely
without wearing a tie. Better still, designers Marc Boyer and
Pierre Coppini have put together a collection that plays by

Continental rules—pieces of ensembles can all be bought separately, clothes from different houses are ordered in complimentary colours that mix but *don't* match, the cuts are subtle and very adaptable, and there are lots of different textures to make everything much more interesting. It's *'le weekend'* as opposed to 'the country' look—an informal mood that isn't taken to extremes. And if you don't quite know how to go about exchanging your jeans-jumper-and-shirt or jeans-polo-and-safari-jacket for the new look, Les 2 Zebras specialise in providing you with a basic wardrobe of perhaps five pieces that will blend with the clothes you already have, update them, and carry you through a season with *brio*. One of the mainstays will be Marc Boyer's own pure cotton shirts in bonbon colours, rich natural textures, plain and patterned in plaids and stripes. Another will be the shop's choice selection of trousers—the most important part of a fashionable man's ensemble, and usually the most difficult. Here you'll find trousers that capture the up-to-the-minute mood and line without interpreting them too severely—trousers that no one will stare at, but everyone will appreciate. Go on to choose from this Spring's collection in a basic colour range of natural, beige, pale grey, *eau-de-Nil* and khaki green spiced with sienna red, banana, pale havana and dashes of bright primary shades. The fabrics are linen, canvas, poplin and pinwhale cord turned into pleated and military trousers, big soft shirts with small collars, gentle unlined blazers, desert jackets with a Foreign Legion flavour, raglan-sleeved reversible fly-fronted golf blousons, pure cotton knits, specially dyed Fruit of the Loom T-shirts and lace-up crepe-soled shoes in all the season's colours. Use this zebra crossing if you want to get into style.

Sample range—all prices approximate:

**Classic shirts**, button and French cuffs, sizes 14½-16½, **casual shirts** in sizes S, M, L: from £11 to about £25. Specially dyed Fruit of the Loom **T-shirts**, about £3. **Trousers** in French sizes 36-46, from £16 to about £35. Classic **jackets and blazers**, from £50-£80. **Casual jackets** in sizes S, M, L, from £40-£60. **Knits** from £16-£30, including pullover blouson with ribbing at collar, cuff and hip, £30. **Shoes** in French sizes 39-44, crepe-soled lace-ups specially dyed to tone with the clothes. In canvas, from around £25; also in leather and suede.

**Lillywhites** Piccadilly Circus, SW1   01-930 3181
Mon. 9.30-5.30, Tues.-Fri. 9-5.30, Thurs. 9-7, Sat. 9-1
Telegrams: *Lillysport*, London SW1
(Access, American Express, Barclaycard, Diners, Eurocard)
By appointment to Her Majesty the Queen, outfitters

Founded by a member of the Sussex cricketing family in the year
badminton was invented, Lillywhites is an Elysian playing field
for sportsmen of all ages. You'll need a bit of spirit to get round
the shop, as it's laid out along the lines of a modified Sandhurst
assault course. But as you sprint round corners and scramble up
stairs, you'll find kits and gear for everything from judo and
scuba to quoits and croquet. Lillywhites pride themselves on the
sheer scope of their merchandise—at least thirteen sorts of tennis
racquets, twenty makes of skis—four styles of cricket boxes!
Service is another strong point—you can have your racquets
restrung, your skis wedged, your rugger shirts and cricket
sweaters run up in club colours. Lillywhites even bring ski
instructors from the Continent at the start of the season, to serve
as consultants in the winter sports departments. Their world-wide
mail order service has sent skis to Australia and diving gear to
underwater diamond miners in West Africa, and Lillywhites'
'Look-In' sport and leisure magazine is available free on request.
The sporty look is in fashion at the moment but Lillywhites are
rather keener on sport itself, so don't expect stylish clothes for
sitting around on yacht decks, tennis courts or ski terraces. What
you *will* get is serviceable sportswear at extremely reasonable
prices. Look out for hardwearing pure wool sweaters in the
sailing department, pure cotton rugby and football shirts
unclaimed from special orders and offered for sale at bargain
prices, flared cricket trousers by Duncan Fearnley—as worn by
the West Indies team. There are lots of budget lines that are very
useful if you're just taking up a sport, and Lillywhites have their
excellent own-label lines in the medium price range. The younger
staff all seem to lead sporting lives themselves and the senior staff
are virtual encyclopaedias of sport—everyone is keen to help!
Lillywhites' sales are very good value, but you won't get your
savings without a bit of sacrifice—the summer sales invariably
start during Wimbledon week!

Lillywhites' 'Look-In' magazine, two issues a year, sent free on
request. Autumn edition: athletics and winter sports. Spring

edition: golf, tennis and cruise wear. Lillywhites sales: second week in January and first week in July.

A sample of the sportswear and equipment at Lillywhites, with approximate prices:

# Golf

Golfers get the prize for the most whimsical wardrobe in sportswear—bright plaids, plus fours, snazzy shoes and wildly hilarious hats. All matching up to shirts and sweaters embroidered with the private bestiary of sport—rampant lions (Pringle), bears (Hathaway), panthers (Slazenger), alligators (Lacoste) and eagles (Lyle & Scott).

**Trousers:** the brightest checks are in the Johnnie Miller range, the smartest tartans are by Pringle and Morton Knight, and the best pockets for holding lots of tickets, tees, and scorecards are tucked into Lillywhites' own plaid and check trousers. In sizes 30-42, prices from £15.50-£19.50.

**Plus twos:** a slimmer version of plus fours, always in big checks. For the correct look, wear with long wool socks, deerstalker hat and Grenfell walking jacket. Sizes 30-42, £45; Morton Knight plus twos, £19.95.

**Jackets:** walking jackets in poly-cotton Grenfell cloth, several styles from £35. Pro golf jacket for wearing before and after play, £29.95. Morton Knight's very popular showerproof with over-trousers, to wear over regular gear on a wet day, £41.90 the set.

**Also:** V-neck sweaters from £8.25 for acrylic to £8.95 for Pringle lambswool, and hats, gloves, socks, clubs, balls, tees.

# Cricket

Generations of players have put Lillywhites to the test, and this department comes up tops every time. Sweaters and slipovers to order in club colours, prices depend on colours and the amount of cabling. Caps also made to order in club colours.

**Trousers:** in waist sizes 28-44, 29-34 leg in all sizes. Prices from £9.95 for Fred Perry in polyester and Sarille rayon to £10.95 for flared Duncan Fearnley trousers.

**Knitwear:** in a range from Courtelle to pure wool. Plain sleeved pullovers from £8.30-£13; with colour trim. From £15. Plain sleeveless slipovers from £7.50-£11; from £12.95 with colour trim.

**Also:** shirts from £8.95; nice deep Australian style caps, in a range of colours, £2.95, full range of bats, balls, and protective clothing.

# Skiing

The pride of Lillywhites, with everything you could possibly want. Ski wear in stock from October 1st to the end of March, with emphasis on coordinated suits instead of separates. Up to twenty makes of skis, lots in the new shorter lengths. Bindings fitted on the premises.

**Ski Wear:** in sizes 36-46, from £35-£120. Sample range: Finnish suits by Story Design, in this years ecru story, mainly one-piece. Newest addition is the down-filled gilet from Head and H.C.C. Smart three-tone suit by Heinz Zinke, in green and navy Therm Elastic trimmed with white; jackets £35, trousers £22. Swiss suit by Henri Charles Colsenet, with jacket that zips on to salopette trousers, £120; matching hats and gloves extra. Swiss suits by McGregor in royal and navy, with salopette trousers and jacket with stretch panel, £120; matching sweater £30.

**Also:** skis, boots, poles, hats, sweaters and goggles.

---

# Tennis

Tennis takes over from ski wear on April 1st, and holds the selling floor until the end of September. The range of tennis wear goes all the way from serviceable to the stylish, and the selection of racquets is absolutely smashing.

**Shorts:** in sizes 28-44, by Fred Perry and others, prices from £7.50-£9.95. Fabrics include pure cotton, crimplene, polyester and polyester and cotton or wool blends; whites and solid colours.

**Shirts:** prices from £6.95 for plain white shirts in pure cotton. White shirts with navy and sky blue trim, £6.95.

**Knitwear:** sleeveless slipovers from £6.95; pullovers from £7.95; cardigans from £8.50; warm-up jackets from £10.95 approximately.

**Fashion Coordinates:** by Fila White Line, in two styles. Borg: pinstripes on white, trimmed with red/blue or green/blue. Shirt:

£14.95; shorts with special snap at waistband to hold small handtowel, £18.95; towel £2.25. Borg tracksuits, £42 approximately. Panatta; whites with same colour trim but no pinstripes; prices about £1 less than the Borg ranges. For both: coordinating sweaters from £26; velour towelling jacket, £34; wristbands, £1.95 for 2. Coordinates by Head, made in Germany, shirts, £15; and shorts, £19; both approximately.

---

# Racquets

Racquets for squash, tennis and badminton—the largest selection in Britain—at prices from £5.55 for a junior racquet to £115 for a Slazenger Phantom. Lillywhites stock those *hard-to-find handmade Davies tennis racquets* from America, and other makes include Dunlop, Grays of Cambridge, Cresta, Wilson, Head, P.D.P., Yonix, Fischer, Donnay, Starmaster, Tretorn, Ascot, Oliver, Carlton and Vicort. *Racquets can be restrung in gut or synthetic in two to three days*—prices on request. **Also:** all bags, hold-alls and accessories.

---

# Sport Shoes

**Squash:** in sizes 5-12. Kingswell Squash Shoes, £6.95. Adidas Barrington, £11.95.

**Tennis:** in sizes 4-10. Lillywhite Match, £2.95. In sizes 3-14: Adidas Nastase, £11.95; Adidas Stan Smith in leather, £15.25. Dunlop Green Flash, £5.50.

# Athletics

**Rugby:** jerseys in sizes 38-44 in a range of colours, from £8.50. Shorts in waist sizes 28-40, in white, black or navy pure cotton with button fly and side pockets, £4.95.

**Football:** goalkeeper's sweaters in nylon, £4.95; and cotton, £5.25. Jerseys in sizes 26-42, mostly in hard-wearing nylon, in plain colours, stripes and diagonals, from £3.95. Shorts in black or white cotton, nylon shorts in a range of colours, from £3.65. Black umpire's shirt with white collar and cuffs, £9.25. Football scarves from £1.90.

**Tracksuits:** in sizes 36-44. A selection from £7.95 to £29.95, in crimplene, nylon, cotton, pure wool and blends. Range includes popular Millington suits; plain colour suit laced with white or yellow, £17.25; two-tone suit, £17.95; both with straight or flared leg. Adidas rain suits in nylon, to wear over track suit or shorts when running in the rain: trousers and jacket, £9.75 each. Hooded training tops from £8.25.

# Sailing

Nothing for swanning on the Squadron lawn, but everything for sailing in fair or foul weather.

**Sweaters:** traditional Guernsey sweater, close-knit and very warm, in navy, ecru and red pure wool, sizes S-XL, £17.95. Ribbed oiled sweater in pure wool, round or polo neck in navy or ecru, sizes XS-XL, from £10.50. Stripey French fisherman's sweater, all colours £17.10. Norwegian sailing sweaters in speckled navy and white, sizes XS-XL, £12.00. Traditional fisherman's smock in navy or blue sailcloth, without pockets, £3.25.

**Trousers:** in waist sizes 28-40. Sailcloth trousers in navy and rust, £9.95; terylene slacks in navy and light blue £7.25.

**Shoes:** dinghy sailing boots with non-slip soles, £5 approx. Laced top boots with non-slip soles for offshore sailing, in navy, £12.95. Blue canvas sailing shoes, non-slip soles, £3.95.

**Also:** wet weather gear by Henri Lloyd and others, Rukka PVC weatherproofs and Johnsons Waterproofs, Evetts new 100% waterproof smocks, jackets and high bib trousers, all with welded seams, approved by the Royal National Lifeboat Institution, and one-piece suits and jackets by Musto & Hyde.

---

**Lock & Co** 6 St. James's Street, SW1   01-930 8874/5849
Mon.-Fri. 9-5, Sat. 9.30-12.30
Telegrams: *Lockhatter*, London
(Access, American Express, Barclaycard, Diners)
By appointment to His Royal Highness the Duke of Edinburgh, hatters

---

If English history were written as a play, many of the costume credits would read 'hats by Lock & Co', for this proud firm sent Nelson to Trafalgar in a hat with a specially fitted eyepiece, supplied the hat that Wellington wore at Waterloo, made Oscar Wilde a floppy velvet hat to go with his knickerbocker suit, created the elegant Ascot topper, and presented the nation with that badge of British manhood—the bowler. Headgear for history-in-the-making can be found in the shop in the shadow of St. James's Palace occupied by the firm since 1765, but there's nothing old hat about Lock's. You can still find the most classic of toppers and bowlers, called 'Coke hats' here in the memory of the client for whom the first was made—but Lock have expanded into the leisure market with characteristic enterprise, and their range of casual and non-town wear will give a pleasant surprise to customers who have not called in recent years. There are trilbys, golf caps, riding hats and deerstalkers in the Sherlock Holmes style, as well as jackets for town and country, and a selection of ties, scarves, gloves and brollies. American visitors will be familiar with Lock hats through Brooks Brothers shops, and Lock also sell through outlets on the Continent, but the ready-to-wear is exclusive to London, and you'll get the best selection of hats here.

All hats are available in ready-to-wear or made-to-measure, and Lock retain individual measurements and records of transactions, so you can write to them for replacements year after year. For made-to-measure, allow an additional £2 and the following times for delivery: felt hats and bowler hats, ten to twelve weeks; tweed hats, eight to ten weeks; top hats, three to four weeks.

Sample range and prices:

**Hats:** bowler hats in hard fur felt, £15.75 for light and medium weights, £18.75 for hunting weight. Panama hats in two styles, £12. Velvet hunting caps from £17.50. Birkdale tweed hats, £11. Fairway cap in a range of tweeds, £7.75. Stylish Bermuda straw hat with a 3¼in brim, £7.50, tweed Deerstalker hat with or without earflaps, £11. Wide-brimmed velour hat £20, fur hats in different skins and styles from £20.

**Ready-to-wear garments:** specially tailored for Lock by Rodex of London in sizes 36-46.

**Jackets:** tailored tweed jacket for town or country, from £50. Classic double-breasted blazer in navy blue worsted, £76.

**Accessories:** silk bow ties from £3.50, silk ties from £7, a range of silk and cashmere scarves from £14.50, gloves from £6, belts from £4, silk covered umbrellas made to order.

# Henry Maxwell & Co  177 New Bond Street, W1

01-493 1097

Mon.-Fri. 9-1 & 2-6, Sat. 9-12

Telegrams: *Maxwellboot*, London W1

(Access, American Express, Barclaycard, Diners)

By appointment to Her Majesty the Queen, bootmakers

Behind the doors of Henry Maxwell & Co., bootmakers and spurriers, lies a timeless world of officers and gentlemen, patent pumps and spats, and a green, green England where the port is always vintage and the hunting fields stretch on forever. The feeling of security reflects Maxwell's insistence on maintaining standards of craftsmanship, excellence and service that have largely disappeared elsewhere—their handmade shoes and boots are in a class of their own, and you can appreciate the work that goes into them by watching the white-aproned craftsmen in the inner room carefully shaping the wooden lasts by hand. You can also see them hand-repairing shoes—one of the last proper repair services in London. Life Guards and showjumpers come here to choose their spurs from one of the largest and best selections in the world, and everyone pauses to admire the glass-fronted cases that hold collections of antique spurs, shoes and boots—a spur made for Napoleon has pride of place in one cabinet, while another displays a pair of needlepoint slippers worked by Queen Victoria for the Prince Consort. In addition to their spurs and made-to-measure footwear, Maxwell stock ready-to-wear shoes for men, leather goods and accessories, a fine selection of drinks cases, riding crops, and a range of items like deer bones and boot hooks which will gladden the heart of the connoisseurs for whom this shop is meant.

All prices exclusive of VAT

## Made-to-measure boots for men and women

Hunting boots in waxed calf leather, £254; show jumping boots in box calf, £248; hunt boots with brown tops, £306; polo and field boots from £322; wellington boots from £200. **Made-to-measure shoes for men:** two months required for delivery, from £125. Styles include: fringed-tongue golf shoes, brogue saddle shoes in two-tone leather, laced and tasselled Swedish shoes, classic full brogue in brown or black calf, patent pumps with bows, patent dress shoes, monk's shoes and casual slip-ons in brown and white. **Made-to-measure slippers:** in velvet decorated with own monogram, fox head, or choice of

223

designs in several colours, £99.
**Made-to-measure shoes for women:** from £148.
**Ready-to-wear:** a small choice selection of fine bench made shoes for men, classic styles, sizes 8-10, from £45. **Shoe and boot accessories:** deer bone for boning up hunting boots; boot hooks for pulling on your boots; boot jacks for removing your boots yourself—available in portable and upright; wooden boot trees and wooden shoe trees; jockey boot lifts to ease the leg into the boot, £23 a pair; upright Victorian-style boot jacks in mahogany, £185. **Also:** a variety of shoe care kits, top quality shoe polish, canvas boot carriers, ready-to-wear spats, shoe horns, belts, riding whips and crops, walking sticks, men's umbrellas, men's and ladies wallets, leather accessories and a range of drinks cases that will delight the Rover and stirrup cup set. **Shoe repair service:** comprehensive shoe repair service—soles, heels, riding boot repairs, re-topping, and alterations. All repairs done by hand on the premises. **Spurs:** a vast selection with hundreds of pairs in stock, including general riding spurs, hunting and showjumping spurs, military dress spurs and regimental riding spurs.

---

**Piero de Monzi** 68-70 Fulham Road, SW3   01-589 8765
Mon.-Sat. 10.30-7
(Access, American Express, Barclaycard, Diners)

---

The ambiance is very *le tout Paris*—Rome—London. The people are the kind you meet at smart parties. Short glasses of rich coffee are brought out to keep you company. But whatever its resemblance to a private club, this is also one of London's *smartest* shops. When it comes to classic Continental elegance, no one rivals Piero de Monzi. The clothes are all from Italy and France—jeans and casual jackets by New Man, fine leather jackets by McDougal, *superb* knitwear, shirts, suits, trousers and shoes specially made for the shop. Subtle colours and fine textures run through the collection, and the clothes must be tried on to be fully appreciated—besides the beautiful cut, you'll notice the excellent finish and quality of the fabrics. You'll also find the most elegant raincoats and pinstriped suits in town, and you won't get a better suede blouson anywhere else, though you could pay twice the price. The clothes are expensive, but their classic style and quality make them excellent investments. Definitely a place for those who have arrived.

Sample range—all prices
approximate:

**From the special Piero de Monzi collection:** in sizes 36-44, **Suits** from £165; jackets from £119; sweaters from £21. In sizes 26-34: **jeans** from £21; **trousers** from £32. **Shirts** in sizes 14½-16½, from £24. **By New Man:** jeans in sizes 27-34: from £21 for cotton, from £31 in velvet. Casual jackets in sizes 36-44, a range, including cotton jackets from £49. **Leather jackets by McDougal**, from £109: suede jackets from £119. **Shoes by Rossetti**, in sizes 7-10½, from £59.

---

# Piero de Monzi's Cerruti Shop 72 Fulham Road,
SW3    01-589 8208
Mon.-Sat. 10.30-7
(Access, American Express, Barclaycard, Diners)

---

Next door, Piero de Monzi's elegant new shop where you can see Cerruti's entire *collezione fortissima* at its best. This season's look: jackets narrower at the hip, broader at the shoulder, with thin lapels to wear with tapered trousers, and shirts with button-down collars. Lots of smart summer suits in gabardine and light wool, unlined cotton jackets, beautifully soft, for casual wear.

Sample range—all prices
approximate:

**By Cerruti: suits** from £195; **blazers** from £119; **raincoats** from about £75; **coats** from £195; **sweaters** from £37; **trousers** from £38; **shirts** from £26; **hats** from £65; **ties** from £14; **belts** from £19. Also, **cabans,** carcoats and fine designs in suede and leather.

---

# Moss Bros 21-23 Bedford Street, WC2    01-240 4567
Mon.-Fri. 9-5.30, Thurs. 9-7, Sat. 9-1
(Access, American Express, Barclaycard, Diners, Eurocard, Interbank, Mastercharge)

---

Garden parties at the Palace and coronations at the Abbey, hunt balls and horse shows, diplomatic receptions and formal weddings, cocktails at the Savoy and strawberries and cream at Ascot—how could England's finest hours happen without the marvellous firm of Moss Bros, gentlemen's outfitteres extraordinary? This unique shop is like a favourite uncle who can always produce the right thing at the right time—who else could have supplied all the top hats for the Ascot scene in **My Fair**

**Lady**! And the Covent Garden premises are like the houses favourite uncles live in—comfortable and rambling, full of interesting corners and surprises. *Now that the man-about-town look is back in fashion, Moss Bros is the place to find stiff-fronted or soft collarless shirts in cotton, with separate wing collars, at half the price you'd pay elsewhere.* Moss Bros's famous *Hire Service* provides peers' robes, velvet court suits, military uniforms, morning suits and toppers, tailcoats, opera cloaks, fancy dress, Highland dress with skean dhu and sporran, and a hundred other items from cummerbunds to shoes and spats. You can hire them for a day, a week or a month, buy them new, *or purchase them from the hire stock at substantially reduced prices*—one of the best bargains in town. More bargains are to be found in the Special Offer Room that old-timers know as 'Ginger's'—there's a contantly-changing selection of good second-hand clothes, remainders and oddments, and lucky visitors can find second-hand Saville Row suits and Thirties clothes at Thirties prices. The Hire Service is just a part of Moss Bross, who have amply earned the right to call themselves 'the complete man's store'. The **Bespoke Tailoring** department offers made-to-measure shirts, suits and military uniforms at extremely reasonable prices, and the **Livery Department** outfits chauffeurs, porters and waiters from top to toe. Moss Bros pioneered quality ready-to-wear in England, and they have a vast selection of dependable clothes for dress and casual wear. Moss Bros's shoes and hats give particularly good value for money; there's a shoe repair, cleaning and valeting service to keep your wardrobe in proper condition, and *a ski department where skiiers can buy or hire everything for the slopes.* And if that weren't enough, Moss Bros also have one of the best and biggest riding and saddlery departments in the world. There are riding jackets and scarlet evening dress coats, breeches and jodphurs, bradoons and snaffles, saddles and bridles, horse and stable equipment, polo wear, Pony Club books—and Moss Bros's own complimentary booklets 'How to enjoy the Horse Show' and 'Correct Dress for Horse and Rider'. Moss Bros have always provided *good quality at sensible prices*, and the personal service and attention they give have earned them the deep affection of countless customers. Try Moss Bros!

## Hire Service

All hire items are for sale, and if you decide to purchase, the hire charge will be refunded. Moss Bros advise that it is perfectly correct for the morning coat to be black or grey, for the waistcoat to be black, grey or almost any other colour, and the trousers striped, dark, light and even shepherd's plaid—they have them all. The young fashion 'One Up' range is available here and in Moss Bros's other London branch at 21 Lime Street, EC3.

Sample range and prices:

**Morning wear:** black morning suit, £8; grey morning coat, waistcoat, striped trousers and top hat, both £10.50. Grey morning suit in the 'One Up' range £11.50. Grey top hat £1.95; grey spats, £1.25. **Evening wear:** shawl collar baratgea dinner jacket and trousers, £7.50. White dinner jacket and black dress trousers, £8.50. Dress tail suit and white waistcoat, £10.50. 'One Up' velvet dinner jacket and dress trousers, £11.25. Pink dress coat, white waistcoat and dress trousers, £13.50. **Highland Dress:** Kilts, £4.15. Prince Charlie, Montrose and Kenmore doublets from £6.75. Complete Highland outfit, **including skean dhu**, £16.50.

## Mens' Bespoke Tailoring

**Suits:** in fine pure wool, worsted, silk mohair and other fabrics, many weights and colours. Fabrics are bought in pieces rather than in bolts to keep the cost down. Delivery time—five to six weeks for two fittings, three to four weeks for one fitting. Prices from £150 for two-piece suits, from £175 for three-piece suits. Also bespoke military uniforms—prices on application. **Shirts:** made-to-measure shirts with single or double cuffs, neckband or attached collar. In poplin, Sea Island and Oxford cottons, silk; Viyella and voile. From £28.95 for

poplin to £34.95 for silk. Delivery time—two to three weeks.

**Shoes:** an excellent selection in sizes 7-10. Range includes crepe-soled chukka, £29.80; leather-soled kid moccasins in black or tan from £21.99; classic black, tie brogues from £29.50 and tan brogues from £22.70. For evening, leather-soled patent slip-ons, £23.95 and patent tie shoes, £18.80. For riding, box calf boots, £76.80 and mahogany top boots, £96.80.

**The Special Offer Room:** a constantly changing selection of bargains, including waistcoats from £2.50, suits from £12, shirts from £1, trousers from £5 and overcoats from £15.

**Hats:** black top hats (silk finish) sizes 6½-7⅞, £65; soft felt hats, £1295; bowler hats £19.95; Panama hats, £9.95; tweed deerstalker hats, £8.95. Also all officer's hats for men and women in the Services.

## Riding clothes for Men

**Riding jackets:** tweed riding jackets from £59.50; jackets in cavalry twill from £69.50. Member's scarlet hunt coat from £177; dark grey hunt coat from £153. **Breeches:** stretch riding breeches from £21; white stretch breeches, stretch jodphurs and stretch riding trousers, all from £22. **Also:** field mackintosh from

£45; hunt waistcoats from £25; reinforced hunting hat from £72.56; reinforced riding bowler, £24.95; string backed hogskin gloves, £9.95; rubber riding boots, £17.50; jodphur boots with elastic side, £21.40 and with strapped side, £27. Ivory silk hunt stocks, £5.50. And complete riding wear department for women with hacking jackets from £35.

**Stylish Shirts:** in cotton, stiff-fronted and soft-fronted collarless shirts, in sizes 14-17, £12.50 and £8.95; **wing collars**, £1 each.

---

## Maxfield Parrish  4 Woodfall Court, Smith Street, SW3
01-730 4867
Mon.-Fri. 10-6, Sat. 2-5
(American Express, Barclaycard)

---

*'Where can I get something really special made-to-order in suede or leather?'* When it comes to fashion, that's the question men always ask first, and the answer is—**Maxfield Parrish**. The look is sporty, casual, free and easy—blousons, big loose shirts, gently tapered trousers, unconstructed jackets—all the clothes that sum up the new relaxed mood in menswear. The emphasis is on 'fashion' rather than on 'leather', and the fine supple skins simply enhance the effortless style of Nigel Preston's designs. You'll find all the little details that make such a difference—shirts gathered at front and back yoke, linings in plain or check Viyella, loose jackets with gentle blouson gathers at the back to give a better shape if you wear them unbuttoned, real shirt plaquet cuffs for the stylish turnback look. Waistcoats are back in a big way, and Maxfield Parrish have superb models in *three* styles—plain, or with single- or double-breasted revers—in suede or leather with smart striped fabric backs, to go with summer's stripy shirts and linen trousers. If you're looking for *the coat of the season*, don't miss the long leather motoring duster—plain, unbelted, with patch pockets and shirt collar—perfect with tweeds, twills, knits, long scarves and a jaunty tweed flat cap. You can go casual in suede or leather jeans topped with a suede T-shirt, be conservative in a classic leather trench, or kick over the traces in leather jodphurs and a fitted riding coat with buttoned back vent. The leathers come in black, bittersweet brown and brick, the suedes in subtle shades of sage, smoky biscuit, tan, taupe, natural and brown that bring out the best in pure linen, cotton, silk and wool, and give casual clothes a new dimension of luxury.

Clothes **made-to-measure:** allow one week to ten days for delivery. Sample range—all prices approximate:

Classic leather trench, about £175; long leather motoring duster, £250. Suede hacking jacket lined with check or plain Viyella, £115; fitting fitted riding coat with back button vent, £160. Unconstructed shirt with blouson detail at back, two flap pockets, £85. Jeans in suede or leather, about £80-£85; suede T-shirts, £65. Waistcoats in three styles, £35. Leather jodhpurs with zips at calf, £85; single-breasted boxy leather blazer, £110. Trousers with two side pockets, gently tapered legs; £75-£80 in suede, £85 in leather; big loose shirt with two patch breast pockets, shirt collar and shirt plaquet cuffs, in suede, £95.

---

## Penhaligon's  41 Wellington Street, WC2   01-836 2150
Mon.-Fri. 10-6, Sat. 10-1

By appointment to His Royal Highness the Duke of Edinburgh, manufacturers of toilet requisites

---

Toiletries for the most elegant men in the world. For prices and description see separate listing in 'Convent Garden' section.

---

## Retro  229 Kings Road, SW3   01-352 2095
Mon.-Sat. 10.30-6.30, Wed. 10.30-7

---

Men are usually neglected by the nostalgia specialists, but at Retro you'll find a whole room full of great looks from the past. The speciality is the pure American Fifties look—clothes for cruising down Main Street on a Saturday night, for dancing to the juke box at Hamburger Heaven, for watching double bills at the drive-in movies. There are Cub Scout and Boy Scout shirts with badges that say 'Schenectady, New York' and 'Jacksonville Beach, Florida', real Little League baseball shirts and glorious bowling shirts with team names like *Cazzy's Cotillion Lounge* and *Foy's Dinette Center* emblazoned across the back. For the Big Man on Campus image, try the college letter sweaters and cardigans, or the fraternity sweaters embroidered with Greek letters. The jacket collection is particularly good with lots of blousons in that distinctive Fifties marron colour trimmed with contrast stitching and piping, 50's draped jackets, fringed buckskin jackets, leather hunting jackets and the occasional satin jacket embroidered with dragons and mottos—souvenirs of the Vietnam War. Wear them with pleated-top or tapered-bottom trousers—lots of hot plaids and turnups—in fabrics like flannel, gabardine, tweed and cotton. This summer, come in for one of their Hawaiian-print shirts in blazing sunset colours—and don't forget the plastic keyrings, rabbit's foot lucky charms and printed ties to complete the look. Most of the clothes come from America, everything has been cleaned and pressed.

Sample range and prices:

**Shirts:** Boy Scout and Cub Scout shirts from £5-£7; Little League shirts from £7; short and long-sleeved Hawaiian-print shirts, some actually made in Hawaii, from £11.50-£12.50; bowling shirts from £6. **Trousers:** in sizes 28-36, all about £9.50. **Jackets:** leather zip-front hunting jacket, £25; leather jackets with knit shawl collars from about £15.50; leather flying jackets from £25-£45; embroidered Vietnam jacket, £10.50; fringed buckskin jacket, £15; Fifties draped jackets from £22.50. **Sweaters:** college letter sweaters and cardigans from £9.50; fraternity sweaters from £7.50; ski sweaters from £7. **Also:** printed ties from £2.50-£4.50; plastic keyrings from 25p; rabbit's foot charms from 50p.

---

**Saint Laurent**—Rive Gauche 84 Brompton Road, SW3
01-584 4993
Mon.-Sat. 9.30-6, Wed. 9.30-7
(American Express, Barclaycard, Diners)

**Saint Laurent**—Rive Gauche 73 New Bond Street, W1
01-493 0405
Mon.-Sat. 9.30-6, Thurs. 9.30-7
(American Express, Barclaycard, Diners)

---

Yves Saint Laurent's ready-to-wear collection of international good looks—casual and sporty clothes, formal and evening wear. The Rive Gauche total look is a real fashion plus—clothes and all accessories to wear with them, scarves to shoes, underscored by the same design thinking. Spring collection in the boutiques from the end of January, autumn collection from mid-July. Prices are the same as in Paris since duty came off last July. Clothes in sizes 34-44.

Sample range and approximate prices:

Shirts from £19.90, jackets from £80, suits from £150 and ties from £12.

---

## Sign of The Times  17 Elystan Street, SW3   01-589 4774
Mon.-Sat. 10-5.30

---

If you have champagne tastes on a beer budget, kit yourself out at Sign of The Times. Saint Laurent jerseys for £3, Missoni sweaters for £10, blazers by Valentino and Saint Laurent for £18 and Turnbull & Asser shirts for £4 are just a few of the high flying bargains you can find here, along with goodies like Biba blousons at £3 and Brooks Brothers overcoats at £10 that will thrill nostalgic collectors. If your tastes don't run to high fashion, you can opt for jeans at £4 or a judo kit at £10, and if you fancy a bit of glitter, you're in for a real treat. Many of the clothes on sale have come from pop stars, actors and showbiz satellites, and you can have stageclothes worn by 10 C.C.—black satin shirts trimmed with eau-de-Nil and pink—for £10, Eric Clapton's gold-embroidered jackets, or Elton John's football shirt. Stock turns over every day, so it's worth coming in often and taking the time to have a thorough look around. If you don't find anything in your size, you can pick up Hechter, Lanvin and Saint Laurent ties at about £3, and Sign of The Times are always happy to consider anything you'd like to place on sale yourself.

---

## Ronnie Stirling  94 New Bond Street, W1   01-499 2675
Mon.-Sat. 9.30-6, Thurs. 9.30-7

---

Stirling Cooper Jasper are the young fast fashion specialists, always quick off the mark to give you what you want—in fact,

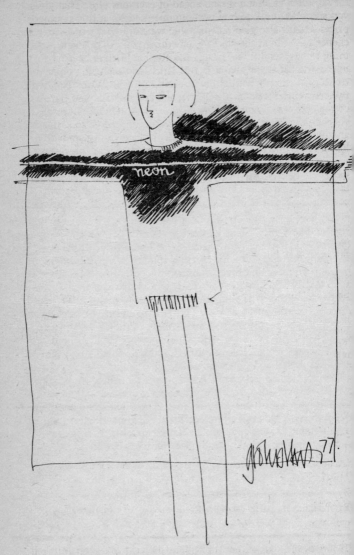

*By George Hostler at Ronnie Stirling*

they're often at least a season ahead of everyone else. That gives you an opportunity to buy next summer's looks at this summer's prices—but it also gives anyone who wants to be a trend-setter a chance to get in at the start of something big. A linen suit is *the* thing to be seen in this Spring, and Ronnie Stirling have unconstructed jackets with narrow lapels and matching tapered trousers in rumply natural linen for around £50. Wear them with two-tone correspondent shoes or schoolboy sandals, and pure cotton shirts with small button-down collars. There's a casual collection in beige, khaki, grey or cream polished cotton; shirts and overshirts with trousers to match, jackets with plain cotton lining and a smashing flying suit. From early Spring onwards, you'll find plenty of light T-shirts and heavier stripy T-shirt knits. Like the women's shop, the men's shop have special high fashion capsule collections throughout the year, and its worth coming in at least once a week to see what's new. Next Autumn, you can look forward to subtle stylish tweeds galore, lots more suits, dashing macs and fine knitwear—*good looks at very good prices*. Clothes by Stirling Cooper Jasper are also available at Take Six branches, but you'll get the biggest selection here.

Sample range and prices:

**Shirts and overshirts** in sizes 1, 2, 3, or S, M, L, in a range of natural fabrics from £9.95. **Blousons** from £14.95-£27.95. **Trousers** in sizes 28-34, in a range of styles including pleated, tapered and military with zipped pockets, from £14.95 to £25. Polished cotton flying suit, £38. **T-shirts:** plain, £2.50—stripy knit T-shirts, £9.95. **Linen suits,** from £50.

---

# Simpsons 203 Piccadilly, W1  01-734 2002

Mon.-Sat. 9-5.30, Thurs. 9-7
Telegrams: *Simperos*, London
(Access, American Express, Barclaycard, Diners, Eurocard, Mastercharge)
By appointment to Her Majesty the Queen, outfitters
By appointment to His Royal Highness, the Duke of Edinburgh, outfitters

---

1936 was the year of the Abdication, the year Margaret Mitchell wrote *Gone With The Wind*—and the year Alexander Simpson

*By Ben Frankel, in Khaki cotton piped with white*

made it possible for men to kick over the traces and throw their braces out of the window. Until then, the basics we now take for granted—neckband shirts with attached collars, casual two-piece lounge suits, light body-fitting underwear, suits and socks that don't need suspenders, simply didn't exist. Working with the company founded by his father Simeon, Alexander Simpson developed the self-supporting DAKS trouser with half tunnel belt that made braces and waistcoats obsolete. His next step was two-piece DAKS lounge suits, followed by new look shirts and underwear to go with them. The result was nothing less than a fashion revolution. The Piccadilly shop was built as a showcase for the DAKS collection, and you can date modern menswear from the day it opened its doors. Complete comfort, beautiful fit and a thoroughly modern classic style have been the hallmarks of DAKS clothes since the very beginning, and DAKS range now includes blazers, jackets, rainwear, topcoats—even DAKS jeans! Simpsons are tops when it comes to the little attentions that make all the difference—when you buy a DAKS blazer, you can choose from a selection of four different buttons, including one with a tiny Eros of Piccadilly motif. Although the DAKs collection has pride of place, there are plenty of other reasons to visit this fine shop. Go to the bright leisurewear department for exciting free and easy fashions by designer Ben Frankel. It's a total collection, with trousers, shorts, knitwear, anoraks, shirts and the *smartest jackets and safari suits in town*—perfect alternatives to a suit and tie. You feel completely relaxed the moment you get into the clothes—and you look as great as you feel. Everything is sold separately, and part of the fun is putting yourself together. The ground floor shirt department is particularly good, with an accent on the classic, and lots of subtle styles. Simpsons maintain a well-bred interest in fashion trends, and change the setting of the popular block stripes slightly every year, sometimes wider or closer together, so you can look perfectly correct without being *vieux jeu*. All shirts have a full straight cut with generous tails, most have French cuffs and there are lots of hard-to-find specialities like superfine pure cotton poplin shirts, and shirts in striped Oxford cloth. The classic look is the strength of the knitwear department as well, and you'll find lambswools, Shetlands and two weights of cashmere in all the blue, heathery and oatmeal shades that suit men so well. Simpsons always have the smartest sportswear in London. From October to April the sportswear department has superb skiwear and accessories by Head, Bognor and Hechter, and in summer the department bursts into high fashion tennis whites, by Head, Lacoste and Sergio Tacchinni. The shoe department has an extremely smart selection with lots of non-lace casual styles, the underwear department has everything from slender cotton briefs to pure cotton button front shorts. You can take lunch or tea in Simpson's Clover Room restaurant, and for a snack or simple drink try the Madison Bar, a perfect meeting place for friends. Also visit the Simpsons barber shop for hair cuts, shampoos, shaves, frictions, beard trims, singes, facials, restyles, manicures, chiropody, pedicures, after-shaves. Appointments are not always necessary, except on Saturdays and Fridays and during lunch hours.

Simpsons pride themselves on service, and here are a few reasons why.

*Export Department* handles forms for foreign visitors who are exempt from the 8% VAT. The minimum order is £25 but, unlike some other shops, Simpsons make no charge for this service.

*Making to order.* DAKS suits can be made to order, in standard sizes only, after you select the cloth from a range of samples. Allow 6-8 weeks delivery.

*Shoe Repairs*, complete shoe repair service, particulars on request.

*A Postal Order Service* is also available and no postal or packing charge is made for goods except for items in catalogues under £25. No VAT is included in overseas purchases. Special insurance is automatically taken out on all goods over £200 or overseas deliveries.

*A Delivery Service* operates Monday to Friday, delivering all around central London.

There are *Interpreters* for twenty different languages.

## The DAKS Collection

In sizes 36-50, short, regular, long and extra long, some fuller fittings. **Blazers** in navy, black or brown, single-breasted from £65 and double-breasted from £79-£119. **Sports jackets:** in a range of fabrics from £65-£205. **Trousers:** in waist sizes 36-46, four length fittings in a range of fabrics, from £27-£47. **Suits:** in range of fabrics, two-piece suits from £89, three-piece suits from £119. **Rainwear:** in a range of styles and fabrics, from £39.

## The Ben Frankel Collection

Two collections a year, March-April and

August-September. All clothes in sizes S, M, L, and XL. The Spring 1978 collection features jackets and matching trousers in textured fabric, lots of tartans and plaids. Ben Frankel excels at casual jackets, so look for his new blouson jacket with knitted cuffs and zip front, button fastened at neck in tartan plaid, and another blouson with drawstring waist, knitted cuffs, low front yoke and two tartan pockets. All the jackets team up with a new brushed denim trouser with an elasticated half waist and tapered bottoms.

## Also

**Evening Wear:** in sizes 36-48. Single breasted Tuxedo with shawl collar, £89, to wear with braid trimmed trousers, £39; Single-breasted dress suit in wool and mohair with satin bound cuff buttons and satin lapels, £109; single-breasted velvet jackets in black and several colours, £63; velvet suits, £125. **Leather and suede:** a selection in shirt, safari, classic jacket and sporty blouson styles; leather and sheepskin coats from £200. **Knitwear:** in sizes 36-46, a few 48's and 50's Shetland crew-neck, £12; V-neck

lambswool sweater, £16; roll collar sweaters, £17; slipover, £13.50; cardigan, £23.50; cashmere V-neck and crew neck pullovers from £40; cashmere roll neck sweaters from £43; cashmere cardigans from £55 and slipovers from £28; pure wool Pringle shirts from £16. **Shirts:** in sizes 14½-17½, a few 18's and 18½'s, short, regular and long fittings. Bengal striped or block striped fine cotton poplin shirts, both £15.50, with white collar and cuffs; striped Oxford cloth shirts, £21; superfine pure cotton poplin and Sea Island cotton shirts, £16.50; dress shirts from £15.50; silk shirts from £32; viyella shirts from £11.95. **Also:** all-leather shoes in sizes 6-12½ including a few 'H' widths. By Bally, Church, Simpsons own label and Clarks sport and leisure shoes. Hats in sizes 6¾-7½, specially made for Simpson. Tweed caps, hats, Panamas and bowlers.
**Sportswear:** two-piece ski suits from £100, Salopette suits from £80; tennis wear from £25 for matching sets; single shorts from £13; single shirts from £11; tracksuits from £19.50; designers sportswear by Head, Hechter and Lacoste.

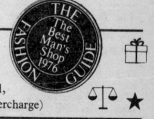

**Take 6** 362 Oxford Street, W1
01-499 9909
Mon.-Sat. 9-6, Thurs. 9-8
(Access, American Express, Barclaycard, Carte Blanche, Diners, Eurocard, Mastercharge)

This is the shop that makes women jealous—the shop that's

*At Take Six*

almost too good to be true! Take six good reasons why Take 6 are the unchallenged leaders of fashionable young-ready-to-wear; top looks, rock bottom prices, constant change, wonderful colours, the best inexpensive suits in town and a smashing sense of style. Take 6 have their own suit, shirt and leather factories—because they control the production there are no middleman charges, and they can get hot looks into the shop, start to finish, in just four weeks. That's where the Take 6 design team win top marks—you can count on them to have the new looks you want, almost before you want them! Take 6 was the shop that put good looks within everyone's reach, and they've had an enormous effect on the industry as a whole. Sidney Brent was the first to start the production of European style in India, leading the way for the rest of the trade. Innovations of this kind are part of the reason why Take 6 can keep their prices so low, and although they could easily charge twice the price that they do, they refuse to jump on the escalator. As Sidney Brent explains, 'Take 6 is for the *intelligent* shopper. We give them what they want, at the price they want, with no stupid snobbery!' As a result, Take 6 has an amazingly varied clientele—all types, backgrounds and ages—with nothing at all in common except knowing a good deal when they see it. A fast fashion pace is what makes Take 6 so exciting—the suit department changes over completely at least twelve times a year and it's change-change-change in the casuals, so a shop looks completely different every time you drop in. This season Take 6 goes back to nature in style. Shirts are looser, more casual, with softer smaller collars, in checks and stripes laced with tiny sparkly threads. Natural textured cotton is the fabric of the season—the more it creases, the better it looks. Trousers are tapered and longer, breaking *on* the shoes—for a real fashion touch, wear them rolled up loosely instead of hemmed. Jackets are unconstructed, effortless, beautifully relaxed. Wear them with the collar turned up, the sleeves pushed back—however you wear it, it's *got* to be beige. There are casual flannels to mix with suits, lots of easy overshirts, long loose blousons and reversible jackets. The Take 6 leather and suede collections deserve a special star of their own, the casual collection a whole constellation. Ladies used to ask 'why isn't there a Take 6 collection for us?'—now the smart ones just come in to buy. Last season's top choices: hacking jackets from £25 and smashing fly-fronted riding macs at £29.95. And there's great news for the visitors who are always asking 'why can't we buy Take 6 abroad'— a *Take 6 International Collection* will be launched this fall! Eleven years at the top and no sign of stopping, Take 6 is the best thing that's happened to men!

Sample range—all prices
approximate:

**Knitwear:** in sizes S, M, L; a
good selection in lambswool and
Shetland, from £5.95; pure
cashmeres from £19.95.

**Suits:** in sizes 34″-44″; summer
suits from £27.95; winter suits
from £29.95; most suits under
£50.

**Suede and Leather:** jackets and

coats, all natural leather, from
£19.95. Average price, £35-£40;
long trench coats about £70.
**Raincoats:** a selection, including
rubberized fly-fronted mac,
£29.95.

**Also:** shirts, T-shirts, trousers,
ties, scarves—everything but
shoes.

Other Take 6 shops in London at 140 and 477 Oxford Street, 90
New Bond Street and 66 Wardour Street, W1; 19 Kensington
Church Street, W8; 69 Kings Road, SW3.

---

# Washington Tremlett 41 Conduit Street, W1
01-734 4236
Mon.-Sat. 9-6

Washington Tremlett has just what a lot of men are looking
for—the Seventies version of the J. D. Salinger look. It's Ivy
League cool in a new relaxed mood—always smart, but wittier
and more interesting than ever before, with a few wry touches of
Ivy League humour. If you've been wondering whatever
happened to the coat, hurry in to see Washington Tremlett's
collection—the best clutch of coats in town, in stock all year
round. There are wrapover coats in wool and alpaca, cuddly as a
bathrobe and smart as a trench, casual *young* trench coats cut high
under the arm so you *don't* have to wear them with a jacket and
*the raincoat of the season*—fly-fronted, single-breasted, slender and
long—an aristocratic version of a dustman's coat. There are flying
jackets, fencing style jackets in quilted heavy leather, reversible
macs with classic cream on one side for days when you want to
play safe, tiny stripes on the other for the day you decide its time
to be different. And there are leather trench coats, long leather
coats with deep fur revers and a shape like Mae West, real riding

*By Malcom Levene for Washington Tremlett*

macs with inner straps for the legs, jackets and blousons galore.
Go on to suit yourself beautifully, in very special Ivy League
styles designed for Washington Tremlett by Malcom Levene.
There are beautifully-cut slender double-breasted blazers that do
lovely things for the shoulders, subtle tweed business suits with
hacking style jackets, evening suits in needle and elephant
cord—a refreshing change from velvet—and lots of three-piece
combinations in flannel, tweed and cord. This summer, look out
for light silk mixture jackets in soft blue and white stripes,
unconstructed textured jackets, lots of linen, shirts with smaller
collars, bow ties in the new smaller size. All very 'U'—and no
doubt very You.

**Washington Tremlett** also at:
1 Burlington Gardens, W1    01-493 1242
Mon.-Sat. 9-6.
Inn on the Park Hotel, Park Lane, W1    01-493 7796
Mon.-Sat. 9.30-7
Britannia Hotel, Grosvenor Square, W1    01-499 0188
Mon.-Fri. 9-6, Sat. 9-5.

**Coats:** in sizes 36"-46": alpaca and
wool wrapover coat, £189; classic
heavy tweed with raglan sleeves
and fly front, £199; young casual
trench, double-breasted, cut high
on the arm, £145. Classic holster
belted trench in cashmere and
camel, £159. Full raglan tweed
coat with button cuffs, high
collar, £119. Raglan fly front with
tie belt and jet pockets, very
smart, £149.

**Raincoats:** double-breasted classic
in rubberized gabardine, £89;
fly-fronted dustman style mac,
£119; green khaki gabardine
trench coat with light buttons,
£125.

**Leather and suede:** leather
double-breasted trench, very soft,
with quilted lining, £269. Dark
leather coat with fur collar, yoke
back, £329. Sheepskin blouson
with zip front, ribbed knit trim,
£179. Soft suede button-up

blouson, knit collar and hem,
£159. Black leather blouson lined
with sheepskin, £189.
Pigskin-textured leather blouson,
zip front, £145. Quilted leather
fencing jacket, £175.

**Suits:** in sizes 36"-46". Business
suit with hacking jacket, lined
trousers, £169. Three piece suits
with plaid jacket, cord trousers
and flannel waistcoat, £179. Smart
business suit in dark flannel, with
two flap pockets and waistcoat,
£200. Evening suits in needle and
elephant cord, £149. Soft tweed
three piece suits with the soft
Savile Row look, £159. Tweed
**jacket**, £89.50; big check
two-button jackets, £119. Two
button summer jackets, in silk
mixture, around £125. Cashmere
jacket with hacking vent and
leather buttons, £149. Navy
blazers from £129; cotton jackets
from £69.50; cotton suits from
£100.

# Turnbull & Asser

71-72 Jermyn Street, SW1
01-930 0502
Mon.-Fri. 9-5.30, Sat. 9-1
Telegrams: *Paddywhack*, London SW1
(American Express, Barclaycard, Diners)

A perfect shirt is a joy forever—as are Turnbull & Asser,
dispensers of gentlemanly bliss. *T & A make the best, most
beautiful shirts in the world*—handsome statements that say all the
things that matter, in a private language of quality and style.
Take 'T & A blue' for starters, a magical mid-blue of their own
devising, quite the nicest blue you could treat yourself to. And
who but T & A could have created the 'City shirt' in stripes or
checks, with white collar and cuffs, and a wonderful air of
distinction. There are stripes by the thousands, checks by the
score, but never any prints—in the view of the house, *there is no
such thing as a good print for a man's shirt*. Buttons come in white
or smoked pearl *only*—and it is *not* done to do up the bottom of
the three cuff buttons on a T & A shirt. The collars are simply
magnificent—bold three-inch collars that square the shoulders,
carry the shirt, give you that dashing on parade look. And the
cut, of course is perfection itself. All of T & A's fabrics are
specially woven for the house, and they only use shirting silks
from their own silk mill. True spun *crêpe*, twice the weight of
ordinary silk and the best under the sun, it gets *better* the more
you wash it. T & A gave stripes to the world, and this is where
you see their subtle artistry at its finest. There are Roman stripes,
Bengal stripes, block stripes, stripes classic and new. By varying
the width and colour of individual stripes, one design can lead to
a hundred variations, and often does—an exciting rainbow of

243

delights. The colours are specially dyed to T & A's order, in every shade you could possible wish to wear. You can even have pyjamas, dressing gowns, nightshirts and shorts, all in the stripes of your choice! There's variety aplenty to spice up your lifestyle—and so many ways to wear a T & A shirt. Try Bengal stripes with a dotted tie, multi-block stripes in black, white and grey with a grey flannel suit. For a spot of fun, pick checks to go with a dinner jacket, or choose a pleated evening shirt in *eau-de-Nil*—next to cream and white, the smartest shade to wear with black. For men who like to travel light, there are switcharound shirts to suit every purpose—gingham check shirts with white collar and cuffs, inner white gauntlet, button flap pocked faced with white. For business, wear it in the usual way with a navy suit and tie. For casual wear, slip on cord or white duck trousers, unbutton the shirt to show the gingham check *inside* the collar, turn back the cuffs to show the inner white gauntlet, unbutton the flap pocket and you're away. For the ultimate in casual throwaway elegance, look out for *the shirt of the season*—T & A's officer shirts with a difference, in fine khaki poplin with white collar, inside gauntlet and cuff. If you want to simplify your wardrobe, remember that in today's world, a few good shirts and an immaculate blazer will take you anywhere—and T & A have superb single and double-breasted blazers that set off their shirts to prefection. You can count on T & A for the little touches that quality and style are all about. This is the only place in the world where you can have ties in *thirty-six ounce silk*; all ties are cut on the true bias, and hand-slipped so they never lose their shape. The wool shirts all have collars lined with cotton, so they never rub. T & A will refit a shirt with white collar and cuffs in forty-eight hours, and they have the best selection of bow ties anywhere, over three thousand at all times. You can pamper yourself with luxurious silk gowns and pyjamas made to order, just like those Noel Coward loved so well. And now that the man-about-town look is back in fashion, you can come to T & A for wing collar shirts, *piqué* dress shirts and silk carnations to wear in your buttonhole. *Dear* T & A—what would the world be without them!

**Ready-to-wear shirts** in sizes 14½-18 (modified): poplin from £15-£20; voile, £20-£25; silk from £35-£45. **Dressing gowns:** silk dressing gowns from £100; cotton robes from £45; cotton kimono wraps from £45. **Pyjamas:** in cotton, £27; in silk, from £80. **Nightshirts**, plain cottons, from £25. **Boxer shorts**, in cotton, £5; in silk, £12. **Bow ties** from £3.50. **Wing** collar shirts, £20.

## Turnbull & Asser  23 Bury Street, SW1   01-930 0502

Mon.-Fri. 9-5.30, Sat. 9-1

**Made to order** shirts, allow six to eight weeks. Poplins from
£21-£25; silks from £40-£50; shirts in voile, Oxford cloth, Sea
Island cotton, from £25-£30. **Also made to measure:** cotton
pyjamas, from £35; silk pyjamas, from £95; cotton nightshirts
from £40. **Ready to wear suits** in pure wool worsted, West of
England flannel, wool and mohair, from £175. Ready to wear
sports jackets in tweed and cashmere from £100-£150, slacks from
£40.

# CHILDREN
# AND MOTHERS

*At Babyboots*

## Babyboots at Boots 150-152 Putney High Street, SW15 01-788 6191
Mon.-Sat. 8.45-5.30, Fri. 8.45-6
(Access)

Boots are walking away with another winner—a stylish range of children's clothes to supplement their fine baby foods and toddler's toiletries. In all baby matters, Boots have always been people you could trust, so when it comes to young good looks, don't think twice about following in their footsteps. Boots aim to give you *fashion and value*, and their collection shows a definite trend away from the traditional and ordinary designs that have dominated the children's field for so long. Instead, they offer clothes that will appeal particularly to young mothers who have grown up in the jeans and Laura Ashley generation. Babies can start off with flower print angel blouses cut like artist's smocks, and this summer children up to the age of five can look forward to *three* minifashion collections from Boots. There are military and safari styles in khaki, pretty frilly pinafores and fresh dainty smocks, a whole sporty wardrobe in primary colours, with lots of drawstring tops and trousers. Little girls can enjoy high fashion fabrics and trims—lots of pure cottons, cheesecloths, *broderie Anglaise*—and delightful *broderie Anglaise* baby caps, just 99p. Little boys get a lot of attention too, with khaki fatigues, tracksuits that look like combat jackets, little stripe-trimmed boxer shorts with T-shirts to match, all at very competitive prices. Boots aim to provide *everything for the under-fives*, and they do—right down to nightgowns, swimwear, fluorescent Glo-Boots and Christmas specialities, like last year's Rupert Bear suit—check trousers, red sweater and scarf, just like Rupert's, for £7.50. You can even buy Baby Deer children's shoes, cloth books and toys. Research has shown that women visit their chemist at least once a week, but it doesn't need any research to see that with the choice available at Babyboots, it makes good sense to get everything for baby here in one go.

Sample range—all prices approximate:

**0 to 3 months:** white christening dresses, £3.45; *broderie Anglaise* caps 99p.

**3-9 months:** shortsleeved strawberry print dress in pure cotton, BDO3, £1.99. Spots and stripes dress, in pure cotton, brown or blue on white, £1.99. Pretty red pinafore-front dress, in paisley and flower print, trimmed with *broderie Anglaise*, £2.45. Cream dress with peasant motif

249

print, red ribbon trim, £2.35. Pure cotton angel set, flower print top with red yoke, and red panties, £2.99. For little boys: white stretch terry playsuit and T-shirt, trimmed with candy stripes, £2.80; stripy rompers, £1.65; stripy dungarees, £2.15. Very special little girls party dress: in Regency-striped seersucker overprinted with roses, ruched top and lace trim: £2.15 for ages 3-9 months, 9-18 months; £2.25 for 9-18 months, 18 months-2 years, 2-3 years.

**9-18 months:** small blue and white dot dress with white puff sleeves, *broderie Anglaise* trim on skirt, £2.45. Stretch terry top and stripy shorts for boys, £2.85.

**18 months-2 years:** pure cotton dresses with puffed sleeves, lace-trimmed neck, floral and stripe prints, £3.15; cheesecloth dresses with ruffles at neck, cross-stitch print, £2.10. For boys, brown dungarees with tartan trim, £3.10; green two piece trimmed with white racing stripes, £3.99; blue shorts and dishcloth look top, £2.80.

**2-3 years:** summer dresses in solids with smart contrast trim, £3.99; dresses in big windowpane checks, square neck, ruched bodice and puffed sleeve, £2.99. Long party dresses with mandarin collar, inset floral border, £5.25; also for ages 3-4. Handknit-look cardigan with wooden-look buttons, £2.99. For little boys, green dungarees, £3.10; white or red boxer shorts with stripe down the side, 99p; pyjamas, £2.99.

**3-4 years:** jolly nightie with puff sleeves, full length transfer print of dancing squirrels, bunnies, frog and bears, £2.90. Smock-look dress with ruffled neck, £2.90. Warm anorak with solid body and hood, stripy yoke and sleeves, £5.55. Little skirts with elasticated waists, gathered or pleated. £1.75. Boys swimming trunks from 85p.

**4-5 years:** blue cheesecloth dress with bell sleeves, *broderie Anglaise* trim and flounced skirt, £4.75. Long dress in gingham with ruffled collar, band of flowers or checks on skirt, £4.65. Aran-look cardigans with toggle fastenings and tie belt, £2.99. Boat-necked shirt sleeved sweaters with cotton-and-silk knit look, £2.15. For boys, denim-look trousers with ticking stripes and patch pockets, £2.65; khaki trousers with elasticated back and two side pockets, £2.50.

---

**Bally**  9 Sloane Street, SW1   01-235 2582
Mon.-Sat. 9-5.30, Wed. 9-7
(Access, American Express, Barclaycard, Chargex, Diners, Mastercharge)

---

Children love the Bally salon where they can scramble up a hill of green cushions, scrawl in coloured chalk on a blackboard wall, enter painting competitions—and get *the smartest small shoes in town*. Bally specialise in *grown-up fashion footwear scaled down to size*—strappy sandals, classic brogues, shaggy *après-ski* boots, all the season's best looks—just the thing for getting the wee ones off on the right foot. And that includes wee ones of any age—the high fashion shoes go up to the equivalents of women's size 6 and men's size 7½, *a real find for dainty-footed shoppers*. Little ladies can look forward to a dazzling summer in Bally's new sling-back open-toe mules on curved cork or bamboo wedges, schoolgirl sandals on tiny jump wedges and ballerina party pumps with slender wraparound ankle straps. Small men-about-town can keep in step with casual soft moccasins, sporty braid-trimmed chukka boots and elegant lace-up brogues, and toddlers can drum their heels in white calf boots or snappy tricolour T-bars by Babybotte of France. Bally also have D.D. Doré Doré tights, cotton ankle socks by Bonnie Doon and the excellent Start-Rite collection of classic shoes and sandals with built-in support under the instep—*so* important for growing feet. Don't forget to enter the painting competitions, held *during school holidays*: for this year's dates, ring Bally.

Sample range—all prices approximate:

**High fashion collection:** elegant mules with sling back and open toe, on cork or bamboo wedges, in sizes 24 (age 3) to 34 (age 12); about £10. Schoolgirl sandal on tiny jump wedge, sizes 27 to 36: about £22. Ballerina party pump with wraparound straps, sizes10-41, about £22. For little boys: elegant moccasins for ages 6-14, about £22. Sporty suede chukka boots with striped braid trim, about £12-£14. Bally Swiss brogues with punch detail: laceups in sizes 36-42 and slip-ons in sizes 34-42, from about £25. **Start-Rite** shoes for ages 1 to 10; C, D and EE fittings. Sample range: Colette, 1 bar shoe with stitched trim, sizes 6-1½, about £6.50. 1 bar patent party shoes from about £6.70; double bar shoes with punch detail, about £6. Boy's buckle loafers, sizes 9-12, about £6.50. **Toddler's shoes** by Babybotte: soft white calf lace-up boots, sizes 18 (under 1 year) to 22, £12.50; also small black patent and two tone shoes. Rubber soled laceup ankle boots in red, white and blue, from about £18.50, sizes 21-28.

***

**Great Expectations** 46 Fulham Road, SW3   01-584 3468
Mon.-Sat. 9.30-5.30

***

If you want to wait in style and bloom while you're doing it,

*By Jennifer Hocking for Great Expectations*

urry to this pretty converted conservatory—London's first *high fashion* maternity shop. Exclusive designs have been commissioned from Jean Muir, Bill Gibb, Gordon L. Clarke, Jennifer Hocking, Yuki, Juliet Dunn, Ann Buck, Julia Fortescue, Yvonne Langley and John Bates and you can expect all the flair of their regular collections with subtle concessions to flare. There are sparkly party frocks, pleated shifts in fine wool challis, Liberty print peasant outfits, boatnecked smocks in pure silk jersey, lots of evening dresses—things you'll want to go on wearing long after the baby has arrived. You can pop in as soon as the diagnosis is confirmed, because there are lots of specially selected models from the designer's regular collections to see you through the early stages, and aromatherapeutic creams and oils by Marguerite Maurey to help you keep your skin supple from the start. Great Expectations also have their own collection of smart day separates, maternity night wear by Night Owls and delightful presents to make baby feel at home—teddy bears, *appliqué* cot quilts, monogrammed baby linen by Eximious, heart-patterned 'pretties' by Nina Campbell, antique silver christening presents and charming knitted cushions by Veronica Franklin.

Sample range—all prices approximate:

**Great Expectations separates:** skirts and trousers, from about £50; **designer models** in a range of styles and prices, including draped jersey top by Yuki, £66; day dresses by Jennifer Hocking, £59.

---

**Kickers** 126 Kings Road, SW3   01-584 9608
Mon.-Sat. 10-6
(Access, American Express, Barclaycard)

---

*Who loves ya, baby? KICKERS!* Kickers have always put a lot of heart into their bright buoyant children's shoes, and the kids-Kickers combination has been the love story of the Seventies, *J'aime Kicker-tu aimes Kickers-il/elle aime Kickers* stylish childrens' favourite French conjugation. So this season Kickers give children a chance to wear their heart on their sleeves, their soles and their backs with the new J'aime Kickers collection. Start off with the new hearts-and-flowers shoes—in white canvas, with grass and daisies round the sides, a red dot under the left heel, a green dot under the right, and a heart under

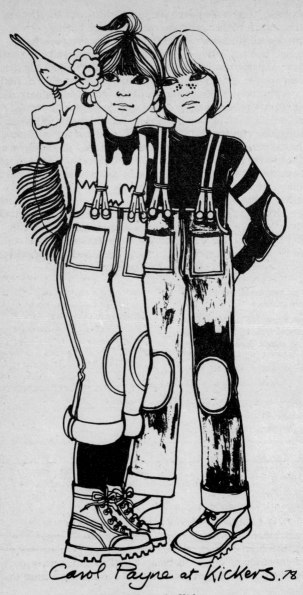

Carol Payne at Kickers. 78

By Carol Payne for Kickers

each instep. There are J'aime Kickers T-shirts and shoebags to match, a great soft Kickers shoe cushion to cuddle up with at night, and lots of loveable Kickers classics in new colourways. You can have the sporty canvas Kickers in lemon and green, red with green, smart white with slate grey; casual Nubuck slip-ons and lace-ups in oxblood red, sage green and sandy beige as well as the primary brights. **Biggest news of all—the Kickers collection of children's shoes** by Carol Payne, the designer who created Kids in Gear back in the Sixties. These are real gambol, rough and tumble clothes with tearaway style; cord and khaki blousons with dungarees to match, **skateboard sweaters** with racing stripes on the shoulders and leather pads on the elbows—just the thing to wear when hotdogging on a special Kickers skateboard! There are more Kickers accessories than ever before—small Kicker shoes on a cord to wear around the neck, plain and Asterix pencil cases filled with coloured pens, satchels in several sizes and socks specially dyed to go with the shoes. You can hand Kickers on from one child to another as easily as a used Aston Martin—and since Kickers isn't just puppy love, children can look forward to Kickers shoes for grown-ups.

Sample range—all prices approximate:

**Shoes** from size 21 (about 1 year). Canvas sandals from £8.95; sporty canvas laceup shoes from £9.95; new rubber rainboots from £6.50; high boots from £20; casual leather shoes from £15.95.
**Kickers clothes** by Carol Payne, in sizes 1 year-10/11 years: canvas and cord blouson, £9.95 and matching dungarees, £10.95. Skateboard sweater, about £5.95. **Kickers accessories:** Kickers skateboard, £29.95; Kickers sweatshirt, £5.95; and T-shirt, £3.95. Kicker shoe on cord, 60p; pencil case full of coloured pencils, £5.95; small satchels from £5.95; J'aime Kickers shoebags, £1.95.

---

**Rowes** 170 New Bond Street, W1   01-734 9711
Mon.-Fri. 9-5.30, Sat. 9-5
Telegrams: *Dusexia*, London W1
(American Express, Barclaycard, Carte Blanche, Diners)
By appointment to Her Majesty the Queen, outfitters

---

Creators of the sailor suit that launched three generations of sea-going princes, Rowes give fortune's darlings the chance to splash out in style. You can have the famous 'Windsor woolies', navy knits with sailor collars, and clothes in the best English tradition—handsmocked frocks, small tweed jackets, riding clothes and barathea coats. If you prefer an international look, Rowes have an excellent collection of Continental childrens clothes by leading houses like Cacharel who specialise in making smaller versions of their grown-up fashion designs. You can expect exactly the kind of things you'd love to wear yourself and usually can't find in London—halter-topped dresses in Tahitian pareu print, *très chic*, cream lace-trimmed blouses to wear with brown velvet pinafores, *molto elegante*. There's a **new baby department** with baby dresses in cream wool for winter and Liberty prints for summer, Buster suits, handknitted matinee jackets and hand embroidered traditional nightdresses in fine cotton lawn—so much nicer than modern sleepers. On the main floor budding young men-about-town will find **the best selection of young men's trousers in London**—a whole wall of smart trews in velvet, tweed, cord, flannel, linen, cotton, denim, gabardine and seersucker—all with special knits that mix but don't match in the sophisticated Continental style. Rowes shoe salon is at the rear, with a choice selection of beautifully made classics—T-bars, button bars, brogues and party patents—even **small fur-trimmed mules** and **two-tone spectator shoes**. Downstairs, look out for smart dressing gowns, children's Fairisles and cashmeres, formal grey suits, tweed hacking jackets and, to order, velvet shorts and jabot blouses in the Lord Faunteleroy style. Bring the children along when you come—it's never too early to teach them what good taste is all about.

Sample range—all price approximate:

Age range: 0-14.

## For babies

Hand finished barathea coats from £30 in 6 months size. Little boys buster suits with hand smocking, from about £40. Bright velours sleepers, from £10. Traditional lawn nightdresses, from £9.

## For little boys

Harris tweed jackets from £30 for 3 year old size; hacking jackets from £40 for aged 6 size. Velvet jackets from £45 for aged 6 size. Viyella shirts and pure silk dress shirts, from £20. Windsor woolies for ages 2-5, from £12 for age 2. **Trousers** in sizes 3-16; all wool trousers lined. From £23 for age 5 in flannel, from £23 for age 5 in cord. **Shoes:** a selection, including slipons for age five from £21.50; laceups from £10.50 for size 5, from £12.50 for size 1½. Baby boots from about £6.50.

## For little girls

Flower girls dresses to order; long velvet pinafores, £68 for aged nine. Riding wear to order. A selection of shoes starting from £6.50 for baby button bars; fur trimmed mules, from £4.50-£6.50. Button bar shoes from about £15; Pretty things by Cacharel, Le Bourget and others, cord, tweed and cotton skirts, Liberty print dresses, velvet pinafores, beachwear, lots of separates.

---

## Sign of The Times   17 Elystan Street, SW3   01-589 4774
Mon.-Sat. 10-5.30
(American Express)

---

As the cost of children's clothes soar to ridiculous heights, canny parents are coming to Sign of The Times for second-hand children's clothes at bargain basement prices. Many of the pieces have been lovingly cared for by Chelsea nannies, and you'll find *cachet* labels like Hechter, Rocking Horse, Kriziababy, Biba and Harrods, lots of useful classics like school raincoats and long party dresses. There are new clothes as well—**end-of-line and sample stock from Meeneys**, available here at half the original price or less. The collection goes from toddlers to teens, and there are separate collections of second-hand clothes for men and women—just the thing for stylish young dressers in the difficult fourteen to fifteen age group.

Sample range—all prices approximate:

Hechter knit romper for age two, £4. Saks baby coat in pale pink eyelet cotton, £1.40. Rocking Horse crossover knickerbockers, age four, £4. Biba lambswool polo pullover, age four, £2. Harrods Harris tweed coat with velvet collar, age eight, £6. Long party dresses, ages six and upwards, from £5-£6. Plush-lined baby's anorak with braid trim, £4. Sweaters at about £2 and under; pure cotton hand smocked romper, £5; Harris tweed coat for age ten, £14; school raincoats from £4.

---

## Tiger, Tiger   219 Kings Road, SW3   01-352 8080
Mon.-Sat. 10-6
(Access, American Express, Barclaycard, Diners)

---

Every day seems like Christmas here in London's most lovable toyshop, and children's eyes light up as brightly as tigers in this treasurehouse of delights. No childhood fancy has been forgotten, from swords for small swashbucklers to Cinderella slippers in little girl sizes, and there's a splendid dressing up cupboard full of masks, false beards and noses, funny hats, fairy wands, non-toxic face paints and costumes for Halloween, rainy days, fancy dress parties and dreary Aunt Dorrie's annual visits. Cuddly beasties gambol in the windows—camels, corgis, King Charles spaniels, old friends like Mrs. Tiggywinkle, tiny bugerigars, giraffes nearly six feet tall—and elegant Afghan hounds for children of the Sixties! Puppet theatres large and small wait in the wings, and chorus lines of marionettes hang from the ceiling—the Pelham collection, Punch and Judy, grinning green dragons, knights in golden armour and a shocking pink ostrich that lays a golden egg. There are toy forts, farms, garages and aerodromes, dolls houses in every style from Regency to Metroland, complete fashion collections for best-dressed dolls, a tremendous selection of tiny furniture and *objets* that will enchant miniature collectors and collectors of miniatures, lots of pretty presents priced at about £1 and *seventy-two* baskets of pocket money toys, stocking fillers and party favours priced from just 10p. Best of all, there are lots of *real* toys, toys made like they used to be—exclusive specialities by English craftsmen, fine toys from France and Italy, Edwardian-style wicker dolls prams, old-fashioned hobby horses, carved wooden Noah's Arks, Victorian style dolls dressed up in Liberty prints and *broderie Anglaise*, place settings of tiny china packed in wicker hampers, Yorkshire skipping ropes with antique cotton bobbin handles, magical rocking horses with the dust of Elidor on their hooves and a sparkle in their eyes to remind you—'*second on the right, and straight on till morning.*' Even the most jaded adult will walk out of Tiger, Tiger lighter in heart than in pocket.

Sample range—all prices approximate:

**Dolls houses:** Lundby dolls houses wired for electricity, £13.95; with units to add on: garage, £7.65; living unit, £6.60. New large Lundby doll house, £24.75. For collectors: Welsh thatched cottage, £74.84; Tudor cottage, £63; gingerbread cottage, £54. Sturdy Georgian houses in plain wood, to paint and decorate yourself, in three sizes: £39, £62 and £81. **Toy forts and farms:** farms from £7.84-£8.82; lavish manor farm, £22.50. Western style forts, £7.84-£11.70. **Toy garages:** from £5.44-£8.64. **Toy castles:** romantic French castle with three turrets, £12.83; castle with five turrets and a drawbridge, £21.29; Border stone castles, from £21.38-£32.08. **Toy shops:** from £7.50 for simple models to £50.99 for collector's pieces. **Puppets:** glove puppets from 95p to £7.99; Pelham puppets from £2.70-£29. Knight in golden armour, two sizes, £2.80 and £4.75; pink ostrich puppet, £15.99. String puppets from £6.28. **Dolls:** superb selection, including rag dolls from £5.85-£11.70; Jane Walsh Angland dolls from £3.51; Victorian style 'Emily' dolls by Anne Wilkinson, £3.92. Doll's china sets in wicker hampers, place settings for two, £4.11; for four, £5.84; for six, £7.02. **Doll's prams:** a selection, including Edwardian style wicker pram, £41.85 and denim pram, £13.50. Charming family of grey and brown mice dressed in Edwardian costumes—nanny in frills, Daddy in a Norfolk jacket, Great Uncle in academic robes, from £4.50. **Dressing Up:** costumes from £5.93-£9.40, including dragon, clown, lion, cowboy, Red Indian, medieval and eastern princess outfits. Non-toxic face paints, 40p. **Cuddly animals:** from £1.58-£3. Carved wooden Noah's Ark, £15; Yorkshire skipping ropes, 95p. Old fashioned hobby horses, many lengths and sizes, £2.23-£10.71. **Rocking horses:** baby rocking horses with back support, £10; nursery rockers with woolly mane, from £22. Fabulous large rocking horses on pillar stand or bullrockers, copies of Victorian models, in dappled grey or pure black: bullrockers, £175.88; pillar stand models, £182.58. Pony-sized versions: £113.97 for bullrockers, £125.36 for pillar stand. Furry Pegasus rocker, £148.50; in pony size, £59.96. **Also:** puzzles, games, dolls furniture, dolls clothes, lots of lovely mobiles, Fisher Price toys, and an *excellent book corner* with Puffins, Beatrix Potter and Pooh books, Richard Scarry picture books, Barbar books by Jean de Brunhoff, Dr. Seuss books, and rag books for toddlers.

---

## Westaway & Westaway 65 Great Russell Street, WC1

01-405 4479

Mon.-Fri. 9.30-5.30, Sat. 9.30-12.45

---

The classic English look is a firm fashion favourite with smart children everywhere, and Westaway of Bloomsbury have woollies, tartans and all the trimmings for putting on the style—at *wonderful bargain prices*. Only pure natural wools are used—lambswool, Shetland, and cashmere; you can have Shetland sweaters in sixty different colours, tartans in scores of different setts. Special fashion buys include children's Fairisle sweaters, tiny cashmere cardigans and tartan waistcoats with matching tam o'shanters. If what you want isn't in stock, you can place a special order, and Westaway will send it anywhere in the world.

Sample range—all prices approximate:

**Knitwear:** from sizes to fit a one year old child. **In Shetland:** crew necks from £5.75; roll necks from £5.90; V-necks from £5.90; cardigans from £5.95 for two year olds to £7.25 for crew necks, £7.50 for roll- and V-necks and £7.75 for cardigans for nine to ten year olds. **Fairisles:** a selection with Fairisle banding round the shoulders: Fairisles for age two from £7.95. **In Lambswool:** a selection, including boys lambswool cardigans for ages three to four, £7.75; for age ten, £7.75.

**Cashmere:** a selection, including cashmere cardigans for ages two to three, about £12-£13; cashmere crew neck pullovers for ages six to seven, about £14. Also, hats, scarves and gloves.

**Tartan:** tartan kilts from £4.95 for 1 year old to £8.50 for a ten year old. Tartan waistcoats, about £5.40. Tartan trews, from £2.95 for a one year old to £4.95 for a ten year old. Matching tams, £1.95. Boy's tartan ties, £1. Children's capes with matching kilts, from £10.95. Tartan dressing gowns, from £12.95.

---

# Westaway & Westaway  29 Bloomsbury Way, WC1
01-405 2128/0497
Mon.-Fri. 9.30-5.30, Sat. 9.30-12.45

---

Just around the corner, Westaway's fabric shop where you can buy fabric by the yard, for making up into little girl's dresses or little boy's blazers. Tartan from £5.10 per metre, special clan tartans from £6 per metre, tweeds from £6 per metre, suiting fabrics from £10 per metre.

---

# The White House  51-52 New Bond Street, W1

01-629 3521
Mon.-Fri. 9-5.30, Sat. 9-1

---

The aristocrat of the children's specialists, the White House have pampered three generations with baby and children's clothes fit for princes and princesses, **the finest in the world**. White House babies start life in antique Victorian cots trimmed with handmade lace or soft muslin, see the world for the first time from a coach-built 'Rolls-Royce' of prams, and drift off to sleep in handsmocked wool nightgowns wrapped in pure cashmere shawls. Even the font is a less daunting experience when dressed in cascading White House christening robes of plumetis and handmade lace. The White House has an international reputation for its exquisite handworked specialities—everything from handsmocked crawlers in cream satinised cotton to elaborate Greek Orthodox christening robes and handknitted jacket sets scattered with hand-embroidered roses. There are more delights in store as the children grow up, for the White House party clothes are absolutely magnificent. Little boys can have short velvet trousers and pintucked lace-trimmed shirts just like fairy tale princes, little girls have their choice of summer and winter long dresses, or ravishing sugar and spice organdie frocks threaded with pretty ribbon. And best of all are the fabulous barathea coats, the ultimate classics, with fine pintucking and handworked trim on collar and cuffs. The White House also have Continental sportswear, fine knitwear including cashmere shirts with pullovers to match, ski wear, small gabardine suits, party bags and capes to match the party dresses. The service is impeccable, and customers have their special assistants who serve them year after year. If the White House had a motto, it would surely be 'nothing is better than the best', and that is true of everything within its doors. There's everything in a good beginning—and this is the place to start.

Sample range and approximate prices:

**Matinee jackets** for babies: jacket with mittens, bonnet and bootees to match, handknitted and embroidered with rosebuds on the cuffs and waist, onto the buttons, bonnet, mittens and bootees, from £33. Antique Victorian cot, trimmed with real lace or spot muslin from £695 for large size and from £450 for small size. **For Boys:** short velvet trousers from £23 worn with pintucked lace trimmed shirts from £35. **For Girls:** cotton organdie party dress with ribbon and Dorothy bag to match from £115; superb negligees in pastel Florgalle, handsmocked round neck and sleeves from £80. **Coats:** barathea coat, with fine pintucking and handworked trim on collar and cuffs, handmade buttons, from £155.

# Young Finland  4 Halkin Arcade, SW1
Mon.-Fri. 10-5, Sat. 10-3

Few shops are as much to young tastes as Young Finland—children love sweets and cuddles, and Young Finland's collection of kitten-soft clothes in lollipop colours always go down a treat. Pride of place goes to an exceptionally well-considered range of *separates in pure cotton and velvety velours* for children from birth to age seven—skirts, trousers, shorts, tops, pinafores, dungarees, jumpsuits, summer T-shirts, beach pants and bikinis. There are no frills or whimsies, and the collection's considerable appeal is based on beautifully simple cuts, superb fabrics and delicious colours that are just right for the Favourite Colour stage. The basic range in solid red, blue, brown, green and yellow is supplemented every season by separates in toning stripes and prints, and there's an outstanding selection of *dungarees and pinafores in denim and pure cotton twill* in stock all year round. Everything has been designed with complete comfort in mind—there are none of the tight bindings, difficult fastenings or scratchy textures that children dislike, and all of the pieces have gently elasticated waists. Practicality is another important consideration—all the separates are machine-washable, and come with a very generous length in the hem. In winter Young Finland have a fine selection of hardy outdoor and ski wear, and in summer this is the place to come for the long-sleeved cotton T-shirts that are usually so hard to find. Other specialities include exclusive handknits designed to complement the separates, and one of the best selections of *pure cotton socks* in town. So if you want all the usual objections to Getting Dressed to melt away, pop in here. Children may not know about Fashion, but they certainly know what they like.

Sample range—all prices approximate:

**In velours: Jumpsuits** with zip up front, long or short sleeves, several styles, ages 2-7, from £8.90 for age 6 months to £15 for age 7. **Skirts** with elasticated waists, short day skirts and long skirts for parties, for ages 2-7; from £5 for short and from £10 for long. **Pinafore dresses** for ages 0-3, from £5. **Dungarees** with bib, for ages 1-5; from £7.50. Shorts, for ages 6 months to 7, from £3. Velours **tops** in matching or contrast colours, long sleeves, from £5.90 to £8.90. **Trousers** for ages 1-7, from £6. For babies;

long-sleeved **all-in-one-suits** from £5, **baby dungarees** with attached feet, from £5.25.

**In pure cotton:** pure cotton **polo neck jumpers**, ribbed and plain, for ages 0-7; from £2.30 for age 0, from £3.45 to age 7. Long & short **summer T-shirts**, for ages 0-7, from £2. **Vest and pants** Matching vest and pants, sold separately, for ages 0-7, from £1.35 the set for age 3 months. **Bikinis** for ages 2-7, from £3. Little beach pants, for ages 3 months-7, from £1.25. Excellent selection of denim and cotton twill dungarees, for ages 1-6, from £8.50. Matching **pinafore dress**,

from £8.90 in 1-2 year old size.
Pure cotton socks, long and short
lengths, for ages 0-7; from 75p.

**In pure wool: exclusive
handknits** specially designed to
complement the young Finland
collection. Sporty casual styles,
including little pinafores, dresses,
overshirts and jumpers. Small
selection in stock, can also be
knitted to order—allow two
weeks. Prices vary accordingly to
style and age, but a matching set

of jumper, hat and gloves will cost
about £9.

**Also:** a good selection of hardy
high quality outdoor wear,
including real **ski wear** and lighter
**outdoor suits**, for ages 1-7. Ski
jackets from £16, jacket and
dungaree ski suits from £25. Very
amusing **braces**, with colourful
straps printed with stars and bon
mots and clasps shaped like little
hands, from £2.50.

---

**Zero Four Plus** 53 South Molton Street, W1    01-493 4920
Mon.-Fri. 10-6, Sat. 10-5
(Barclaycard, Mastercharge)

---

At Zero Four Plus, fashion conscious children can follow the
latest looks and colours as closely as their parents do across the
street in Browns. Most of the clothes are from France and
Italy—the pick of the children's *prêt-à-porter* collections—and the
rules of the game change every season, just like they do with
grownup styles. Trousers, for example, are **in** this year; dungarees
definitely **out**. And be warned: when summer comes, the smart
child will **not** be seen in anything that isn't pastel or white. The
clothes have a definite bias toward the sporty look—'Jap' style
dropped panel skirts, Fairisle waistcoats and loose cotton shirts,
with lots of shorts and towelling blousons for little boys. Even
specialities made for the shop in England have a decidely
Continental feeling—Liberty print sundresses without any
smocking, bikini bottoms without any tops. If you dress your
children at Zero Four Plus, they'll never feel out of place if you
have to drag them off to St. Moritz or St. Tropez at a moments
notice.

Sample prices and approximate
prices:

**Footwear:** shoes from £12, boots
from £15, leather sandals from £8
and canvas espadrilles from £3.
**Tops:** blouson type jackets, in
cotton and towelling, from £15;
T-shirts from £3 and baby
T-shirts from £2; baggy cotton
shirts from £9. **Dresses:** frilly

263

dresses with lace in pale colours and white, from £20; sundresses in Liberty prints from £13 or Cacharel sundresses from £13-£15; long jersey T-shirt dress for the beach, from £8. **Skirts:** 'Jap' style on the hips and pleated all the way round, from £12. **Trousers:** bermuda trousers, below the knee, from £10; baggy bermudas with pleats in front, from £10; cord, velvet, tweed, in tube style, from £14. **Knitwear:** chunky knit cardigans with simple designs, from £15; patterned flecky sweaters from £11; Fairisle waistcoats from £12; plain polo necked sweaters for babies to 12 years, from £3. **Baby clothes:** Viyella nightie, with rabbit applique, £6; babygrows from £5.

**Also:** cotton socks, plain and striped, from £1.50; straw hats from £3; petit bateau underwear from £1.80; braces from £3.

# DESIGNER'S
# SKETCHBOOK

*By Julia Grahame for Charles Grahame Lingerie*

Danny Noble

*Bill Gibb*

*Richard Nott for Peter Barron*

*Mulberry, Sketch by Antony Kwok*

cotton voile
and lace

silk tweed
and lace

Andrea
Burrow
'78

*Andrea Burrow*

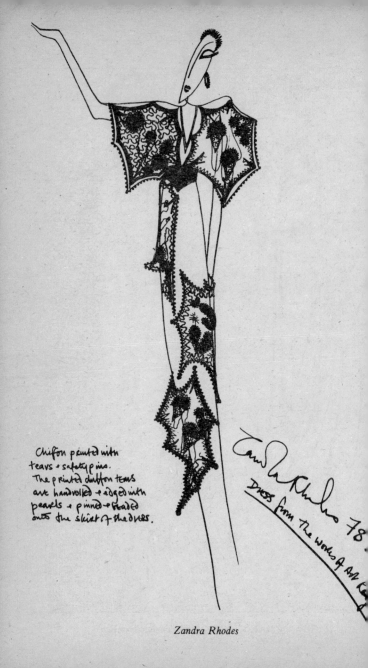

Chifon painted with
tears & safety pins.
The printed chiffon tears
are handrolled & edged with
pearls & pinned & beaded
onto the skirt of the dress.

Zandra Rhodes 78.
Dress from The Works of Art Fair

*Zandra Rhodes*

Wendy Dagworthy Spring 1978.

Wendy Dagworthy

ROS
TERRILL

Sheridan Barnett

Spring 78 · 26·6·77                    Shelagh Brown

*Shelagh Brown*

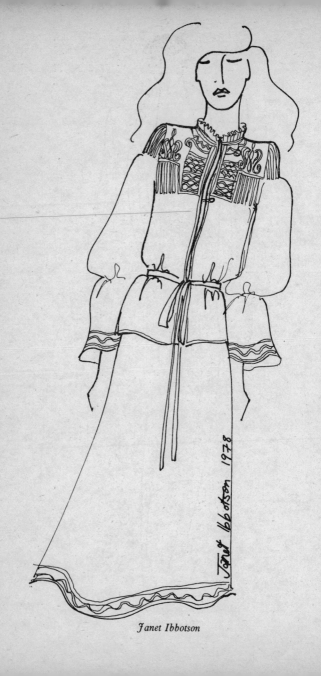

*Janet Ibbotson*

*Bruce Oldfield*

Jaime Ortega

Paul Smith Spring 78

*Paul Smith*

*Juliet Dunn*

*Paul Howie*

Gordon L. Clarke

*Ninivah Khomo*

BLACK CRÊPE
JERSEY.

Jean Muir
'78

*Jean Muir*

*Maureen Baker*

Shirt 90

Trousers 81

Victor Herbert

*Gina Fratini*

wool crepe
silk print.

DA 820
coatdress

BA 818
Blouse

SA 811
Skirt.

*Pauline Wynne Jones*

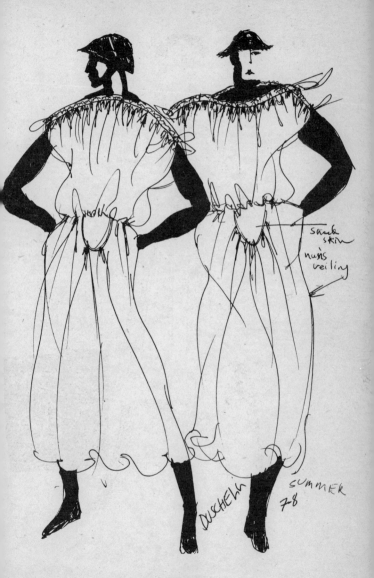

*Tony Duschell*

CARDIFF
NOTTINGHAM
OXFORD

## Apropos  39 St. Mary Street, Cardiff
0222-34434

If this jewellery shop opened in London, it would be everyone's
favourite within a week. Apropos specialises in modern jewellery
in 9ct and 18ct gold and sterling silver, in a price range that has
no equivalent in London. Many of the pieces have been specially
designed for the shop by top jewellers like Jane Allen and Cathy
Stephens, and you can have anklet chains made to order in 9ct
gold. Chains are a speciality—Blecher, S-link, Venetian, Prince of
Wales chains, every design under the sun, in lengths from fifteen
to thirty-six inches. There are lots of exceptionally pretty rings
including Russian wedding rings, engagement and wedding rings
and a superb collection of watches by Michael Heuer, Roy King,
Raymond Weil, Quilbe and Nepro—the smartest digital watches
on the market. The shop is beautifully appointed, the pieces
displayed with great style. London could learn a lot from Apropos
and so could you. If you write for particulars, they will do their
best to fill mail order requests.

Sample range and prices:

**Rings:** specialising in modern
engagement and wedding rings.
Diamond engagement ring by
Cathy Stephens from £63.
**Watches:** Michael Heuer, 17
jewel Swiss movement, smart
stainless steel band, from £62;
smart tank watch by Raymond
Weil from £30. **Also:** bangles and
bracelets, earrings, anklet chains,
lighters including Dunhill, key
rings and gold or silver ingots.

## Carmelle  Central Square, Cardiff  0222-22959/54

Carmelle has the largest selection of high fashion handbags
outside London—and the smartest selection anywhere in England,
everything from soft Enny bags and sophisticate designs by
Pistore of Italy to marvellous applique day and evening bags by
Stephanie Wood and Barbara Maertens. The range of fashion
jewellery stands up to the best London can offer, including
designs by Grosse, Dior, and Trifari, with lots of gold-plated
pieces that look like the real thing. Linked up with top London
shop Chic of Hampstead, Carmelle have top designer day and
evening wear and all the accessories you could possible want,

including vamp style Italian umbrellas and an exceptional collection of leather goods. Look out for the very special Italian styled English made executive cases with fitted interiors—a lizard case with combination lock is priced at only £159.

Sample range and approximate prices:

**Handbags:** beautiful appliqué clutch bags by Stephanie Wood in snakeskin interwoven with Liberty prints and wools for day wear from £45; Barbara Maertens clutch bags in soft suedes with leather edges and unusual appliques designs—spider's web, sunsets, delicate floral designs, from £25. **Jewellery:** from £2-£100. **Also:** day and evening wear, shoes and boots, belts, sunglasses, ties and scarves, perfumes and toiletries, umbrellas, leathergoods, tights, gifts.

---

## Monsieur Z  35 St. Mary Street, Cardiff  (0222) 30072
Mon.-Sat. 10-6

---

A sleek, smart and stunning men's shop, Monsieur Z offers a superb hats-to-shoes selection of Continental good looks spiced with Anthony Hendley's new look designs, and classic shirts by Ingram and Richard Jones. The emphasis is on the beautifully groomed casual clothes that the Italians do so well. Look out for beautifully cut linen trousers in beige, camel and khaki by L'Uomo, linen and cotton trousers with matching blousons by Ghedini, and fine wool knitwear by Gabicci, Raffaello and Nani Bon. To go with the clothes, Monsieur Z have luggage, belts, cufflinks, toiletries by Dunhill and Yves Saint Laurent, small leather goods, and one of the best selection of smart men's shoes in England, by Carlos Gonzalez, Kilvestar, Bally, Zapata & Da Vinci, D'Amico Mario Luciano and Vincenzo. This summer the Monseiur Z collection will be more exciting than ever before, with Anthony Hendley's openweave natural cotton boat neck shirts, and casual openweave T-shirts by Peter Werth.

Sample range and prices:

**Shirts:** in sizes 14½-16½; soft Viyella over-shirt by Anthony Hendley from £27; polyester and cotton shirts from £12; short sleeve shirts from £6.25 and open-weave designs including T-shirts from £2.35. **Trousers:** in sizes 28-26, linen in several colours from £17.95; corduroy trousers in black, charcoal, rust and spice from £19.50; cotton trousers in pastel colours from

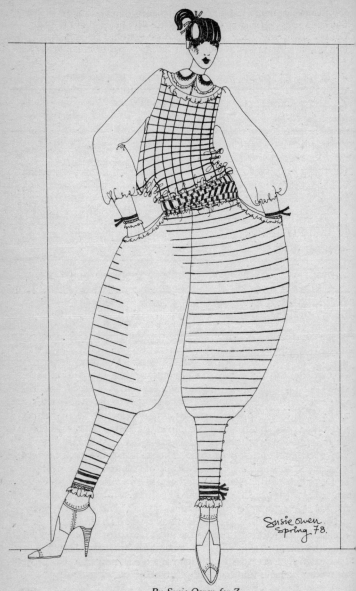

Susie Owen.
Spring. 78.

*By Susie Owen for Z*

£30. **Knitwear:** from £15-£40.
**Shoes:** in sizes 6-11 and by Carlos
Gonzalez, Kilvestar, Bally, slipons
in four colours from £30; two-tone
brogues from £22; canvas slipons
from £10; boots from £35-£42.
**Also:** executive cases, belts,
cufflinks, perfumes and luggage.

---

# Z   38 St. Mary Street, Cardiff   0222-30072
Mon.-Sat. 10-6

---

Z specialise in young designer looks with all the accessories to
match;—clothes by Cherry Frizzell, Amariaggi, Anthony
Hendley, Ann Buck and many others, the Young Enny collection
of handbags, patchwork and printed suede bags by Keybags of
Scotland, coloured tights to go with everything, top shoes, boots
and sandals, and Rive Gauche perfume by Yves Saint Laurent.
**Best of all,** you can have smashing outfits in fine Welsh tweeds
made to order by Susie Owen, one of the bright new fashion
names to watch!

---

# Pennyfeathers   29 Shakespeare Street, Nottingham
Tues.-Sat. 10.30-6

---

Birds who love nostalgic feathers should lose no time in flocking
here. These specialists in pretty things from the past have a
collection as snappy as any in London, at prices that are really a
snip—*less than half what you'd have to pay down south.* Elaborate
white cotton Victorian nighties with lace-trimmed Cavalier collar
and cuffs are just £8, long *crêpe* evening dresses and silk kimonos
start at £7, and children's lace-trimmed pinafores at only £3.50.
Better still, Pennyfeathers will delight anyone nostalgic for the
way nostalgia-hunting used to be. The stock has not been savaged
by dealers, so you have a kaleidoscope of colours, prints and
styles to choose from and the clothes come in *wearable* sizes—10's
and 12's—instead of the 14's and 16's that swamp the London
market. Everything has been cleaned, pressed and mended when
necessary, and there's a full alteration service. The collection
ranges from Victorian times to the 50's, with a particularly good
selection from the 20's and 30's including extravagant hats,
beaded bags, Deco shawls and long and short French kid gloves.
In winter you can find handknitted Fairisle pullovers and

295

cardigans, big 50's mohair sweaters, and 40's and 50's tweed suits with pleated skirts and padded shoulders. The summer collection includes peasant blouses with smocking and embroidery from £4, little strappy shoulder-tie tops made in 30's crepe and chiffon for £3.75 and a garden of silk flower-print day dresses from £7. You'd be pound-foolish not to take advantage of penny-wise prices like these—the money you'll save will cover the cost of a day-return ticket to Nottingham, and still leave you handily in pocket.

Sample range—all prices approximate:

**Skirts:** 50's taffeta skirts, pleated and circular, from £3-£6; tiered skirts in printed *crêpe*, from £5-£6.

**Dresses:** silk day dresses, from £7-£11; long *crêpe* evening dresses, from £9-£12.50; velvet day dresses, rom £6.

**Robes:** chinese embroidered silk robes, from £8; kimonos from £7.

**Nightgowns:** Victorian white cotton nightdresses trimmed with lace, from £5; satin nighties trimmed with lace, from £2-£5.

**Blouses:** 20's to 50's blouses in *crêpe*, satin, chiffon, cotton and printed silk, from £1.75-£5. 30's silk blouses trimmed with lace, from £4-£6. Collarless cotton shirts, £2.50.

**Also:** children's lace-trimmed **pinafores** from £3.50; lace-trimmed **camisoles** from £3.74; **camiknickers** from £1, long printed silk and crepe scarves from £2.50. For collectors: **Victorian ensembles** in excellent condition, a black silk satin day dress with shirred front and flounced skirt for £8, and a complete nursemaid's uniform in grey with a pintucked bib and blue and white striped pinafore for £9.50.

---

**Paul Smith**  10 Byard Lane, Nottingham    (0602) 48105
Mon.-Sat. 10-6
(Access, American Express, Barclaycard, Diners)

---

The opening of the Paul Smith shop at Barney's in New York last autumn was the sensation of the season, and Paul Smith is being tipped in all the top places as **the** new menswear designer, the man with the look everyone wants. Which comes as no surprise at all to London's smartest men, who've been slipping off to buy their clothes in his splendid Nottingham shop. **The trip is worth every minute, every penny and more; you can expect to be swept off your feet.** The service is delightful, the presentation superb; outfits are displayed with all the accessories to make it easy for you to put yourself together, and there are tasteful touches like burnished copper type faces spelling out the price of everything in the windows. As gifted a buyer as he is a designer, Paul Smith has assembled a knitwear collection that comes as a revelation to anyone used to London costs—Aran sweaters for £17; blue and white fisherman's jumpers £14 and classic cricket pullovers with navy trim for £12—all in pure wool, and beautifully made. There are accessories like canvas toolbags with suede straps for just £10, silk ties and beautiful bench-made shoes, but the best thing of all in Paul Smith's new collection—**a stunning interplay of pure silk, wool and cotton in the most exciting colours and textures to hit the fashion world in years.** There's not a single dull surface, flash shade or sloppy shape in his wonderfuly imaginative collection that creates a completely new kind of relaxed male chic. There are three basic tops—a two-buttoned double-breasted jacket with low-draped single breasted lapels, that looks just as good when worn unbuttoned, and gives you the style of the classic double breast with all the freedom of the single. The second jacket is similar, except for a zipped breast pocket and zipped cuffs—and the sleeves are lined with finely striped silky fabric, to add a bit of dash if you wear them rolled back. The third is the height of casual simplicity—an easy untailored five-button jacketshirt with shirt collar, straight back and sleeves and three front pockets. You can have the jackets in slub-, woven or Oxford cloth-textured wool and silk blends, in tobacco, taupe, cream, oyster, moss, sage green, *eau-de-Nil* and several blues, blended with natural backgrounds. Wear them with trousers in the same fabric, with solid coloured trousers in pure linen or cotton drill—or with snappy zip-pocketed cotton drill Jamaica shorts. The shirts are a whole collection in themselves—scores, in shades that sweep across the spectrum. There are classic shirts with small soft collars in traditional windowpane checks washed with completely contemporary colours, linen-finish cotton and pure linen casual shirts with roomy inverted-pleat flap pockets, easy short-sleeved heatwave shirts in beachtowel-striped cotton, superb pure silk shirts in handwoven textures and rich shades, or in a dazzling selection of fine stripes that look like miniature rainbows. And that's not all—there are pure cotton T-shirts specially dyed to go with the collection, and a whole range of specially-dyed knits in woven and waffle textured cotton and wool, that add another dimension to the layered look. Everything works with everything

*At Annabelinda*

else, nothing matches too exactly, the prices are good and the clothes are smashing—what are you waiting for? Paul Smith's designs are available in top London men's shops, but you'll get the best selection, service, and prices here.

## Annabelinda 6 Gloucester Street, Oxford (0865) 46806
Mon.-Sat. 10-6

Only in the city of inspired dreamers could a shop like this exist. Tucked away by the stage door of the New Theatre, Annabelinda create gowns that will sweep you through the looking glass into a land of pure romance. Imagine yourself in Camelot or Samarkand, see yourself as a Medici princess, a sultan's favourite or the sweetheart of a Duke, and let these specialists paint your portrait in the stuff that dreams are made of. There are rustling silks and shimmering satins, Liberty prints, luxurious velvets and chiffons light as a sigh, in a harlequinade of jewel colours. You can have anything you like—plaits, pleats, piping, brinding, antique braid, scalloping, quilting, handpainting and embroidery, as finely worked as a Durer etching. Annabelinda's special dresses are vaguely medieval, Renaissance or Russian in style, thoroughly romantic in feeling. The made to order dresses start with a consultation—you can go through folios of sketches, or simply describe what you'd like, and they'll submit sketches for your approval. All clothes are designed and made on the premises, and you can follow the progress of your gown as Medici princes followed the works specially commissioned from goldsmiths and painters. The handwork and details are superb, with a sensitive feeling for fine points—all the dresses are done up with loops and buttons, and there are no zips at the back or sides. You can have evening dresses, wedding gowns, bridesmaids frocks, coats, capes and children's clothes made to order in two to three weeks, and there's a lovely ready-to-wear collection that includes peplum-top velvet suits trimmed with Liberty peacock print chiffon, bias cut pinafores, Liberty print dresses with velvet bodices, cuffs and hems, swirling skirts and cossack tunics. If you cherish your dreams and love clothes full of fantasy, this is the place for you.

Sample range—all prices approximate:

**Special orders:** dresses from £75, wedding dresses from £85;

handpainted tops from £79.50. Sumptuous silk chiffon layered ensembles lined with silk, about £180, other prices on consultation. **Ready to Wear:** in sizes 8-18. Velvet peplum suit with peacock print trim; jacket, £49.50; six panel skirt, £49.50. Silk shirts from £22.50; cossack tunic in silk, £25. Liberty print dresses with velvet bodice and trim, about £65. Bias pinafore dresses, from £29.50 short, from £39.50 long. Skirts from £29.50 short, from £39.50 long.

---

# A.N.I.—Art Needlework Industries 7 St. Michael's Mansions, Ship Street, Oxford
Mon.-Sat. 9-4.40

Heinz Edgar Kiewe has devoted over forty years to researching, rescuing and re-establishing traditional knitting and needlework, and his shop is full of tantalising threads you can follow back to your ethnic roots. This is the place to find Aran knitting patterns over 1300 years old, patterns using the 'Norman rib' stitch adapted from 12th century garments, patterns and wool for Guernsey and Jersey fishermen's sweaters, designs for traditional Scandinavian sweaters and legwarmers, Fairisle patterns reprinted from the Thirties, patterns for rural smocks, Jacobs and Romney Marsh fleece and many more fascinating things. 'Spinning a yarn' is much more than a figure of speech here, for traditional patterns are full of poetry, symbolism and history, and the shop has an exceptional collection of books and essays dealing with everything from the links between Berber carpets and Icelandic sweaters to the folkloric motifs of Saxon Transylvania. Those who prefer practice to theory will find a stunning selection of *pure wool yarns specially spun and dyed for A.N.I.*—hard-wearing handspun Harris tweed yarn for fishermen's sweaters and socks, rich North Country Double Knit Skiwool with a high lanolin content for natural insulation, combed and carded scoured white Skiwool for home dyeing and spinning, warm light Shetland 2-ply that knits to any 3-ply pattern, soft lace-ply and one-ply wool for baby clothes and boudoir shawls in delicious shades like peach and *eau-de-Nil*, pillow lace thread and the country's largest selection of authentic Bainin Aran wools. The quality and colours are peerless and you can go on to dip into large boxes of old embroidery transfers or sort through A.N.I.'s magnificent collection of *exclusive handpainted tapestry designs*. Mr. Kiewe was instrumental in the revival of the Renaissance Florentine Flame (bargello) stitch in 1951, and A.N.I. has *the finest selection of*

*Florentine patterns in the world.* The complete tapestry range takes in everything from Szekely patterns that came to Europe with Attila the Hun to modern designs by Jean Lurcat of Aubusson. Look out for a *fleur de lys* design by Marie Antoinette, a rose pattern adapted from a waistcoat belonging to Henry VIII, William Morris designs, Caucasian and Kirman nomad patterns, Chippendale and Verdure motifs, Coptic studes, 'Medieval designs, early American patterns and designs from the Chinese Imperial Court. To go with them, A.N.I. have specially-dyed tapestry wool *chapelets*—'rosaries of shades'—colour-matched to original tapestries of the period. And if that doesn't needle you into action, you can select from a ready-to-wear collection that includes Aran handknits, Harris tweed shooting socks and hand-embroidered rural smocks in pure linen. Delightfully old-fashioned in many ways, A.N.I. is very much a shop for the future as Mr. Kiewe is particularly interested in passing on his lore and skills to young people, children of the plastic and synthetic generation of whom he has long despaired. *This is the best needlework shop in the country, and one of the finest in the world.* No one who appreciates the good things in life should miss a visit, and if you can't call in person, A.N.I. have a *world-wide mail order service.*

Sample range—all prices approximate:

## Wools

Fine Shetland 4-ply fleece, 39p per oz. Scoured white pure Skiwool, £1.76 per lb. Double knit wools in natural shades and colours, ideal for Guernsey and Jersey sweaters, in 2 oz hanks, 72p per hank. Shetland 2-ply, knits to any 3 ply pattern, just use one finer needle than given in the pattern, 39p per oz. Light Shetland lace-ply, 60p per oz. Double Knit Skiwool, high lanolin content, in natural shades, colours, marls and mixtures, 31p per 25 gr. Handspun Harris tweed wool, fine colours, 38p per oz. Piebald Jacobs fleece, £1.76 per lb, Romney Marsh fleece, £1.96 per lb. **Báinín** Aran yarn from 48p per 50 gr. Also, the best yarns from houses like Emu, Twilleys, and Icelandic Lopi. Exclusive tapestry wools, from 14p per skein; chapelets of wool, approximately 48 in each chapelet, from £6.72.

## Also

Crochet thread, in sizes 1-150, sixteen thicknesses, from 52p per ball. Embroidery cotton from 18p per skein. Handpainted tapestries, sizes from 12″ to 36″ and 72″, prices from £8 to £80. Knitting needles; every size and shape, including hard-to-find nos 15 and 16 and circular needles.

# Knits

Harris tweed socks and stockings, £2.27 and £4.27 the pair. Aran sweaters for men, and women, cardigan, polo and crew-neck styles, from £28. Aran sweaters for children, to order, from £16. Shawl-collared cardigan in Norman stitch, £36. Knit hats from £2.88 and mittens from £3.35. Guernsey and Jersey sweaters, from £32.77. Hand-embroidered traditional rural smocks, in cream only, from £45.

**Books:** an excellent selection, including Civilization On Loan £11.50, The Sacred History of Knitting £3.80, and Charted Peasant Designs from Saxon Transylvania £5.90, all by H. E. Kiewe. The Principles of the Stitch by his neice Lilo Markrich of the Textile Museum in Washington D.C., £5.20. Knit Your Own Norwegian Sweaters by Dale Yarn Co, United States Patchwork Pattern Book by Bannister and Ford books on Florentine stitch, rug making and many more.

# PICK OF
# THE POST

## Universal Beauty Club  167/169 Great Portland Street, London W1E 3QZ

A pound and the price of postage are your passport to good looks with a difference. Basically, the club offers members six packs of beauty and body preparations every year, at £2 per pack plus postage and packing. Each pack contains about six items by leading makers like Helena Rubinstein, Dorothy Grey, Bonne Bell, Revlon and Rose Laird, in regular not 'sample' sizes. If you were to buy the same items direct from a shop, you could easily pay twice the price and more. The contents have been fully tested by the club, and every pack introduces you to something extra special, like body shampoo or facial masks. Better still, there's a Beauty Guide in every pack that explains what everything is and how and why to use it in a comfy down-to-earth style that sweeps away a lot of the mystique about beauty, but leaves you a lot of magic to play with. All the products are widely available, so if you find something very much to your liking, you'll have no trouble obtaining it locally. And you can be sure that you're keeping up to date with the best of the new developments in beauty.

## E.M. Wools  58 Elm Road, Leigh On Sea, Essex Southend (0702) 75518

Knitting is a piece of cake in this tiny slice of a shop stacked from floor to ceiling with Phildar yarns from France. Phildar are known on the Continent for their high fashion colours like bois de rose, grenadine, lupin and morille, and for their exceptionally stylish designs for men, women and children, presented in glossy magazines that leave the English equivalents far behind. However, Phildar are also fairly hard to find, and are not at present available throughout the country. So dedicated knitters who have purchased Phildar pattern books on holidays abroad will be delighted to hear that E.M. Wools have virtually the entire Phildar collection, will mail Phildar yarns and pattern books anywhere in the country, and can place special orders for anything that isn't in stock. Best news of all for those who don't know a knit from a purl—**you don't even have to do the knitting yourself!** If you see something you like in a pattern book—*anything from a Phildar model to a Thirties Fairisle* *pattern*—you can write for an order form, fill in the relevant measurements and colour details, enclose the pattern where applicable, and E.M. Wools will have it knitted for you in Phildar yarn for a cost of 30p per ball of yarn used, plus the price of the yarn! With sweaters knitted to period patterns turning up in all the top nostalgia shops at very fancy prices, E.M. Wool's special service gives you a chance to make some great bargain buys. You can also have baby and children's clothes knitted to order, and E.M. Wools have a crochet service as well, at a cost of 40p per ball used, plus the crochet thread! Allow 21 days for delivery of garments, and 14 days for delivery of wool and cotton.

## Sundancer P.O. Box 798, London SW15 1TD

Fashion may be off-the-shoulder and getting more so by the minute, but for bare to be beautiful, all those naked wrists, necks and earlobes need an extra bit of shimmer. Chunky necklaces or jokey jewels won't do. What you need is delicate interesting pieces of **real** jewellery that you can wear with everything, from morning to night. Pretty things don't have to cost a fortune, and they certainly won't if you get them from designer Nick Rodwell at Sundancer. His speciality is liquid silver—tiny cylinders of real sterling silver or rolled gold—made up into delicate chokers, bracelets and earrings, plain or combined with semi-precious stones in all the fashion colours. The choker necklaces cost £5.50, and you can have chokers with pink rhodonite beads—perfect for this season's pastels—chokers with brown tigers eye to wear with natural linens, black jade to wear with summer's smartest evening dresses, coral to set off a sun tan, mother of pearl to wear with frilly *broderie Anglaise*. There are some very special necklaces for sweethearts—set with a small coral heart, or with a lovebird in silver, natural shell or mother-of-pearl. Most of the necklaces and bracelets have matching earrings for pierced or unpierced ears at £3.45—lovebirds, stars, doves, moons and tiny fish, in silver and semi-precious stones. A matching set of bracelet, choker and earrings will cost you less than £15, and make you look a million. Nick Rodwell's designs have been featured in top glossies like **Cosmopolitan,** but you'll have to see the complete range to appreciate all the possibilities. The right sort of jewellery makes all the difference, and at prices like this, you can't afford to say no. Write to Sundancer, and a fully illustrated brochure will be sent free by return.

## Tuppence Coloured Brookside Cottage, Stour Provost, Nr. Gillingham, Dorset   Tel: East Stour 630

No one who shopped their way through the Sixties has ever forgotten the clothes with the Foale and Tuffin label—exciting, bright, full of enthusiasm and originality—and just as wearable now as they were ten years ago. Today Sally Tuffin and Monica Renaudo design the Tuppence Coloured collection of sew-yourself clothes for children and grownups—a choice selection that will please anyone who appreciates quality and good design. The shapes are simple, but the clothes have real style—traditional smocks in corduroy, cord jerkins lined with fur fabric, smocked blouson dresses, little cord lumber jackets to wear with quilted Liberty print trousers, and superb reversible quilted Liberty print dufle coats for adults. Whenever possible, only natural fabrics are used, and very fine ones at that—pure cotton, Liberty Print Jubilee cotton and wool, and Liberty Print pure wool Varuna. You can expect lovely texture and colour contrasts, little luxuries like real wide-whale cord instead of the cheaper, stiffer pincord, lavish pockets in all the right places, pretty trimmings and ties. Made up yourself, the clothes are slightly less expensive than similar models in top children's shops, but price is not the main consideration. Remember the old saying **'penny plain, and tuppence coloured'?** You can easily pay less for children's clothes than Tuppence Coloured charges, and you can easily pay more—but you will be hard pressed indeed to find clothes at any price with the style and charm of these. This is your chance to have real designer clothes at very fair prices, so if you appreciate the good things in life, send for the current catalogue right away.

Sample range—all prices approximte:

From the current catalogue: traditional smock in corduroy, from £8.50 for ages 1-4; from £7.50 in Liberty Print Jubilee. Blouson dress in Liberty Print Jubilee, from £6.50 for ages 1-4; £16 in adult sizes. Corduroy lumber jacket, from £7 for ages 1-4; from £8 in quilted Liberty Print Jubilee. Adults reversible quilted Liberty Print coat, £22.

# HAIR

## Ricci Burns  94 George Street, W1   01-935 3657
Mon.-Fri. 9-5, Sat. 9-12.
Also at: 151 Kings Road, SW3   01-351 1235/6
Mon.-Fri. 9-5, Sat. 9-12

If you've never dared to ask your hairdresser **'make me
beautiful'**, take heart—glamour is alive and well at Ricci Burns.
**You're** the centre of attention in this salon, where the object is to
make you look marvellous, not just neat or trendy. Ricci Burns
has a designer's flair and an actor's appreciation of style—he
thinks in terms of total looks, and adores individuality. 'It doesn't
take money to look good', he says—'all it takes is confidence. Be
**definite,** throw your shyness away. Get to know yourself, know
what you like—don't just copy!' The salon offers an exceptionally
wide spectrum of techniques and looks, anything you could
possibly want, so you can really indulge in being yourself. You'll
learn a lot about glamour as well, because Ricci Burns is an
expert on the subject. 'I like people who've made an effort. Who
haven't just thrown on a pair of jeans. Vulgarity and being too
casual are the same. Be the strange magical lady you are, use your
hands, your eyes, the way you move, your clothes, your perfume,
everything about you—to express your femininity. Make your
hairdresser **want** to do your hair, ask his advice, use your time
with him constructively.' His stylists make every effort to draw
you out and put you at ease. They sit and talk with you, don't
just go straight to the head and start cutting, and even if its your
first visit they'll go on talking as they work, building up a rapport
that makes it easy to ask all the questions you want. If you ask
Ricci Burns himself, you're in for a real treat—he loves to change
people's image, redesign their looks, tell them how to make
everything work together. 'Do one thing at a time' he says, 'if
you emphasize the hair, the makeup must be light and soft, the
clothes crisp and simple.' If you want to be beautiful—and what
woman doesn't—this is the salon for you. As Ricci Burns says—
**'In life, if you want something enough, and try, you'll get it.'**

Sample range—all prices
approximate:
Cut, blow dry and shampoo with
Ricci, from £14; cut, blow dry
and shampoo with top stylists,
Anthony or Laurence, £10.26;
cut, blow dry, shampoo with

other stylists, £7.02. **Perm** from
£20.50; conditioning rinse, £3.90;
highlight, half head, from £18.50
and from £30.50 for full head;
tinting £12.60.

308

## Cadogan Club 182 Sloane Stret, SW1   01-235 3814/5
Mon.-Fri. 9-5, Sat. 9-12 (women)

You don't have to be proposed and seconded to make an appointment at the Cadogan Club, but there are so many clients who come in at least once a week that the atmosphere is definitely clubby—in the most convivial way. The club is small but choice—like the best diamonds—and there is a beauty salon under the direction of José and three trained manicurists to look after you while you sample a menu of healthy salads and fruit juices. In the hairdressing salon, directors Aldo and Patricia emphasize the cut and the condition of the hair. They use all the Redken products as well as Fermodyl, a fine new conditioner from Belgium. The clientele includes visitors from abroad who only stay in London for a fortnight or so each year and make a special point of going to the Cadogan Club each trip.

Salon prices: all prices include
VAT

Patricia and Aldo, cut £5 and shampoo and set, £4. Other stylists, cutting from £3.80, shampoo and set, £3 and blow dry £4.15. Permanent wave £13, Highlights from £25, Tinting from £8.50, Manicure from £1.75, Pedicure from £3.50.

## Colombe 8 Motcomb Street, SW1   01-235 3286/7
Mon.-Fri. 10-6, Sat. 10-5

Diamonds aren't what they used to be—today a shiny head of hair is a girl's best friend, and her next best friend is Colombe. The stylists are Celine, Karen and Trevor, and the salon has a special elegance as soft as the dove it's named for. There are delicate peach and cream tones throughout, the atmosphere is peaceful and pleasant, and there are little touches like a terrace to sit on in summer and the prettiest shampooing room in town. Women who come to Colombe are pampered shamelessly—and they have a wonderful time. The Colombe cuts are subtle, the perms soft, the look completely feminine, with plenty of bounce and shine. There are no crazy colours, no extreme styles. Colombe concentrate on bringing out the beauty of the hair, and making it the primary focus of attention. There are pure shampoos with deliciously delicate natural fragrances like Lemon Grass and Jasmine, superb conditioners and natural conditioning treatments that will make your hair lovelier than you ever thought possible. The final result is a beautifully relaxed understated elegance that you'll find nowhere else.

Sample range and prices:

Celine cut, £8.50 and set, £5.50; Karen cut, £7.50 and set, £5.50; Trevor cut, £7.50 and set, £5.50. Stylists, cut and set, £3.50 each.

Perms from £15, henna from £7.50; half-head highlights from £15. Colombe shampoos and conditioners, £3.50 each.

---

**Molton Brown**  58 South Molton Street, W1   01-493 6959, 01-629 1872
Mon.-Wed. 10-5, Thurs.-Fri. 9-5.30, Sat. 9-Noon

---

When is a hairdresser not a hairdresser? When it's Molton Brown. Hair being *worked* in coordination with clothes and makeup is what Molton Brown is all about—a completely integrated total look in which colours, shapes and textures are repeated and counterpointed from top to toe. Far from being contrived, it's the most natural thing in the world—or as Michael says, 'Do you ever see just a head floating into a salon?' Subtlety is the basis of the Molton Brown method—the subtlety of one-directional drying that lifts the hair naturally, of forward graduation cutting that gives a softer and more original look, of delicate tints and highlights feathered lightly around the ears or over the forehead to accentuate the fine points of the face. Another Molton Brown speciality is the square fringe, cut high and well away from the side of the face, that focuses interest on the eyes, gives the face a new balance and stimulates new possibilities for makeup. Cut is only the beginning at Molton Brown—hair is twisted, marcelled, bound in silk, coiled in loops, coaxed with crochet hooks, sleeked back with slides, laced with overnight dyes, embellished with pompoms, threaded with beads—suddenly hair is *exciting*, and you'll find your fashion self-image extended and expanded in ways you never dreamed of before! Imagine a straight mid-length blonde bob washed with the faintest grey highlight, hanging free except for a strand to one side bound in blue grey silk braid and marcelled at the tips, worn with a blue grey Corine Bricaire layered ensemble that repeats the same texture contrasts, and silvery grey-blue eyeshadow that picks up the wash on the hair! Imagine a short roll of hair just above the forehead, bound in silversmith's wire, worn with a silvery camisole, pearlised eyeshadow and a tan. Imagine a chignon of hair looped around the head like swirls of honey, silk braid woven through the hairline all the way around, matching the colours and shape of a slouchy, stripy Sonia Rykiel cardigan. Imagine a marcelled square finge bob and a long cream evening dress, five of Molton Brown's 'magic circles' in scarlet silk worn just over the forehead, three cream circles worn as chokers repeating the theme, a cream and a scarlet circle worn high on the arm, a cream and scarlet circle on one wrist, and a scarlet circle round the ankle. Imagine yourself *beautiful*! When this spring's collections were shown in Paris, the model's hair tied with pompoms created an enormous stir—but Michael had begun to refine his total styles seasons before. Don't miss Molton Brown—the salon that's creating a *new dimension of fashion*!

## Special Notes

Upstairs at Molton Brown, the newly extended wholefood restaurant, with a pleasant summer garden atmosphere and the best quiches in town. Downstairs at Molton Brown, a small boutique with all the Molton Brown products—rosemary and canomile shampoo, conditioning hair cream and rinse, and the super seaweed setting lotion, with anti-static properties that will keep your summer plaits and chignons sleek. The products are available singly or in delightful fabric purses, pouches, rolls and bags.

Sample range and approximate prices:

**Molton Brown products:** camomile shampoo and rosemary shampoo, from £1.10; seaweed setting lotion from £1.20; conditioning hair cream, £1.75; conditioning hair rinse, £1.40; elm and lemon hand-care, from 95p; aromatic hair oil, £1.20. **Hair:** Michael, cut £8 and set £7; creative director, cut £7 and set £6; top stylists, cut £6 and set £5; senior stylists, cut £5 and set £4; stylists, cut £4 and set £3.50; tinting from £9; highlights from £27 for whole head; henna treatment from £12.50; perms from £15.50; trichology from £4 for Molton Brown treatment and from £10 for a course of 3 treatments. **Men's salon** cut and shampoo from £6.50; blow-dry from £3.50

## Smile (Men and Women) 15 Brompton Road, SW3
01-589 8355/8334
Mon.-Fri. 9.30-6.30, Sat. 9.30-12.30

Variety is the spice of life at Smile, where you can treat yourself to a feast of looks and colours in a salon done up like a Deco brasserie. It's a wonderful place for people-watching, because Smile have the most imaginatively dressed stylists and widest repertoire of hair styles in London, with a clientele to match. The house philosophy is 'anything goes as long as it's well cut', and it's an ideal salon for people who *enjoy* being themselves. You can have everything from Hollywood glamour and *avant-garde* crops to a simple half-inch-off-the-ends. Pop stars, producers, actors, teachers, secretaries, the old and the young all come here for looks that suit their tastes and lifestyles perfectly. The open plan decor, large windows and relaxed friendly ambience are a world away from the claustrophobic atmosphere of many London salons, and although Smile have an international reputation for stunningly original high fashion styles, you will never be intimidated or pressured into a look you don't want. Visits begin with an exceptionally good wash using Smile's own detergent-free preparations—*the best shampoos in town*. If you want a completely new image, book yourself in for one of Keith's striking creations or one of Leslie's extravagantly feminine styles. You can have subtle sets of highlights, soft perms, henna and conditioning treatments, special occasion styles with hair slides and combs, elaborate chignons, asymmetric sweeps, shaggy cuts, sexily uncontrived natural looks and all the very latest hair fashion trends. Nothing is too much trouble, and you'll be showered with good advice like 'centre partings are almost always unflattering', 'cream rinses only untangle the hair, they don't strengthen it like conditioners' and 'when you wash your hair, concentrate more on rinsing than on working up the lather'. Be sure to buy enough Smile shampoo and conditioner to last till your next visit. You're bound to be back soon because the salon is a fascinating part of the London scene, a pulse point for all the newest looks and feelings. Visits are as exciting as they are enjoyable, and you'll walk out looking and feeling great—just like you do when you smile.

Sample range—all prices approximate:

**Women:** cutting and drying, £7.05; cutting and drying with Leslie and Keith, £8.50. **Men:** cutting and drying, £6.25; cutting and drying with Keith and Leslie, £7.65. Permanent Wave, £13.05. Highlights, whole head, £23.65 and £14.45 half head. Tinting, £10.80. Manicure, £1.50. Bottle of special shampoo, detergent-free, 85p. **Absolutely the best shampoos in town.**

---

## Strands (Men and Women) 62 Duke Street, W1
01-629 5169/5622
First and last appointments: Mon.-Wed. & Sat. 9-4.30, Thurs. & Fri. 9-5.30
(Access, American Express, Barclaycard, Mastercharge)

---

Strands by Strands are as rich as pure silk—soft and shiny, rippling with colour, cascading into curls at the slightest shake of the head. It's the limpid look without the limpness of old-fashioned precision cutting—a buoyant feeling for shapes instead of edges, for soft curls and long upsweeps that turn nature into art. As fashion leaves jeans, T-shirts and the starkly natural look behind, Strands is the place to find styles that go with satin frocks, velvet cloaks, fascinating scents—all the little things that show you know you're someone special. 'C' is the key to the salon's approach—exciting combinations of cut, colour and condition, constructive use of hair textures, creative styles that change into day or evening looks with the flick of a comb. For special occasions, try the elegant asymmetric upsweeps finished off with gentle steam crimping, or the graceful twists that loop back on themselve like poured honey. Strands treat hair as working capital in the beauty bank, and you won't get any asset-stripping back-combing, burning or bleaching. Here your good looks start with you—your bone structure, your life style and your hair—seen *before* a shampoo. Strands use graduated cutting and soft perms to give subtle lifts and shapes to every hair type from flyaway to heavy, and add another dimension with their exclusive La Maur conditioning preparation. Try the moisturising bone marrow treatments for dry hair, the gamma quotient for bleached and overprocessed hair, or the marvellous multi-purpose organicure. Colour is used the way cosmetics should be, for shaping and gentle high-lighting—no flattening matte colour washes or distracting carnival shades. And beauty doesn't have to stop at the hairline, because you can go on to choose pure cosmetics from the La Maur collection. When you go to Strands you know you'll come out looking lovely, and it's no accident that

313

they have lots of London's top models as regular clients. Downstairs in the men's salon, you can lounge on soft leather sofas, browse through piles of magazines and look forward to **the best men's cuts in town.** Come here for styles that make the most of the texture and movement in your hair, bringing out all your natural assets. You don't leave Strands looking like you've just been to the barber, and because the styles are completely natural, you can leave your locks to take care of themselves. As the icing on the cake, Strands are particularly good at shaping sideboards, trimming beards and dealing with thinning hair.

Sample range—all prices approximate:

**For men:** cut and blow dry, £4.30. **For women:** cut and blow dry, perm, £15; full head of highlights, £18. **Special preparations:** Bone Marrow treatment, £2.50; conditioner, £2.75; Apple Pectin Shampoo, £1.40; Organicure general skin treatment for skin, scalp and hair, £1.75; all by La Maur.

# BEAUTIFUL PEOPLE
PLACES

**Elizabeth Arden**  20 New Bond Street, W1   01-629 1200
Mon.-Fri. 9-6, Sat. 9.30-12.30
By appointment to Her Majesty the Queen, suppliers of cosmetics
By apppointment to Her Majesty Queen Elizabeth the Queen Mother,
suppliers of cosmetics

Miss Arden built an empire by putting ladies in the pink and
keeping them there, and the London salon has always been a
favourite with connoisseurs of beauty. Many of the techniques
were devised by Miss Arden herself, but there's nothing
old-fashioned about the treatments. Miss Arden was the originator
of the health-and-beauty approach to good looks, and the new
keep-fit regimes that are being introduced in other salons have
been part of the Arden method since the Twenties. Salads were
simply *not* fashionable until they were served at the Arden Maine
Chance health farm. Miss Arden had an unrivalled genius for
knowing how to bring out the best in her clients, and apart from
health and grooming there was a third factor in her method that
is possibly the most important of all—*complete relaxation.* When
you enter the red doors of the salon you are leaving the world
behind, and nothing will intrude on your privacy for the duration
of your visit. Today, when there are more pressures and stresses
than ever before, Arden is the only salon that understands the
importance of being easy. The famous Arden facials are nothing
less than sheer bliss. Everything is gentle, hushed and calm, and
the treatments are given in individual treatment rooms on the
most comfortable contoured couches in the world. The
movements were devised by Miss Arden and are administered by
the best hands in the business. At the end of an hour you are
relaxed from head to toe, completely revived and glowing with
well-being. No aspect of beauty is overlooked at Arden—there are
two hair salons, Vibro therapy treatments, Ardena wax baths,
Slendertone treatments, wax manicures, a new depilation
treatment to remove unwanted hair, chiropody, eyelash-tinting,
pedicures, steam cabinets, makeup lessons and a splendid new
solarium for Ultra-violet and Infra-red treatments. The infra-red
treatment with body massage will soothe all your cares away, the
Ultra-violet treatments will help you build up a stunning tan
gradually. You can spend the whole day at Arden and lots of
ladies do, booking themselves in to a Top-to-Toe treatment or
Maine Chance Day. The best investment for the future is an

investment in yourself, so start here at Arden—its the best salon in town.

Sample range and prices:

Facials from £6.50; special make-up and instruction from £6.75; body massage for 50 min., £7; Top-to-Toe treatment includes restyled hair, shampoo and set or blow dry, a face treatment make-up, facemask and massage with cream-manicure, and body massage, all for £23. Other prices and details of treatments available on application.

---

# Beauty Without Cruelty 40-41 Marylebone High Street, W1  01-486 2845
Mon.-Fri. 10-5, Sat. By appointment only

---

*Il faut suffrir pour être belle*—but you're not the one who's suffering. Thousands of wild and domestic creatures are sacrificed to the beauty industry every year—and some species, like the Himalayan musk deer, have been pushed to the brink of extinction. If you can't face the reflection in your makeup mirror, then hurry along to *Beauty Without Cruelty*. This unique organization is devoted to providing a *positive* alternative to the choice between ethics and elegance. Everything in their collection comes with their guarantee, 'No animal has suffered to provide these natural cosmetics for you'—preparations are made from pure oils and extracts from herbs, vegetables and flowers, and when they test their products, they test them on *themselves*. The makeup collection has five powder eyeshadows and an excellent pearlised highlighter—though the range is not as comprehensive as that of a large cosmetic house, there are plans for new fashion colours, eye pencils and mascara. There are four blushers, four shades of foundation, an exceptionally fine Avocado Satin Lotion moisturiser and a fine delicate perfume called 'Amaranth'—the mythical flower of perfect beauty that never faded or died. The shampoos come in marvellous mixtures like Lotus Flower and Almond oil, and the soaps are the purest in the world. Beauty Without Cruelty are constantly expanding their range so you won't have to settle for second best looks, and clients have included Celia Hammond and Marie Helvin, two of the most beautiful models to have graced the glossies. This is one place where beauty is more than skin deep. Price list and retail order form available on request from address above.

Sample range and approximate prices:

Face powder, 72p; lipstick, 67p; eyeshadow, 44p; highlighter, 47p; blusher, 44p; foundation cream in tube, £1.02; foundation lotion, 72p; Amaranth perfume purse vial 6cc, £1.80 and 14cc bottle, £4.30; Cucumber cleansing milk, 90p; rose petal skin freshener, £1.03; Avocado Satin Lotion moisturiser, £1.38; shampoos in 155cc botles, 59p.

## Cadogan Club 182 Sloane Street, SW1
01-235 3814/5
Mon.-Fri. 9-5, Sat. 9-12

The most *sophistiqué* of the salons, the Cadogan Club specialise in beautifying treatments de luxe—the unabashedly hedonistic sort that give Continental women their superbly feline gloss and Continental men their cool confidence. None of the little details are omitted, and some of the treatments make the techniques of other salons look positively primitive. The unique Juliette treatment involves the application of tiny fibres to the nails to make them stronger, and there are different massages for toning, relaxing and slimming. All the skin-care and make-up preparations are by Guerlain, the aristocrats of the beauty world, and the luxurious hour-long facials are so popular that you should count on having to book your appointment in advance. The facials begin with a thorough cleansing and toning using different combinations of emulsions and lotions to suit your skin type. Next comes a half-hour massage using the special Guerlain movements, a steaming to remove impurities and a relaxing interval under one of the refreshing Guerlain masks which wash off gently with warm water and temporarily smooth away the fine tension lines. After a final tone, a moisture base, perhaps the new Protective Moisture Base for Dry Skin or the mousse-like creme Secret de Bonne Femme. A complete and totally sybaritic treatment for tired, city skins—both male and female. For ladies, the facial continues with an elegant make-up. Guerlain have exceptionally delicate foundations that give every skin a young flawless look—new this summer their fine colour film, Ultra

Sport, gives the best soft glowing looks under the sun, and last winter all the smartest ladies were using their silky Elysemat. You can purchase all the Guerlain preparations in the salon, so look out for their superb revitalizers Ambrosia Emulsion and Collagena to care for ageing skins, which they advise to begin at 25. Whatever you choose, don't forget Guerlain's Creme Pour le Cou, it's quite simply the best neck creme in the world.

Sample range—all prices approximate:

Facial treatments, 1 hour, from £7; Body Massage from £7; with José or Orita; all other prices on application.

---

## Cosmetics a la Carte 16 Motcomb Street, SW1
01-235 0596
Mon.-Fri. 10-5.30, Wed. 10-7 ★

---

Join London's top models and makeup artists, who come here for **carte blanche beauty**—makeup for your looks and life, **made to order!** At Cosmetics a la Carte, Christina Stewart and Lynne Battley have the most dazzling cosmetics in London—**real fashion makeup.** Everything is made on the premises, and you won't find such superb quality, choice and imagination in any mass-manufactured range. There are seventy-seven lipsticks, a **hundred** eye colours, foundation in eleven basic shades from cream to olive that can be blended to match any skin tone while you wait, and that's just for starters. The lip glosees are almost legendary—they're shiny, non-oily, and they stay in place all the way through a meal. The cream rouges come in shades like Mandarin—marvellous with tweeds, Claret—a warm feminine rose, perfect for the Gigi look, and Nutmeg—**a true shadow that shades the face without leaving any telltale colour behind!** There are six powder blushers, including Flame, Coral and Cerise—**clear** colours that set off dark skins and summer suntans beautifully, and Dusky—a blend of golden pearl and golden brown, the model girls favourite. Their eye colours are creamy powders that blend beautifully, can be applied damp or dry, never go into lines—and last! Three basic palettes are covered with irresistable shades like teal, smoke, mint, amethyst and bright gold, really good mauves which are impossible to find anywhere else, and a real charcoal black—indispensable for the

319

exotic eastern look. There's a fourth spectacular palette of pure primary pigments—scarlet, turqoise, violet and ten others—that top professional makeup artists use to get high fashion colour effects. You can forget about diamonds— the best way to put some sparkle in your life is with Cosmetics a la Carte's **fabulous collection of dazzlers.** For very subtle effects, try **interference pearl** in blue, red or green—it looks like white powder in the bottle, but changes on the skin into the palest of tinted shimmers. The **sparkles** are fine powders that leave a clear colour overlaid with delicate sparkle, available in six shades including an exceptionally gorgeous green. Best of all, there's **stardust**—like pinpoint sequins—in silver and gold. Brush it on your cheeks, arms and shoulders, sprinkle it on your hair—and twinkle like the star you are. On top of all that—**if you're looking for something that isn't in their range, they'll make it specially to order!** Cosmetics a la Carte have a fine skin and body care collection as well. Look out for the new delicately scented bath oil, body lotion and oil, and the very special matte miracle—an anti-shine preparation, soothing and gentle, that you can use on the centre panel of the face under makeup. It really does keep the shine off, and its another models favourite. The salon is relaxed and delightfully friendly—the cosmetics are displayed on palettes so you can stroll in and try them, and they are very free with samples and advice. Every woman can find her own look here, but if you want to make the most of yourself, have one of their makeup lessons. Everything about their approach is positive—they teach you emphasize your good features, teach you how to apply your makeup to model standard, and send you off with your own beauty chart. They also create special makeups for parties, photography, shows and weddings. Another feature of the salon are Judy Nunn's deep cleansing and vitamin E facial treatments that do wonderful things for the skin, body massage by hand, waxing and eyebrow shaping and tinting. There's no place like it anywhere in the world—here's to a beautiful you!


Special note: if you live outside London, you'll appreciate their mail-order service and the newsletters they send out to keep clients up-to-date with new beauty trends and colours. Write for particulars.

Sample range and approximate prices:

## Cosmetics

Powder eyeshadow and highlighters, £1.50; skin tint foundation, standard or blended colours, £3.50/30 grams; Powder rouge, £4; cream rouge £3; lip glosses in compacts, eight shades, £3; lipsticks, £2; translucent powder in a box or compact, £3.50; matte miracle, £2.50; concealing stick, £2.50; makeup sponges, 50p; sable make-up brushes, £2; eye pencils, £1.50; rouge mops, £2.50; cream tint foundation for photographic and special cover, £3.50/17 grams compact.

## Skin Care and Cleansing

Skin nourisher cream with vitamin E, £5; skin soother, £5; vitamin E concentrate, £10; moisturising skin reviver, £5; overall moisture lotion, £4.50; cleansing cream from £3; cleansing lotion from

£2.25; cucumber refresher and birch camomile toner fom £2; dry skin mask with vitamin E and regfining mask, £3; eye balm, £3.50; overnight blemish lotion, £3.50; herb shampoo, £2; conditioning shampoo, £2; bath oil, £8; body lotion, £6; body oil, £6; sun lotion, £6; tan oil, £4; moisture lotion and UV filter, £3.

## Treatments

Half-hour cleanse and make-up, £5; personal makeup design, £6; skin care and makeup lesson, 1½, hours, £10; vitamin E and deep cleansing facials, 1 hour, £8; pre-makeup facial, ½ hour, £4; eyelash tinting, £4; eyebrow tinting, £2; eyebrow shaping from £2; cold wax depilation from £1 for lip or chin to £10 for full leg; oil bleaching, from £1.50 for lip to £4 for half leg; half hour manicure, £2.50; pedicure, £5; full body massage, 1 hour, £8; back and neck massage, ½ hour, £4.

# Dona Alda at Medina  10 West Halkin Street, SW1
01-235 7179
Mon.-Fri. 10-6, Sat. 10-4

Dona Alda's beauty and body oils are exactly what you need for the dynamic good looks of the Seventies. Beauty today means lithe movement, supple bodies, shining skins—a vital new approach to living. Dance and body rhythmics have replaced steam cabinets and wax baths, tight girdles and taut faces held in place with surgical pins are **passé**. Now beauty comes from within, helped by exercise and the pleasant exertions of massage and body care, with fine natural oils and essences. Marisa

Fleischa's fabulous Dona Alda preparations are based on the finest lightest unsaturated oils—good things like avocado, apricot, sesame and almond—that penetrate the skin quickly, preserve the important oil/acid balance and never leave a greasy, heavy feeling. Hand-blended like fine perfumes, the base oils are enhanced with absolutes, citrus oils, essential oils like Bulgarian rose, Clary sage, jasmine, lavender and sandlewood—all pure and fresh. The natural properties of the ingredients are used to good effect—lemon grass and lavender are ideal for troubled skins, mandarin and orange blossom neroli petals or almond and apricot are excellent for very dry skins, sea-plant extract cools and tones the skin while greasy skins benefit from sage, violet leaves and lemon. **These natural oils are far better for your skin and your looks than any water-based moisturiser or synthetic cream.** Dona Alda have a whole range of preparations, and simple treatments you can do yourself. The method of application is as important as the oils themselves—the movements must be as positive and smooth as those of a dancer, the pressure firm but gentle, the movements always circular and upward, giving a **natural lift** to the skin and muscles. You can turn a simple bath into an excellent beauty treatment with Dona Alda's bath oil in four delightful fragrances—floral, citrus, herbal and woody. Use a gentle body brush or a natural sponge, and scrub upwards from the ankles to the collarbones. The movement stimulates circulation and removes dead skin cells as well as surface dirt, and stimulates the growth of new cells, so your skin looks smoother and younger. Used in the same way, even the richest soaps dry the skin. If you prefer showers, it is particularly important to rub the oils upwards, to counteract the downward pull of the shower spray on the skin. After the bath, do not apply talc, as it clogs the pores and makes the skin look matte and old. Instead, dry briskly with a towel and apply Dona Alda body oil in the same upward, circular motions while you are still warm from the bath. Wrap yourself in the towel for two or three minutes; by then the oil will have been absorbed. Besides being excellent for the skin, the process involves the muscles in a gentle natural exercise that is far better for your looks than any beauty mask. Before bed, apply Dona Alda eye oil, lightest of the preparations. It keeps the skin around the eyes from getting papery, and eases wrinkles. The movements should be very delicate, and should not drag or pull on the skin—you'll find it's a super way to remove tension. The eye oil can also be worn under makeup—a perfect base for today's fresh, free and easy beauty. The shop has the complete

Dona Alda range, including sun oil, hand cream, oils for men, the lovely new Marisa perfumes and a superb nail treatment—a blend of essential oils that really do work wonders for problem nails. If you want to be one of the new beauties, come to Dona Alda and let nature take its course.

Sample range—all prices approximate:

**Dona Alda preparations:** cleansing oil, £1.25; face oil, £3; bath oil, £2.30; body oil, £2.95; eye oil, £1.50; nail oil, 90p; Marisa perfumes, £3.75-£8; hair oil, £2.50; lip glosses, £1.75.

---

## Molton Brown  58 South Molton Street, W1
01-493 6959/6629/1872
Mon.-Wed. 10-5, Thurs.-Fri. 9-5.30, Sat. 9-12

---

This is the place to come for easy, breezy beauty—good looks with the light touch and fresh unfussy feeling that's so unmistakably Molton Brown. In fashion terms, this is the most exciting of the London salons because it's part of that top-to-toe, inside-outside total Browns life style. The emphasis is on the completely open, essentially natural look—and the Beauty Room reflects this perfectly. Instead of darkened treatment rooms and closed doors, there are fresh fabric screens, lots of light everywhere, and no little artificial rituals. Because hair and beauty are inseparable, the Beauty room has purposely not been completely isolated from the rest of the salon. You're very much a part of what's happening, and you won't easily fall into the trap of thinking of your looks in parts instead of wholes. It's the most natural thing in the world to go down to have your hair done after a facial, or to come up for a facial after a cut—which is what style is all about. The hour-long facials include eyebrow trimming, deep vapozone cleansing, facial massage, mask and skin toning with Payot or Germaine Monteil preparations. Both lines are light and unfussy, with no over-rich creams or harsh toners. The Monteil treatment includes an exceptionally fine rose skin cream that will keep you fresh as a rose for the rest of the day. This is the place to learn about how to match your haircut with your makeup, how to make the most of your makeup when you vary your hairstyle, how to use powder highlighter to accentuate the highlights in your hair. You can have eyelash and eyebrow dyeing treatments, waxes, massage, manicures, pedicures, a complete top-to-toe treatment and finish up with lunch in the Molton Brown restaurant. Good looks have never been so easy!

Sample range and prices:

Facials £6, and a course of six, £30; cleansing and makeup, £3.75; special makeup, £5.50; body massage £6; lip wax, £1.75; full leg wax, £10; eye and brow dyeing, £6.50 together.

---

# Helena Rubinstein at Harvey Nichols, Knightsbridge, SW1
01-235 5000
Mon.-Sat. 9.30-6, Wed. 9.30-7

---

Up at the top of Harvey Nichols, a newly expanded beauty department offers a solarium, massage and Helena Rubinstein facials using the Skin Life and Bio Clear ranges. The facials last an hour, and afterwards you can go to the Helena Rubinstein counter on the ground floor and treat yourself to the new 'Grecian Earthen Look' for Spring. There are thirty-two new lip colours with matching nail colours, bronze and shimmer tones for cheeks and eyes, to use with the fabulous Rubinstein blusher collection of creams, frosts and sheers—eighteen shades in all, that help you to redesign your face. Top makeup artist Anthony Clavet has devised special make-ups for every face shape and skin tone, and there are special booklets on the counter you can flip through to find your look. There will be another fashion colour collection in Summer, and two new sun preparations, so drop in often and keep up with the exciting new Rubinstein face fashions.

---

# Sanctuary at the Dance Centre 12 Floral Street, WC2
01-836 6544
Mon.-Sat. 10-7

---

If you're fleeing from grim reality, seek sanctuary here. A cross between a Moorish harem and the tropical plant house at Kew, with a dash of Hollywood glamour in the style of Dorothy Lamour, this opulent establishment is a lotus eaters paradise. Lagoons filled with lilies, lap at islands draped with orchids and dripping with vines, little bridges lead to brilliant macaws and parrots perched amid the foliage, divans line the walls. The Sanctuary is part club, part salon, and for ladies only. For £5 a time you can swim all day in a pool with a switch-on waterfall, take saunas, bask in the solarium where infra-red and ultra-violet treatments are laid on, or laze on the couches reading the daily papers and current magazines—all in the nude, if you like. Soap, shampoo and conditioner by Crabtree & Evelyn, towels, lockers, and use of hairdryers and swimsuits are included in the price. There's a vegetarian restaurant serving wholesome hot and cold dishes, fruit juices and homebaked wholemeal breads—not included in the £5. The salon treatments are also extra. They include massage, slimming treatments, pedicures, manicures and facials using Lancome and Orlane preparations. It is not possible to arrange to come just for the treatments. The Sanctuary is one of the wonders of London, a sight not to be missed. If you're getting over an affair, planning one, bored, stale or in need of a holiday, a day spent here will be just the tonic you need.

Sample range—all prices approximate:

**Entrance to club:** £5 per visit, or £40 for 10 visits, £75 for 25 visits and £100 for 50 visits.

**Treatments:** massage, 45 minutes, £4.50; facials, £5.50; pedicure, £2.80; manicure, £1.60.

# DESIGNER'S
# STOCKISTS

## Sheridan Barnett, Shelagh Brown
Office: 15 Macklin Street, London WC2   01-405 2335

### London

Elle, All branches
Crocodile, All branches
Bombacha, Fulham Road
Roxy, Kensington Church Street
Bellville Sassoon, Pavillion Road

### Abroad

Puch & Hans, Amsterdam,
  Rotterdam, The Hague
Lord & Taylor, New York,
  U.S.A.
Zebra, Antwerp, Belgium

## Andrea Burrow   Office: 57 Kenley Road, St. Margarets, Twickenham, Middlesex   01-891 2527

## Browns Studio

### London

Browns Men, 23 South Molton
  Street, W1

### Out of London

Brighton, Cobley's Gog Shop, 33
  Duke Street
Cambridge, Joshua Taylor, Sidney
  Street
Manchester, Manolo's, 13 Old
  Bank Street, St. Anne's Square

### Abroad

**America**
Jerry Magnin, 323 North Rodeo
  Drive, Beverley Hills, California
Maxfield Blue, 9091 Santa Monica
Boulevard, Los Angeles,
  California
**Browns Shop** in Joseph Magnin,
  59 Harrison, San Francisco,
  California
Ultimo, 114 E. Oak Street,
  Chicago, Illinois
Barney's, New York City, New
  York
**Browns Shop** in B. Altman, 5th
  Avenue & 34th Street, New
  York City, New York
Neiman Marcus, Dallas, Texas
Neiman Marcus, Houston, Texas
Britches, 1321 Leslie Avenue,
  Alexandria, Virginia
Butch Blum, 1408 5th Avenue,
  Seattle, Washington

**Australia**
Oliver Plunkett, Jackson Street,
  Turak, Melbourne

ldiz Alexander, King Street,
   Sydney

**ance**

arcel Lassance, Société Daubel,
   17 rue des Vieux-Colombier, 6ᵉ,
   Paris

alerie Point Show, 66 Champs
   Élysées, 8ᵉ, Paris

J.B., 40 rue de la Charité,
   Lyons

eranda, 73 rue de Béthune,
   Lyons

**Italy**

Basile,    Via Solferino, Milan

Top Ten, 2 Via Soleri, Turin

**Netherlands**

Society Shop, 25 Binderij,
   Amsterdam

**Sweden**

Margot Man, Harrington 10,
   Stockholm

**Switzerland**

Zunfthaus Z, Meisen, Zurich

---

**harmian**  Office: Charmian Designs Ltd., 247 Regent Street,
ondon W1   01-408 1855

---

**ondon**

sablanca, 35 Brook Street, W1

sablanca, 9 Hampstead High
   Street, NW3

net Wilson, 11 Beauchamp
   Place, SW3

bell, 44 Baker Street, W1

cienne Phillips, 89
   Knightsbridge, SW1

**Abroad**

**America**

Poir Moir, 1181 Second Avenue,
   New York

**Australia**

Goullet, 51 Bridge Road,
   Richmond, Victoria

---

**ordon L. Clarke**  Office: Medina, 26-29 Maunsel Street,
ondon SW1   01-828 2191

---

**ondon**

edina, 10 West Halkin Street,
   London SW1

athers, 40 Hans Crescent,
   Knightsbridge, London SW1

rrods, Hans Crescent,
   Knightsbridge, London SW1

Harvey Nicholls, Knightsbridge,
   London SW1

Lucienne Phillips, 89
   Knightsbridge, London SW1

Simpsons, Piccadilly, London W1

## Out of London

Darling, 15 Northumberland
    Place, Bath, Avon
Emma Somerset, 9 Stevenson
    Square, Manchester
Harpers, 11 The Promenade,
    Station Road, Edgeware,
    Middlesex
June Daybell, 21 The Promenade,
    Cheltenham, Gloucestershire

## Abroad

**America**
Apropos 1415B East McFadden
    Avenue, Santa Anna, California
    92706
Niemann Marcus, Dallas, Texas

Saks, Fifth Avenue, New York

**France**
Best Seller, 52 Avenue Chausée
    d'Antin, 75009, Paris
Daniel Ho, Societé d'Exploration
    Daniel Ho, 54 Rue de Rennes,
    75006, Paris
Sandra Boutique, 84 Avenue des
    Champs Elysées, 75008, Paris
Adonis, Le Bahia, Avenue
    Princess Grace, Monte Carlo
Perry, 3 Place Esquirel, Toulous

**Germany**
Horn Textil, Neuer Wall, 31-35,
    Hamburg, 36

**Italy**
Galtrucco Lorenzo, Via San
    Gregorio, 29 Milano
Alexander, Rome

# Wendy Dagworthy Limited  43 Berwick Street, (2nd floor), London W1V 3RE    01-437 6105

## London

Bombacha, 104 Fulham Road,
    SW7
Crocodile, All branches
Elle, All branches
Feathers, 40 Hans Crescent, SW1
Parkers, 31 Brook Street, W1
Roxy, 25 Kensington Church
    Street, W8
**Mens Wear**
Adam Owen, 13 Chiltern Street,
    W1
Barnaby's, 18 Kensington Church
    Street, W8
Ebony, 45 South Molton Street,
    W1

Feathers, 40 Hans Crescent, SW
Howie, 138 Longacre, WC2
Stanely Adams, 29-30 Kingley
    Street, W1

## Out of London

Cassidys, 23 Thames Street,
    Windsor, Buckinghamshire
The Clothes Shop, 52 Church
    Street, Weybridge
Frocks, 37 Haverlock Street,
    Swindon
Pat Crowley, 14 Duke Street,
    Dublin
Ricci, Stratford House,
    Shakespeare Street,
    Newcastle-Upon-Tyne

Rosy Vyse, 11 Malcolm Arcade,
Leicester
Scotts, As mens
Trio, 26 Chester Street,
Wrexham, North Wales
Zig-Zag, 19 Cheap Street, Bath

**Mens Wear**
Clangers, 2-3 Wyle Cop,
Shrewsbury
Froggetts, 21 North Street,
Brighton
Manolo Designs, 12 Old Bank
Street, Manchester
Scotts, 8 The Promenade,
Cheltenham, Gloucestershire

## Abroad

**America**
Avventura, Box 85 Sun Valley,
Ldaho 83333 Apropos, Santa
Ana, California
Camel's Hump, 28 Boylston

Street, Cambridge, Mass 02138
Kleids British Clothing Co, 171
Faneuil Hall, Market Place,
Boston, Mass 02109
Kenneth & Cooper, 1728
Chestnut Street, Philadelphia,
Pennsylvania 19103
Fosters of Paris, 21730
Independence Avenue,
Southfield, Mich, 48076
Neiman Marcus, Dallas, Texas

**Europe**
Biba, 18 Rue de Sevres, Paris
7506
Kir, Singel 276, Amsterdam,
Holland

**Abroad**
Seibu Department Store Ltd,
Tokyo, Japan
Squire Shops, 409 New South
Head Road, Double Bay,
N.S.W. 2028 Australia
Greatermans, Johannesburg 2000,
South Africa

---

# Ebony   Office: 45 South Molton Street, London W1
01-629 4721/8500

---

# Sarah Fermi   Office: 43 Regent Street, Cambridge CB2 1AE
(0223) 312048

---

## London

Liberty, Regent Street, Night
Owls, Fulham Road, Courtney,
Brook Street

## Abroad

**Netherlands**
Metz Liberty Shop, 'Leidsestraat,
Amsterdam
Metz Liberty Shop, Plaats 13A,
The Hague

## Gina Fratini Office: 2 New Burlington Place, W1
01-439 4074

## London

Chic, 82 Heath Street, NW3
Lucienne Phillips, Knightsbridge,
  SW1

## Bill Gibb Office: 14 Bruton Place, London W1   01-629 5551

## London

Bill Gibb Shop, 138 New Bond
  Street, London W1
Harrods, Knightsbridge, London
  SW1
Harvey Nichols, Knightsbridge,
  London SW1
Lucienne Phillips, 89
  Knightsbridge, London SW1
Chic of Hampstead, 82 Heath
  Street, Hampstead, London
  NW3
Julie Fitzmaurice, 40 Parliament
  Street, Harrogate, Yorks
Joan Ponting, 160 Broad Street,
  Birmingham 15
Penny Lee, 13 Grove Street,
  Wilmslow, Cheshire

## Abroad

Bongenie Geneve, Brunschwig &
  Cie, 34 Rue du Marche, 1211
  Geneve 3, Switzerland

Barbara Ellmauer, Etchika
  Werner, Kurfurstendamm 138,
  100 Berlin, W. Germany
Boutique Au Grenier, Beatengasse
  4, 8001 Zurich, Switzerland
Modehause Helg, Kramerstrasse
  19/21, 5100 Aachen,
  W. Germany
Julius Herpich, 4000 Dusseldorf,
  Ko-Center 30, W. Germany
Claire Pearone, 2771 Somerset
  Mall, Troy, Michigan 48084,
  U.S.A.
I Magnin, through O Ziegler Ltd,
  12 Great Portland Street,
  London W1
Marshall Field & Co, 111 North
  Street, Chicago, Illinois 60690,
  U.S.A.
Maja, 8 Munchen 2,
  Whittelsbacheplats 1,
  EingangBrienerStrasse,
  W. Germany
Zapata, 4000 Dusseldort,
  Konigsalle 21, W. Germany

# Charles Grahame Office: 47b Ridley Road, London E8
1-254 6525

## London

Harrods
Harvey Nichols
Fenwicks
Top Shop
Bourne & Hollingsworth
Dickens & Jones
John Lewis
Le Trousseau
Fenwicks Brent Cross

Kendal Milne, Manchester
Howels, Cardiff
Claydows, Bradford
Jollys, Bath
Rackhams, Birmingham
Finnigans, Wilmslow
Jane Dowson, Blackburn
Bare Essentials, St. Albans
Joshua Taylor, Cambridge
Kathrine Prasey, Birmingham

## Out of London

Stella Nova, Edinburgh
Eva, Rugby
Warwick House, Malvern
Ricemans, Canterbury
Ellis Barker, Chester
Dingles,
 Bournemouth/Bristol/Plymouth

### Abroad

Monopol, Luxembourg
Kaufhoff, Cologne
Nieman Marcus, Dallas
Galeries Lafayette, Paris
Inno BM, Brussels
Steen & Strom, Oslo

# Victor Herbert Office: G. C. Ultimate, 35 Curzon Street,
London W1Y 7AE   01-499 9613. Showroom: 01-491 3320

# George Hostler (knitwear) 45 Belvoir Street,
Leicester   0533 709163

## London

Deborah & Clare, Beauchamp
 Place
Ebony, Sth. Molton Street

Ace, King's Road
Howie, Long Acre
Janet Ibbotson Ltd., Pond Place
Ritva, Hollywood Road
Ronnie Stirling, Bond Street

## Out of London

George Hostler, Belvoir Street, Leicester

Metropolis, Village Square, Leicester

Pauline, Acorn Road, Newcastle upon Tyne

She, Railway Street, Altrincham, Cheshire

## Abroad

### America

Cuzzens of California, 300 Post Street, San Francisco

Cussens of Houston, 2220 Galleria 5015, West Heimer Road, Houston, Texas

Cuzzens of Dallas, 430 Nth. Park Centre, Dallas, Texas

Cuzzens, Caesars Palace, Las Vegas, Nevada

Cuzzens, Las Vegas Hilton Hotel, Las Vegas, Nevada

Frank Leonard M. Corp. Main Street, St. Thomas, Virgin Islands

Jerry Magnin, Beverley Hills, California

Mike Bain Stores, 8483 Sunset Boulevard, Los Angeles

Sakowitz, 2401 Capital, Houston, Texas

Wilkes Bashford, 336 Sutter Street, San Francisco

---

**Paul Howie**   Office: Howie (Clothing) Ltd, 138 Long Acre, London WC2    01-836 3156

---

## London

Howie, 138 Long Acre, London WC2

Bombacha, 104 Fulham Road SW3

Parkers, 31 Brook Street W1

Roxy, 25 Kensington Church Street, London W8

Stanley Adams, Kings Road, London SW3

Joseph, Sth. Molton Street, London W1

## Out of London

Co-Existence, 10 Argylle Street, Bath

Manolo, St. Anns Square, Manchester

Victoria & Albert, Newcastle

## Abroad

### America

Buffalo Weavers, 60th & 2nd, New York, U.S.A.

Henri Bendals, New York, U.S.A.

Saks, Fifth Avenue, New York, U.S.A.

Stone Free, Madison Avenue, New York, U.S.A.

Bloomingdales, New York, U.S.A.

J. & L. Dallas, Texas

### France

Upla, Paris

Island, Paris

Altona, Paris

Brumes, Nice

Cremieux, Paris & St. Tropez

**Italy**
La-Shopping, Parma
Puppasmith, Bologna

**Holland**
Kir, Amsterdam
Gen. Fashion, Rotterdam

**Switzerland**
Galaxy, Zurich
Jet-Set, Zurich & St. Moritz
The Great Blondino Co, Zurich

**Sweden**
Puss & Kran, Stockholm

**Germany**
Hotch Potch, West Berlin
Bazaar, Frankfurt
Yak, Cologne

**France**
Charlie, Rue de la Republique,
    Antibes, France
Gul & Bla, Paris

**Germany**
Burghard's, Sarrazin Str., Berlin
Daily Blues, Marschall Str.,
    Munich
Manfred Roth, Adelungstrasse,
    Darmstadt.

**Sweden**
Gul & Bla, Stockholm, Sweden

**Switzerland**
Gt. Blondino Company,
    Weldmannstrasse, Zurich
Rose, Hertensteinstrasse, Lucerne

---

# Ninevah Khomo   Office: Medina, 26-29 Maunsel Street,
SW1   01-828 2191 Telex: 8814291 Medina AG

---

# Les Lansdown   Office: 178 Upper Street, London N1
01-359 5044

---

## London

Fortnum & Mason
Lucienne Phillips

---

# Mulberry Company   Office: 4a Ladbroke Gardens,
London W11   01-727 7500

---

## London

Harvey Nichols
Harrods
Jap and Joseph shops
Liberty, Regent Street

Selfridges
Elle shops
Bombacha
Peter Jones
John Lewis

335

## Out of London

Zig Zag, Bath
June Daybell, Cheltenham
Julie Fitzmaurice, Harrogate
Cog shop and Cobley's Cog shop,
  Brighton
His and Hers of Derby
Penny Lee, Wallmslow
Marcus Price, Newcastle

## Abroad

Marcel Lassance, Paris

Upla, Paris
Bob Shop, Paris
Tilbury, Paris
Lo Shopping, Parma, Italy
Biffi, Milan
Neiman Marcus, America
Bloomingdales
Bergdorf Goodman
Saks 5th Avenue
Stewart Ross, New York
Right Bank Clothing
Maxfield Blue, L.A.
Charles Gallay, L.A.
Shiseido, Japan
and everywhere else in selected
  shops

---

**Danny Noble**  Office: 9 Hampstead High Street, London
NW3   01-435 3982

---

**Richard Nott**  for Peter Barron, 40 Clipstone Street, London
W1

---

## London

Harrods, Knightsbridge, SW1
Harvey Nichols, Knightsbridge,
  SW1
Dickins & Jones, Regent Street,
  W1
Selfridges, Oxford Street, W1
D. H. Evans, Oxford Street, W1
John Barker, Kensington High
  Street, W8

## Abroad

**Port Said**
El Shaboury

**Tokyo**
Shulatex

**Athens**
Louise

**Nassau**
Caprice

**Lucerne**
Tricot

**Tripoli**
Warfelli

**Oporto**
Tapatha

**Utrecht**
Pommeterie

## Jaime Ortega

**Jaime Ortega** Office: 34a Goldsborough Road, London SW8 4RR 01-622 9282

## Out of London

Daphne and Jane, Clistonville, Kent

**Susie Owen** Office: 38 Saint Mary Street, Cardiff *Cardiff* (0222) 22959/30072

**Carol Payne** (designs for children). Office: Salt of the Earth Ltd, Kings Acre, Luxulyan, Bodmin, Cornwall Stenalees (0726) 850 820

# Zandra Rhodes

## London

Zandra Rhodes, 14a Grafton Street, W1

Zandra Rhodes Shop in Harrods, Knightsbridge, SW1

## Abroad

**America**

Zandra Rhodes Shop in Marshall Field, Watertower Place, 835 N. Michigan Avenue, Illinois, Chicago

Zandra Rhodes Shop in Marshall Field, 111 North State Street, Illinois, Chicago

Zandra Rhodes Shop in Bloomingdales, 1000 3rd Avenue, New York City, New York

## Paul Smith
Office: 10 Byard Lane, Nottingham, England   (0602) 48105   Telex 377231 ATTN Paul Smith

### London

Adam Owen
Les 2 Zebras
Quincy
Barnaby
Stanley Adams
Ebony

### Out of London

Paul Smith, Nottingham
Gog shop, Brighton
Manolo, Manchester
Marcus Price, Newcastle
Joshua Taylor, Cambridge

L'Homme, Bournemouth
Zig Zag, Bath

### Abroad

Marcel Lassance, Paris
Habitude, Nice
Gul & Bla, Stockholm
Hannes B, Zurich
Barneys, New York
Wilkes Bashford, San Francisco
Jerry Magnin, Los Angeles
Eric Ross, Beverley Hills
Canterbury Tales, Alexandria
Goods Dept, Store, Cambridge, Mass
Dinghy, Miami

## Take 6 International
19 Woodfield Road, London W9 2BA   01-289 1771   Telex 8812026 Takesix

## Pauline Wynne Jones
Office: Halkyn Hall, Pentre Halkyn, Clwyd, Ch8 8HR North Wales   Halkyn 609 from London 0352-88-609

### London

Lucienne Phillips, London
Harrods, London
Chic of Hampstead, London
Shirley Leonard, London
Rolli, London
Crocodile, London
Johnson, London
Ib Jorgenson, London

### Abroad

**Eire**
Ib Jorgenson, Dublin

**America**
Saks, New York
Hirshleifer's, New York
Helga Howie, San Francisco
Gunn Trigere, Beverley Hills
Arthur Roberts, Illinois

338

# RIGHTS AND WRONGS

*A look at which is which, and what to do about it\**

## For the customer

In civil law, your rights as an individual are covered by the Sale of Goods Act 1893—as amended by the Supply of Goods (Implied Terms) Act 1973.

As a customer, the law assumes that you have certain 'implied' rights whenever you make a purchase. These rights are:

1. *That the goods are of merchantable quality.* This means that the goods must be in working order, and neither damaged nor broken. A handbag with a broken clasp or an umbrella that does not open properly is not of merchantable quality.
2. *That the goods are as described.* In other words, a pair of gloves labeled 'size 5' should be that size, and a box labeled 'three handkerchiefs—blue' should contain exactly that.
3. *That the goods should be fit for their purpose.* This refers to a situation in which you specify the requirements of the article you intend to purchase. For example, if you ask for a pair of 'waterproof boots' and are then sold a pair that let in water the first time you wear them, the goods were not fit for the purpose you specified at the time of purchase.

When you buy something from a shop you and the shop enter into a legally binding contract, and as soon as the shop accepts your payment they—and not the manufacturer—accept the responsibility of meeting the conditions of your implied rights. You should make every effort to examine the goods before you make a purchase, but if you do, and discover afterwards that the goods are faulty in any of the above respects, then *the shop is in the wrong*.

## What to do about it

Return the goods to the shop at once—*you are entitled to a refund of the purchase price*. The shop may claim that the responsibility for faulty goods lies with the manufacturer, but under the law cited above it is the shop's responsibility to supply you with satisfactory goods—they can take up their claim against the manufacturer later. *You are not obliged to accept a credit note.* If the shop offers you an exchange or repair you may accept it—but if you do, you will probably be waiving your right to a cash refund under the act cited above.

*This guide to your rights should not be taken as a final and authoritative statement of the law. In the event of difficulties, contact your local Citizen

Advice Bureau, or Consumer Advice Centre, listed in the phone book under your local authority.

## SALES AND MARKED-DOWN GOODS

Under the Trades Description Act 1968, it is a criminal offence for a shop to display a tag like this:

unless the article has been on sale at the original price for at least 28 consecutive days in the preceding six months. If it has *not* been, the shop ought to affix a ticket saying 'last week's price £17, this week's price £9'. Normally, you as a customer would assume that the article on sale was of the usual quality you associate with the shop. Unless the goods are labeled 'soiled', 'imperfect', 'bargain purchase', 'special purchase' or any other phrase that implies 'defective goods', you have the same rights as above—whether or not it was purchased in a sale.

# OUT OF LONDON ADDRESSES AND INDEXES

## Bally shops and Bally outlets
### Abroad

America, Bally, 711 Fifth Avenue, New York

America, Bally, 340 No. Rodeo Drive, Beverly Hills, California

France, Bally Capucines/Scribe, 35 Boulevard des Capucines, Paris

Guam, Caronel, Tumon Sands Plaza, **AGANA**/Guam, U.S.A.

Hong Kong, Lane Crawford, Queen's Road Central, Hong Kong

Hong Kong, Mayfair Co., 92 Nathan Road, Kowloon/Hong Kong

Hong Kong, Asia, 81/B Nathan Road, Kowloon/Hong Kong

Japan, Bally Boutique, Akasaka Plaza, AAkasaka Tokyu Hotel, 14-3, Nagata-cho 2-chome, Chiyoda-ku, Tokyo

Japan, Bally Boutique, Tamagawa Takashimaya Shopping Center, 17-1, Tamagawa 3-chome, Setagaya-ku, Tokyo

Japan, Boutique Bally, Palais Français, Togo-Bunkakaikan, 6-1, Jinumae 1-chome, Shibuya-ku, Tokyo

Philippines, Rustan's, Makati, Manila/Philippines

Singapore, Isetan, Apollo Building, Havelock Road, Singapore

Singapore, Melwani, Singapura Plaza, Singapore

Singapore, Chanrai, High Street Centre, Singapore

Switzerland, Bally Capitol or/and Bally Doelker, Bahnhofstrasse, Zurich

Switzerland, Bally Scheurer, Rue Du Rhone, Geneva

West Germany, Bally, Kurfurstendamm, Berlin

West Germany, Bally, Theatinerstrasse, Munich

## Bentalls
### London
Bentalls, Ealing Broadway, W5

### Out of London
Bracknell, Bentalls, High Street

Worthing, Bentalls, South Street

## The Cue Shop at Austin Reed
### London
Brent Cross Shopping Centre, London NW4

### Out of London
Birmingham, 4 North Court, Birmingham Shopping Centre

Bournemouth, Westover Corner

Bristol, Embassy House, Queen's Road

Edinburgh, 124 Princess Street

Glasgow, 74 Buchanan Street

Leeds, 37/39 Bond Street

Liverpool, 27/29 Bold Street

Manchester, 4 Exchange Street, St. Ann's Square

Oxford, 38 Cornmarket Street

### Abroad
Ireland, 60/61 Grafton Street, Dublin

## Dance Centre
### Abroad
America, Camomilla, 9029 Santa Monica Boulevard, Los Angeles, California

America, The Covent Garden in Bergdorf Goodman, 5th Avenue at 57th Street, New York City, New York

Denmark, Dance Centre Shop, gl kongivej 31, Copenhagen

France, Boutique de la danse, 19 rue de l'Arc-en-Ciel, Strasbourg

Finland, T°°mi Surkku Erkkilä, Huhtasenkatu 32, Tampere

Norway, Ballett Shop, Boks 922, Oslo

Sweden, Dansboutiken, Chalmersgatan 25, Gothenberg

## Dunhill

### London

Alfred Dunhill Ltd., 30 Duke Street, St. James's, London SW1Y 6DL. Telephone: 01-493 9161. Telegrams: *Salaams*, London SW1. Telex: 266914

### Abroad

**America**, Alfred Dunhill of London Inc., 136 South Rodeo Drive, Beverly Hills, California 90212, U.S.A. Telephone 272-6515

America, Alfred Dunhill of London Inc., Water Tower Place, 835 North Michigan Avenue, Second Level, Chicago, Illinois 60611, U.S.A. Telephone: 467-4455

America, Alfred Dunhill of London Inc., 426 North Park Center, Dallas, Texas 75225, U.S.A. Telephone: 691-0191

America, Alfred Dunhill of London Inc., Galleria II, 5085 Westheimer Road, Suite 2650, Houston, Texas 77056, U.S.A. Telephone: 961-4661

America, Alfred Dunhill of London Inc., 620 Fifth Avenue, New York, N.Y. 10020, U.S.A. Telephone: 684-7600. Cables: *Salaams*, New York. Telex: 422843

America, Alfred Dunhill of London Inc., 290 Post Street, San Francisco, California 91408, U.S.A. Telephone: 781-3368

**Australia**, Alfred Dunhill (Australia) Pty. Ltd., 23/25 O'Connell Street, Sydney, N.S.W. 2000, Australia. Telephone: 2315511

**France**, S.A.F. Alfred Dunhill, 15 rue de la Paix, 75002 Paris, France. Telephone: 261-57-58/59/60/61. Telegrams: *Salaams*, Paris Telex: Publi 21311F—Ref. 0106

**Germany**, Alfred Dunhill G.m.b.H., 4 Düsseldorf, Königsalle 28, Germany. Telephone: 32 55 05/32 77 53. Telegrams: Dunhill, Düsselldorf

**Hong Kong**, Alfred Dunhill (Far East) Ltd., Prince's Building, 5 Ice House Street, Hong Kong. Telephone: 243663. Cables: *Dunhill*, Hong Kong. Telex: HX73406 'For Dunhill'

**Japan**, Alfred Dunhill of London Ltd., New Yurakucho Building, No. 12-1, 1-Chome Yuraku-cho, Chiyoda-ku, Tokyo 100, Japan. Telephone: 214 4006. Cables: *Salaams*, Tokyo. Telex: J28515 Salaams

**Malaysia**, Alfred Dunhill of London (Malaysia) Sdn. Bhd., 2 Jalan Tun Perak, Kuala Lumpur, Malaysia. Telephone: Kuala Lumpur 86818

**Singapore**, Alfred Dunhill (Singapore) Pty. Ltd., 9 The Orchard, Orchard Road, Singapore 9. Telephone: 660077

**Spain**, Alfred Dunhill, J. Ortega y Gasset 26, Madrid 6, Spain. Telephone: 275 36 31

At present the Dunhill collection of co-related menswear is available exclusively from the London and Tokyo shops and the Dunhill shop within the store of Les Ambassadeurs, Bahnhofstrasse 64, 8001 Zurich, Switzerland.

## Floris

### Out of London

Birmingham, Rackham's, Corporation Street

Brighton, Hannington Ltd., North Street

Carlisle, L & J Robson Ltd., 46-50 Warwick Road

Edinburgh, Jenners Ltd., Princes Street

Glasgow, R. W. Forsyth Ltd., 1-11 Renfield Street

Nottingham, Jessops, Victoria Centre

Taunton, Hatcher & Sons Ltd., High Street

Tunbridge Wells, A. E. Hobbs Ltd, Mount Pleasant

**Abroad**

America, Colonial Drug, 49 Brattle Street, Harvard Square, Cambridge, Massachusetts

America, Cambridge Chemists, 702 Madison Avenue, New York City, New York

America, Casell-Massey, 518 Lexington Avenue, New York City, New York

France, Diptyque, 34 Boulevard Saint Germain, 5$^e$, Paris

Italy, Ditta Giuseppe Casolari, Corso Mateotti 1, Milan

Italy, Ditta Renato Castelli, 52 Via Frattina, Rome

**Gucci**
**Abroad**

America, 347 North Rodeo Drive, Beverly Hills, California

America, Royal Ponciana Plaza, Palm Beach, Florida

America, 713 North Michigan Avenue, Chicago, Illinois

America, 699 Fifth Avenue, New York City, New York

France, 8$^e$, 350 rue St. Honore, Paris

Italy, 73R Via Tornabuoni, Florence

Italy, 8 Via Montenapoleone, Milan

Italy, 15 Corso Roma, Montecatini

**Jaeger**
**Abroad**

America, in Bullocks Wilshire, 3050 Wilshire Boulevard, Los Angeles, California. **L**

America, Woodlands Hill, Palm Springs, Newport Beach, California. **L**

America, 272 Post Street, San Francisco, California. **L, M**

America, Phipps Plaza, 3500 Peachtree Road, Atlanta, Georgia. **L, M**

America, Water Tower Place, 835 N. Michigan Avenue, Chicago, Illinois. **L, M**

America, 818 Madison Avenue, New York. **L, M**

Belgium, Jaegar at Austin Reed, 33-35 Place de Brouckère, Brussels. **L**

Canada, 557 Granville Street, Vancouver, British Columbia. **L, M**

Canada, Eaton Centre, 290 Yonge Street, Toronto, Ontario. **L, M**

Canada, Jaegar in Ogilvys, 1307 St. Catherine Street N., Montreal, Quebec. **L**

Denmark, A C Illum A/S, Østergade 52, 1001 K Øbenhaun K, Copenhagen. **L**

France, 5 La Croisette, Cannes. **L, M**

France, 8 Avenue de Verdun, Nice. **L, M**

France, 3-5 rue de Faubourg St. Honoré, Paris. **L, M**

Netherlands, Jaegar at Austin Reed, 68 Rokin/71 Kalverstraat, Amsterdam. **L**

Netherlands, Jaegar at Austin Reed B.V., Hoogstraat 16, The Hague. **L**

Sweden, Austin Reed Stroms AB, Kungsgatan 27-29, Gothenburg. **L**

Sweden, Austin Reed Cason AB, Gustav Ad. torg 8, Malmo. **L**

Sweden, Jaegar Hos Austin Reed, Kungsgatan 38, Stockholm. **L**

**L = Ladies,   M = Men.**

346

## Herbert Johnson
### London
Chic, 100 Mount Street, W1 and 82 Heath Street, NW3
Harrods, Knightsbridge, SW1
Harvey Nichols, Knightsbridge, SW1
Simpsons, 203 Piccadilly, W1

### Out of London
Bath, Chloe Fairclough, 17 Green Street
Beaconsfield, Belinda, Station Road
Bradford, Brown Muff, Market Street
Stow on the Wold, Purdey of Stowe, Digbeth Street
Swansea, Elwyn James, 5 Caer Street
Weybridge, The Clothes Shop, 52 Church Street

### Abroad
America, Bergdorf Goodman, 5th Avenue at 57th & 58th Streets, New York City, New York
America, Lord & Taylor, 424 Fifth Avenue, New York City, New York
America, Saks, 611 Fifth Avenue, New York City, New York
America, Neiman Marcus, Dallas, Texas
America, Neiman Marcus, Houston, Texas
Ireland, Brown Thomas, Grafton Street, Dublin
Ireland, Switzers, Grafton Street, Dublin

## Charles Jourdan
### Out of London
Glasgow, Dido
Jersey, Marcel Jacques

### Abroad
America, Charles Jourdan at Bonwit Teller, 9536 Wilshire Boulevard, Los Angeles, California.

America, Charles Jourdan at Joseph Magnin, 77 O'Farrel Street, San Francisco, California
America, 700 Fifth Avenue, New York City, New York
France, 86 Champs Elysees, 8ᵉ, Paris
France, 12 rue de Faubourg Saint-Honore, Paris
France, 5 boulevard de la Madeleine, Paris
Germany, Kö-Center, Konigsallee 30, Dusseldorf
Germany, Theatinerstrasse 27, Munich
Spain, Avenida Jose Antonio, 1, Madrid
Switzerland, 10 rue de la Croix d'Or, Geneva

## Liberty
### Out of London
Edinburgh, Liberty in Forsyths, Princes Street
Glasgow, Liberty in Forsyths, Renfield Street
Manchester, The Liberty Fabric Shop, 16-18 King Street

### Abroad
France, Liberty Chez Peinture, 18 rue du Pré aux Clercs, 7ᵉ
Netherlands, Metz-Liberty Shop, Leidsestraat, Amsterdam
Netherlands, Metz-Liberty Shop, Plaats 13A, The Hague

## Molton Brown Products
### London
Liberty, Regent Street, London W1
Harrods, Knightsbridge, London SW1
Harvey Nicholls, Knightsbridge, London SW1
Savoury and Moore, Curzon Street, London W1

The Neal Street Shop, 29 Neal
Street, London WC2
Designers Guild, 277 Kings Road,
London SW3
**Out of London**
Edinburgh, Comparrisons, 63 This-
tle Street
Nottingham, Peru, 17 Bridle Smith
Gate

**Abroad**
America, Fingers Inc., The Charter
Club, 600 N.E. 36th Street,
Miami, Florida
Canada, The Soap Box, 99 Yorkville
Avenue, Toronto M.5.R., I, CI,
Canada
France, Madame Ancelin, 20 Rue
St. Guillaume, St. Brieuc 22000
Brittany
France, Au Printemps, 102 Rue de
Provence, 75009 Paris
France, Grain de Beaute, 9 Rue du
Cherche Midi, 75006 Paris
Ireland, Arnotts and Co. Ltd.,
· Henry Street, Dublin 1
Ireland, Brown Thomas & Co.
Ltd., Graften Street, Dublin 2

**Penhaligon's**
**London**
David Hicks, Jermyn Street, SW1

**Abroad**
France, Grain de Beaute, 9 rue du
Cherche Midi, 6$^e$, Paris
France, Sena, 29 rue de Condé, 6$^e$,
Paris
France, Upla, 17 rue des Halles, 1$^e$,
Paris
Germany, Baff, 46 Kur-
furstendamm, Berlin
Germany, Art et Decor,
Admiralitätsstrasse 71, Hamburg
Italy, Guiseppi Casolari, 2 via P.
Verri, Milan
Italy, G. Battistoni, 61a via Con-
dotti, Rome
Italy, De Paola Profumeria, 23 via
della Croce, Rome

**The Scotch House**
**London**
7 Marble Arch, W1
191 Regent Street, W1
187 Oxford Street, W1
2 Brompton Road, SW1
122-D Kings Road, SW3
129-133 Kensington High Street,
W8

**Out of London**
Edinburgh, 60 Princes Street

**Abroad**
France, 56 rue de Passy, 16$^e$, Paris

## Shops

## Who's Where

# NOTES

# NOTES

# NOTES

# NOTES

# NOTES

# NOTES

# STOP PRESS

## Look out for . . .

Sizzling good looks at **Burns**, 55 George Street, W1, Lillian Burns' new shop full of very special clothes by French, Italian and young English designers. Expect lots of fashion excitement and a creative approach to style. Day and evening wear, presented in total looks. Don't forget to pop in to Ricci Burns at 94 George Street for a new hairstyle to match.

A new **Gordon L. Clarke shop** in London, for details ring 01-828 2191.

A new **Lucienne Phillips shop** in Paris, for details ring 01-235 2134.

**Dona Alda** facial treatments at Dandelion in Beauchamp Place, SW3.

**Mail Order** copies of **The Fashion Guide 1978,** available from:

....................................................................................................

CORONET BOOKS, P.O. Box 11, Falmouth, Cornwall.
Please send cheque or postal order, and allow the following for postage and packing:

U.K. – One book 19p plus 9p per copy for each additional book ordered, up to a maximum of 73p.

B.F.P.O. and EIRE – 19p for the first book plus 9p per copy for the next 6 books, thereafter 3p per book.

OTHER OVERSEAS CUSTOMERS – 20p for the first book and 10p per copy for each additional book.


Name ....................................................................................................


Address ................................................................................................


....................................................................................................